Arthur C.

Risk Culture an...

Governance

General thoughts:

- Light on human factors/different emphasis on measurements quantified

- Lack of emphasis on test which desired human behaviour embedded

- Lack of emphasis on learning (but share system-wide) forum

Republic p118.

How to make such things happen as industries eg 119
1191/20: Good 119

Risk Culture and Effective Risk Governance

Patricia Jackson

Published by Risk Books, a Division of Incisive Media Investments Ltd

Incisive Media
32–34 Broadwick Street
London W1A 2HG
Tel: +44(0) 20 7316 9000
E-mail: books@incisivemedia.com
Sites: www.riskbooks.com
www.incisivemedia.com

© 2014 Incisive Media

ISBN 978 1 78272 099 7

British Library Cataloguing in Publication Data
A catalogue record for this book is available from the British Library

Publisher: Nick Carver
Commissioning Editor: Sarah Hastings
Managing Editor: Lewis O'Sullivan
Designer: Lisa Ling
Copyeditor: Laurie Donaldson

Typeset by Mark Heslington Ltd, Scarborough, North Yorkshire
Printed and bound in the UK by PrintonDemand-Worldwide

Contents

About the Editor   vii

About the Authors   ix

Foreword   xv

1   Introduction: Understanding Risk Culture and What To Do About It   1
Patricia Jackson

2   Risk Culture: Definitions, Change Practices and Challenges for Chief Risk Officers   25
Simon Ashby, Tommaso Palermo and Mike Power

3   Risk Culture: A View from the Board   47
Louise Redmond

4   The Views of The PRA on Risk Culture and Risk Governance in Banks and Insurers   81
Andrew Bailey and John Sutherland

5   Risk Culture and Risk Appetite: A Regulatory View   103
Michael Alix

6   The Investor Perspective on Risk Culture   123
Peter Montagnon

7   Value Driven Performance Measurement   137
Robert Potter and Miriam Earley

8   Creating a Culture of Success: Reducing the Likelihood of Conduct Failures   161
Brendon Young

9   Internal Audit and Risk Culture   191
    Stephen Gregory

10 Compensation and Risk: Regulation and Design of Incentive
    Schemes   215
    José Luis López del Olmo

11 A View from the Remuneration Committee: Emerging Good
    Practice in the UK   239
    Alan M. Judes

12 Risk Transparency and Risk Culture for Financial Institutions   255
    Sylvie Mathérat

13 The Importance of Data and IT for a Strong Risk Culture   275
    Darren Smith and Andrew Cross

14 The Role of Whistleblowing in Risk Culture and Effective
    Governance   295
    Carol Sergeant

    Index   315

About the Editor

Patricia Jackson advises major financial institutions on risk governance covering areas such as risk appetite, risk culture and stress testing. She is a member of the EY Global Regulatory Network, having joined EY as a partner in in 2004 to lead the banking risk practice. She has led an annual EY/IFF industry survey on risk governance since the crisis. Previously, Patricia was a senior official at the Bank of England and head of the Financial Industry and Regulation Division. She represented the UK on the Basel Committee for Banking Supervision, and is the non-executive deputy chairman and chair of the risk committee of CHAPS Co. Patricia is an adjunct professor at Imperial College, on the council of SUERF and a trustee of the Centre for Economic Policy Research, and has published papers on risk topics and the global financial crisis.

About the Authors

Michael Alix is a senior vice president in the Financial Institutions Supervision Group at the Federal Reserve Bank of New York, where he has worked since 2008. He also leads or serves on management groups that oversee and coordinate the Federal Reserve System's supervision of large, complex financial institutions, and serves on a number of international regulatory bodies, including the Senior Supervisors Group. Michael was previously co-head of the risk and policy function, and has also worked with FRBNY's AIG Monitoring Team. He holds a BA from Duke University and an MBA from the Wharton School of the University of Pennsylvania.

Simon Ashby is associate professor of financial services at Plymouth Business School. He has previously worked as a financial regulator and as a senior risk manager in several UK financial institutions, and remains involved in the UK financial services sector. Simon is a regular speaker at industry conferences and seminars, and provides occasional training and consultancy services to financial institutions and their regulators. He has published many academic papers on risk, regulation, banking and insurance, is a fellow and chairman of the Institute of Operational Risk and has a PhD in corporate risk management.

Andrew Bailey has been deputy governor for prudential regulation at the Bank of England and chief executive officer of the Prudential Regulation Authority since April 2013. He is a member of the BoE's court of directors, the PRA board, the Financial Policy Committee and the board of the Financial Conduct Authority. Andrew joined the Financial Services Authority in April 2011 as deputy head of the Prudential Business Unit and director of UK banks and building societies, becoming managing director of the former in July 2012. He was previously executive director for banking services and chief cashier at the BoE, as well as head of its Special Resolution Unit.

Andrew Cross is director of risk infrastructure at RBS, where he is responsible for providing the risk management function with a variety of services, including risk models, governance, systems and data, as well as people strategy and financial planning. He joined RBS in 2011, having spent a number of years at Credit Suisse. Andrew has spent the majority of his career leading risk management activities in major banks, holds an MA in mathematics from the University of Cambridge and is a chartered accountant.

Miriam Earley is an HR consultant at JLT Group, having worked there since the late 2000s. At JLT, she has helped to introduce a range of strategic initiatives, including succession planning, employee engagement, reward management and career development. Prior to joining JLT, Miriam spent five years at Watson Wyatt, where she was a consultant within their strategic reward team, working on a wide range of projects from job architecture to employee engagement. She holds a masters degree in human resources management from the Smurfit Business School, University College Dublin.

Stephen Gregory is a partner at EY in London, specialising in risk governance and internal audit. He is the leader of their risk, regulatory and internal audit practice, focused on the financial services sector in Europe, Middle East, India and Africa. Stephen has more than 20 years' of experience working with internal audit functions across the globe, and has worked with more than 30 global businesses. His work involves board level governance, risk capability transformation, integrated assurance and internal audit performance. Stephen has advised audit committees and chief audit executives on steps required to address heightened performance standards placed on internal audit functions by global regulators.

Alan Judes is the founder of Strategic Remuneration, an independent reward consultancy based in London, with particular emphasis on corporate governance, incentive arrangements, and equity-based pay. He has been an executive compensation consultant for many years, and was previously a partner at Bacon & Woodrow and head of their executive compensation consulting practice. Alan is a regular conference speaker, has written chapters for several manuals on compensation practice and is author of *Transactions: Share Incentives* *for Employees*. He is a chartered accountant, chartered tax adviser and certified management consultant, and read commerce at the University of the Witwatersrand, Johannesburg.

José Luis López del Olmo is the head of the International Co-ordination and Regulatory Policy Division at Banco de España. He joined the bank in 1994 – passing the official examinations to become a bank inspector. Prior to that, José worked for four years in a commercial bank, where he was responsible for the monitoring of prudential reporting. He has been involved in a number of international policy committees, including involvement in official sector policies on remuneration. He holds a degree in economics and in actuarial studies from the Complutense University of Madrid.

Sylvie Mathérat is deputy director general, Directorate General Operations, at the **Banque de France**, with a focus on the operations and covers markets, financial stability and regulation, payment and settlement systems, infrastructures and banking services. She is a member of the Basel Committee for Banking Supervision and chairs its liquidity group, and is a member of the BIS Committee on Payment and Settlement Systems, the ECB Payment and Settlement Systems Committee and a number of FSB working groups. Sylvie has been director of research and policy for the French Prudential Authority, in charge of Basel II implementation and IFRS application, and has worked on structured finance for a large banking group.

Peter Montagnon is associate director at the Institute of Business Ethics, having previously held senior positions at the Financial Reporting Council, the Association of British Insurers, and as a journalist at the *Financial Times*. He is also a member of the Corporate Governance Advisory Board of the Norges Bank Investment management, a board member of the Hawkamah Institute, Dubai, and serves on the Council of the Royal Institute for International Affairs. Peter is a past chairman of the International Corporate Governance Network and a previous member of the European Corporate governance Forum.

Tommaso Palermo is a lecturer in accounting at the London School of Economics, a position he has held since September 2013. His research focuses on management control systems, performance measurement and risk management, while his teaching focuses on planning and control practices, and the organisational and institutional settings within which risk is managed. Tommaso received a PhD in management, economics and industrial engineering from the Politecnico di Milano in Italy, which explored the links between risk and performance management roles and processes.

Robert Potter is Group HR director and management board member at Hays Plc, with over 20 years of experience working in human resources. Prior to joining Hays, he worked for Jardine Lloyd Thompson Ltd and Société Générale Corporate and Investment Bank as global head of HR. In addition to his role as chairman of the City HR Association, Robert has been the chairman of the HR Advisory Board to the Lord Mayor's City Values Forum. He has an MBA from Durham University and a BA in combined sociology and psychology, and divides his time between London, where he works, and Paris, where he lives with his family.

Michael Power is professor of accounting at the London School of Economics, where he has worked since 1987. He is a fellow of the Institute of Chartered Accountants in England and Wales (ICAEW), an associate member of the UK Chartered Institute of Taxation and an honorary fellow of the UK Institute of Risk Management. Michael is also a non-executive director of St James's Place International and RIT Capital Partners, and holds honorary doctorates from University of St Gallen, Switzerland and Uppsala University, Sweden.

Louise Redmond is a founder director of Risk Culture Insights, as well as holding a portfolio of non-executive director positions, including at Cranfield University and the Government Actuary's Department in the UK. She set up Law Debenture Governance Services, where she established a practice in corporate governance and board effectiveness. Louise was previously the human resources director at the Bank of England between 2004 and 2010, the vice president of organisation effectiveness at GlaxoSmithKline and an executive management consultant at KPMG. She is completing her doctorate in corporate governance at the London Centre for Corporate Governance and Ethics at Birkbeck, University of London.

Carol Sergeant is non-executive director at Danske Bank, Secure Trust Bank and Martin Currie Holdings, and chairman of the BSI Strategy and Policy Committee. She is also chairman of Public Concern at Work, trustee of the Lloyds Register Foundation and a member of the Cass Business School Strategy and Development Board. Carol was previously a senior official at the Bank of England, managing director of the UK Financial Services Authority and CRO of Lloyds Bank. She has been chairman of Simple Financial Products, a member of the high-level expert group on the structure of banking and member of the UK committee on Internal Audit Guidance for Financial Services.

Darren Smith works in the risk infrastructure group at RBS, where he is responsible for oversight of the risk function data strategy. He joined RBS in 1999, having previously worked at Barclays, Westpac and Colonial Assurance. Darren has specialised in risk and regulatory reporting and related systems, data and change management.

John Sutherland is a senior adviser at the Bank of England working for the deputy governor of prudential regulation, and is involved in the supervision of major banks and insurers. He spent 35 years at Lloyds and Nationwide, leading divisions in payment services, retail branches, back-office operations and technology, and was a special adviser in the Bank of England's Special Resolution Unit. In 2011, John was appointed as senior adviser at the Financial Services Authority, and later seconded to the Parliamentary Commission on Banking Standards. He regularly speaks on leadership and risk management, and is an honorary fellow of the University of Exeter Business School, where he received an MBA and an MA in leadership studies.

Brendon Young is chairman of the ORRF Risk Research Forum and founding president of the Institute of Operational Risk, and is a leading expert in risk management and accounting. He has been an advisor to financial institutions, including Moody's and the Financial Reporting Council Board of Actuarial Standards, and was previously director of Arthur Andersen's risk research centre. Brendon has published papers and lectured widely, and was business school associate dean at Birmingham City University. His early career was

in consultancy with Deloitte and later in venture capital, after
initially training in industry with Rolls-Royce aero-engines and
Jaguar Cars, qualifying both as a chartered engineer and a chartered
management accountant.

Foreword

Probably the greatest challenge facing chairmen, boards and top management is how to ensure that the risk culture of an organisation supports its overarching goals. Globally, the financial services industry has been rocked by the 2007–08 crisis and then – from a reputation standpoint, in an even more damaging way – by conduct scandals post-crisis. The development of better approaches to identify unknown risks or unknown pockets of bad behaviour, while at the same time creating a climate where individuals are more likely to behave instinctively in the right way, is of paramount importance. Other industries have also seen failings in the identification or management of risk and individual behaviour.

These are fundamental issues that need practical solutions. The Editor, Patricia Jackson, who has wide experience in the risk management field, has brought together an impressive array of authors to look at the nexus of factors that influence risk culture, and at ways that an organisation can go about strengthening culture. In my view, the role of the board is central, and every chapter covers areas of importance for board members in terms of the tools and frameworks that can influence the prevailing environment and individual behaviour. They also consider how the board itself should operate, looking at the role of board-level conduct committees and how board members should challenge themselves on their own willingness to speak up and question a consensus viewpoint. An important message from this book is the need for openness in debate and a willingness to hear unwelcome messages from the top to the bottom in an organisation.

The book combines thinking on both the "hard" risk management frameworks, such as risk appetite and risk transparency, with the much more demanding "softer" areas influencing individual conduct. Here, it takes a wide view on the role of incentives, looking at informal influences such as reactions from peers to local bad behaviour, and more structural influences such as remuneration frameworks. It also looks at how new forms of monitoring can be established to identify fertile ground for conduct or compliance issues.

Financial services regulators have turned their attention from building capital and liquidity bulwarks to the whole area of risk governance and risk culture, and are starting to set out a roadmap in a number of areas. Their viewpoint is explained clearly in four chapters written by senior regulators drawn from the global regulatory community. This is balanced by chapters written by practitioners: experts in a range of fields, from the role of boards and governance to how values can be established and risk transparency can be achieved. The book also draws on thinking from a wide range of industries, some of which are more advanced in terms of approaches to influence individual behaviour.

With the benefit of hindsight, companies can see clearly where they went wrong in the past. However, the factors that undermine firms in the future will be different, and we need to consider new ways to do things to ensure we are not taken by surprise again.

Sir David Walker,
Chairman Barclays PLC

Introduction: Understanding Risk Culture and What To Do About It

Patricia Jackson

EY

Concerns about risk culture in financial firms, fostered by the 2007–08 financial crisis and perhaps even more by the exposure of many different conduct failings in the industry since the crisis, have propelled the topic to the top of board and regulatory agendas. Sizeable operational problems in some industrial companies have raised similar questions about the safety culture. This book looks at risk culture in the round, covering the fundamental questions that many are asking about the role of the board and senior management in assessing and setting culture, and the enablers that can be used to achieve an appropriate risk culture. The authors come from a variety of backgrounds and countries, and include leading regulators, academics and industry professionals from different fields.

Although it is clear that risk culture must be set from the top of any organisation, it is equally clear that this is not enough to achieve the goal. New mechanisms and techniques are required to ensure that risk culture is embedded in decisions, and there needs to be more intensive scrutiny within firms of wider factors driving behaviour. In some of these areas, thinking in the financial services industry is ahead of that in other industries. This is being driven in part by intensive work in the global bodies, such as the Financial Stability Board (FSB), to enhance risk governance and change culture in the industry. This thinking may well provide a route map for other industries where safety and risk are key considerations and costs of failure in culture can be devastating. However, thinking in industries such as nuclear power can equally provide important insights for financial firms, which underlines the message from this book that risk culture needs to be considered across a broad canvas.

RISK CULTURE

The essence of risk culture is the creation of an environment where decisions by individuals or business lines, and, even more importantly, the Executive Management Committee, will be in tune with the risk goals of the board. In setting those goals, the board and senior management should also consider if the risks are commensurate with the organisation's capacity to deal with the consequences. The ideal culture is one where individuals will instinctively take decisions that are consistent with the risk thinking of the organisation. However, on a practical level, to achieve a good risk culture, risk management needs to be very effective. If senior management does not know that large risks are being run, if appropriate controls are not in place and appropriate procedures are not exercised, if risk expectations are flouted, then no amount of town halls and newsletters on values will create a strong risk culture.

This link between culture and risk management is one of the findings of Simon Ashby, Tommasso Palermo and Mike Power, in the chapter "Risk Culture: Definitions, Change Practices and Challenges for Chief Risk Officers", which reports their research into risk culture. In examining definitions of culture, they find that almost all focus to a significant extent on the behaviour of individuals in relation to risk taking and control, and the effectiveness of risk management processes. Nonetheless, although these aspects feature strongly, ethics and values are also prominent.

In Chapter 4, Andrew Bailey, head of the Prudential Regulatory Authority (PRA) in the UK, with his colleague John Sutherland set out the views of the PRA on risk culture and risk governance in banks and insurers. This highlights the alignment of the PRA's focus in this area with that of the FSB. The FSB, in their April 2014 paper[1] "Guidance on Supervisory Interaction with Financial Institutions on Risk Culture (A Framework for Assessing Risk Culture)", underlined that they were concerned about "the institution's norms, attitudes and behaviours related to risk awareness, risk taking and risk management." In looking at risk culture, the FSB cites an appropriate risk–reward balance consistent with risk appetite, an effective system of controls, quality of risk measurement and control structures as fundamental enablers, and sets out a range of indicators of a strong culture. Andrew Bailey makes clear that the PRA expects "boards to have a firm grip on the risk being run and the forward-looking risks that may arise", and cannot see how this would be possible without the "type of risk culture the FSB promotes being in place."

It is this nexus of norms, behaviours and risk management that makes risk culture a difficult and, for some, nebulous topic. An essential aspect of risk culture is how individuals behave and the decisions they take within the context of the risk environment. Louise Redmond, in the chapter "Risk Culture: A View from the Board" which takes a broad view of the board's role in setting risk culture and influencing risk management, suggests that culture is about individuals: "how people behave, together, to meet their understanding of what work should be done and how".

Risk culture is influenced partly by overall culture but also covers rather different ground. It is about risk behaviour, grounded in general behaviour, and is influenced by incentive structures as well as values, but is also about risk awareness and risk controls. To understand the range of elements that come into play, it is worth looking at how different risk cultures have failed across a range of industries.

UNDERSTANDING RISK CULTURE FAILURE

Risk culture can go off track at many levels in a firm and in many ways. In some cases, it has been because of the strategic decisions taken by senior management and the board. In others, it has been because of actions taken by individuals lower down the organisation without the knowledge of those at the top.

Lack of focus on known but unlikely risks

At a strategic level, a risk culture may fail because of over-optimism, or what the economics literature calls "disaster myopia"[2] – a lack of focus on potential extreme events or poor outcomes, or a belief that they will not reoccur. This was part of the story behind the excessive risk taking in the run up to the crisis in the banking industry. Many firms had large concentrations of risk that had not been fully recognised or had been discounted as a potential risk. An example here was the massive exposure globally to US-generated retail mortgage-backed securities and, through them, to the US housing market.[3] Stress testing was not severe enough, nor was it designed to uncover the risks in the particular concentrated exposures. The belief was that it could not be a problem because house prices would have to fall in every state in the US to underestimate securities backed by large diversified pools of mortgages – but this is what happened.

The general theme across many failures in risk culture is the lack of sufficient focus on low-probability, high-impact events. If a low-probability event could destroy or substantially weaken the firm, efforts to test for it need to be doubled and redoubled, but it may take a new event to provide the imperative. Following a disaster, stress testing (the main tool used to assess risks from extreme events) is made more extreme, but over time complacency slips back in. This is true of many industries. After the Fukushima nuclear disaster, the EU called for a programme of stress testing across member countries, which uncovered the "need for significant and tangible improvements"[4] for most nuclear power plants.

Complacency can also be bred by the fact that the known risk has never crystallised in a particular country, market or industry. Japan had never seen a fall in property prices before the early 1990s, which led to a belief that it would never occur; consequently, over-lending and over-borrowing sowed the seeds for a massive financial crash. The same was true of Ireland before the 2007–08 financial crisis. Likewise, the enquiry after the King's Cross underground fire highlighted a culture of complacency in the UK transport system – because there had never been a fatal fire on the underground, staff had not been given training to deal with one.[5]

Questions every board should address are: how can they know how much risk is being run, how can they ensure that risks are being kept within sustainable levels (ie that the appropriate controls and contingency plans are in place) and how can this state of alertness to risk be maintained as a priority, even in benign periods. Different organisations will have a higher or lower tolerance for risk, and board and senior management may decide consciously to follow a higher-risk path; however, the operative word here is "consciously".

Trade-offs leading to too much risk

A particular strategy may be driven by a search for profit or cost reduction without enough weight being given to the consequent risks. There are strong elements of this in decisions in the run up to the financial crisis. Much of the drive for riskier structured products and higher-risk mortgage lending came from a search for yield, with the risks being discounted too heavily, in part because of disaster myopia (as seen above). This is not just confined to the financial services industry. In their final report, the National Commission on the BP Deepwater Horizon Oil Spill and Offshore Drilling[6] found that BP, Halliburton and Transocean attempts to contain costs had been a factor. Also, Hopkins (2009),[7] referenced in Sumwalt (2013),[8] in looking at train crashes, shuttle accidents and oil refinery fires, found different physical causes but surprisingly similar root causes at an organisational and cultural level. "Mindless cost cutting, incentive schemes that divert attention away from safe operations and failure to consider safety implications of organisational changes."

Trade-offs have to be made in all industries because no organisation can be perfectly safe, but the trade-offs have to be made at the right level and the implications for organisation-wide risk need to be clearly highlighted and discussed. Risks must be adequately debated at board level, and must be in line with objectives. It is important that the board does not sign up piecemeal to different aspects of strategy without having the means to assess or test the combined risk implications. There is a potential slippery slope here. A board could agree to a sequence of individual proposals that standalone appear acceptable, but lead together to an unacceptable build-up of risk. Also, boards and senior management need to consider whether the combined risk is within the capacity that the firm has to absorb the consequences and within the appetite for risk. To assess this, the magnitude of risk must be tested under different scenarios and the implications must be fully assessed, and this assessment must include possible reputation damage that could be long-lasting. The future is not certain, and therefore the possible outcomes as a result of the risk taking need to be assessed against a variety of possible adverse developments.

Failure of senior management to uncover risks

Another reason for lack of action to prevent excessive buildup in risk is that senior management is simply unaware of it. Individuals lower down the organisation may have taken actions (or not taken risk-reducing actions) knowing there are risks, but have chosen not to flag them to senior management. The individual may have taken the view that the risk was implausible (ie, too unlikely to warrant serious consideration), but the board or senior management might well have reached a different conclusion had they been informed.

A technical change in the structured investment vehicles (SIVs) in London pre-crisis left a number of banks vulnerable from a liquidity or reputation standpoint to loss of US commercial paper funding. The vehicles invested in structured products and were funded through US commercial paper. To increase profitability, a decision was taken not to include pre-arranged lines with other banks to supply funding if insufficient commercial paper could be issued. The implication of the change was well understood by those designing the vehicles. However, because they had deemed a drying up of the commercial paper market to be implausible, the risk had not been debated and tested at an organisation level. In the crisis some banks, already under liquidity pressure, had to individually provide large quantities of liquidity to their vehicles or suffer reputation damage by leaving them to go into receivership. HSBC provided $35billion in funding to bailout its SIVs.[9]

A further dimension is that organisations have a tendency to focus on the headline risks, and not sufficiently on more detailed aspects of exposures that could cause severe damage. For example, pre-crisis, banks were stressing their business models for the effect of a recession (although not with the severity needed) but did not stress test the triggers built into the securitisation vehicles they were using for funding. This raises a question about the tools needed to enable management to uncover fault lines in the business. You cannot stress-test something if you do not know about it, but how do you find out about it if individuals have applied their own plausibility test and do not report or highlight it? This means that much more effort needs to be placed on identifying business fault lines (which may be hidden in the technicalities of some products or processes) at a business line, and even business unit, level.

Of course, it may not be in the interests of individuals to alert senior management to risks, given incentive structures. This enhances the need for better risk identification but also underlines the need for alignment of incentive structures with risk management Increased complexity in terms of organisation structure or use of suppliers may make it harder to uncover risks. In the case of the Hatfield Rail crash in 2000, the cause that came to light following an investigation was that over 300 critical cracks had been found in the rails. The problem was known to various individuals before the crash but Railtrack, reliant on maintenance contractors, had inadequate maintenance records to track the risk centrally.[10]

Another issue which is flagged by Bailey and Sutherland (in chapter 4) is that business activities change. A risk that could safely be ignored yesterday, because it was irrelevant given the particular activities, may be critical today because products and activities have altered.

Risk reduction not seen as a priority by employees

Alternatively, individuals might fail to report risks or take risky decisions because they do not see safety or risk containment as a high priority of the organisation – if, for example, they believe that management is focused on revenue and revenue targets, and will not welcome bad news. This impression could be given at many levels in the organisation, and indeed a different impression given by the board (that the organisation is concerned about risks) could be counteracted by the behaviour of middle management.

A signal to the organisation that costs must be cut may be taken as indicating that this, rather than risk control, is the priority. The danger is reinforced because hierarchies can develop, which discourage risk reporting higher up. The space shuttle Columbia Accident Investigation Board came to the view that, at NASA, "cultural traits and organisational practices detrimental to safety and reliability were allowed to develop", and that certain goals in the cash-strapped organisation turned a technical culture into "a culture of production".[11] Dick and Launis, quoting Vaughan, also suggest that a focus on efficiency was an important factor, exacerbated by hierarchy and rule following.[12]

Wider perceptions of goals are important (see Zohar, 2010).[13] In analysing the Washington subway incident, the NTSB[14] found that workers perceived that moving trains on time was the priority of the railway system, and concluded that workers pattern their safety behaviour to meet the demonstrated priorities of the firm's leaders.[15]

Individual risky behaviour

The behaviour of individuals is central to a further range of potential risk culture failings. Individuals may decide to take actions that could bring a firm or organisation into disrepute, or create the risk of financial or reputation damage. This could happen, however strong the risk culture – for example, rogue trading or fraud could take place in many different types of firm, with many different cultures.

It is this area of individual conduct that has undoubtedly created the most reputation damage for the banks post-crisis. This too can have fundamentally different causes. In many cases, individual behaviour has been driven by personal objectives; however, some problems were linked to the strategy of the firm. For example, the sale of personal protection insurance in the UK was being targeted for growth at a firm level given the profits generated. The Financial Services Authority (FSA) suggested that the incentive schemes established to increase sales actually encouraged mis-selling by individuals.[16] Therefore, mis-selling, although due to the actions of individuals, may well fit more into an organisational failure category. Brendon Young in the chapter "Creating a Culture of Success: Reducing the Likelihood of Conduct Failures", highlights the range of mis-selling cases globally, ranging from products being sold to individuals who would not benefit or were unlikely to benefit, to opacity in the products and the sales materials.

Certainly, many types of bad behaviour have had nothing to do with the firm's strategy, with examples here being Libor and FX manipulation, or Stafford Hospital's poor patient care. However, in the realm of individual adverse behaviour, the questions that boards need to address are whether the strategy and incentives could in some way implicitly encourage poor behaviour, through the use of poorly designed targets for example, or fail to discourage it and whether controls are in place to identify issues fast. An allied question is whether the culture deters others from reporting concerns.

The book looks in detail at the ways in which various governance, incentive and control frameworks interact to influence behaviour, and at emerging practice to harness different tools to foster appropriate risk cultures.

ASSESSING RISK CULTURE

The board is ultimately responsible for the risk culture, and this presents a considerable challenge. Stephen Gregory, in the chapter "Internal Audit and Risk Culture" maintains that cultures can be variable: "change the individuals who form part of a business and the nature of risk culture is also likely to change". This magnifies the difficulty. A board not only needs to know what the culture is across the organisation today, but also if it changes significantly in the future or changes in some business units. This is made more challenging by the size and complexity of some organisations. Ashby, Palermo and Power (Chapter 2) give an example of a heterogeneous organisation that has specific "hotspots" that could drive the organisation outside its "safe zone". Gregory refers to the board's needs in terms of "trustworthy information about actual risk culture and its impact on the quality of risk governance."

Many boards are trying to carry out a stock take. Ashby, Palermo and Power note that different types of survey have been used sometimes adapting employee surveys but also using specialist tools designed for the purpose. Gregory sets out one such tool and the range of different aspects that need to be assessed by the organisation – leadership, incentives and employee lifecycle, risk governance and risk framework.

In addition to trying to understand today's culture boards and senior management also need to have ongoing indicators and information on culture otherwise complacency could develop. Redmond (Chapter 3) suggests that at board level a simple measurement dashboard on key performance and risk indicators will enable "rigorous discussion" and looks at how these indicators can be developed. Gregory proposes that one way to achieve ongoing information on culture is through an expanded role for internal audit. One advantage that internal audit has is that, with the cycle of audits of different parts of the firm year in year out, they are well placed to consider culture as a normal part of their role. They can also carry out broader reviews. The FSB in their paper "Thematic Review on Risk Governance"[17] set out how they see internal audit functions providing an independent view on the risk governance framework.

Redmond also highlights that boards need to challenge and assess their own culture – collegiality may deter non-executive directors from challenging risky proposals, and boards in general may pay too little attention to risk.

CREATING AN APPROPRIATE RISK CULTURE

There is no one identikit risk culture that is appropriate for all organisations. But as mentioned earlier risks taken must be commensurate with the organisation's capacity to deal with the possible consequences, including reputation damage. How can this be achieved? How can a board, or the board and senior management, influence culture? Interestingly, Ashby, Palermo and Power look at how risk culture change programmes depend on what is being emphasised. If ethics are the focus, workshops and mission statements take centre stage. If incentives are seen as the driver, then performance management programmes become central to the solution. They also highlight how many programmes involve structural change – for example, creation of central risk units. The message of this book is that there are a wide variety of elements that need to be considered, and a focus on only one or two avenues is likely to lead to disappointment.

Risk appetite

The common feature of the cases of failed culture at an organisation level is that risks taken on led to losses or reputation damage that exceeded the amount the board would probably have thought acceptable *ex ante*. In some cases, this was because of "risk creep" – the accumulation of risks to an unacceptably high level. In all firms, regardless of industry, decisions have to be taken regarding risk–reward trade-offs, but this is most acute in financial services where the core product is risk. This has led to thinking in the industry on how a framework can be created to ensure that risks taken are in line with board thinking, and do not simply grow to an unsustainable point. For this to be possible, the board's appetite for risk has to be set out in a way that is clear enough for decisions (and aggregate implications for risk profile) to be tested against it. Clear decisions on trade-offs can then be made. If a strategic change would bring forward-looking risk above the set appetite, then either the risk appetite or the strategy has to be changed. In either case it forces an overt decision to be taken.

This is at the heart of the risk appetite approach that is being promoted by the FSB.[18] Ashby, Palermo and Power argue that risk appetite and risk culture are two sides of a coin, and risk appetite is indeed in some sense an expression of expectations around culture.

Redmond, in Chapter 3, also suggests that culture is an intangible phenomenon that boards have to make tangible, and risk appetite is one way in which this can be achieved. As Andrew Bailey and John Sutherland put it, "this means that the board must be able to write down the risk it is happy for the bank to take and the controls that are required."

To fill this role, risk appetite must be much more than an expression of different values and expectations. It has to have real bite in terms of clear metrics that can be controlled against and monitored. This alone will not be enough to deliver a strong risk culture, but it provides a framework against which decisions can be tested and controls can be assessed. Risk appetite is an essential foundation for an effective culture, but the effectiveness of the risk appetite framework also depends on the wider culture. Management must buy into the concept that this is how risk will be managed and decisions taken. Risk transparency needs to be designed so that risks can be tested against risk appetite.

Michael Alix from the Federal Reserve Bank of New York, in the chapter "Risk Culture and Risk Appetite: A Regulatory View", makes the point that risk appetite is not of itself a new concept, but that the role seen for it has become greatly enhanced, and in particular the regulatory focus placed on it has shifted gear. The FSB framework set out by Alix starts with risk capacity. Senior management and the board must decide on the organisation's capacity to absorb loss or other consequences if the risk crystallises, and this presents the upper bound of risk that can be taken. The risk appetite must be set well within this using a mix of quantitative and qualitative metrics. One metric should be a common lingua franca that can be applied across risk types. This is a change for the industry where, in the past, in many cases, either qualitative comments were used or so many quantitative metrics that decisions could not really be tested against the appetite – a decision would be likely to pass some and fail others. The emphasis on having at least one common metric across different business units and risk types is also important. A metric such as forward extreme loss enables risk appetite to be compared across business lines and risk types.

The essence of the framework is about holding people throughout the organisation to account to keep risk within the risk appetite. The appetite must be embedded into business units and decisions tested against it. The banks are making considerable progress, but many firms have some way to go before the impact across the business reaches from top to bottom. Ashby, Palermo and Power refer to research conducted to look at how financial services firms view risk appetite, and found the impact on thinking was very different in different organisations.

To be effective, the risk appetite must cover non-financial risks as effectively as financial. This is creating particular challenges. In terms of risk measurement, the more established risks – credit and market – are much more convincingly measured and understood than issues around conduct or legal risk and infrastructure risk. This is in turn starting to drive thinking on how to develop metrics for non-financial risks to show if they are rising.

The technique of influencing risk taking through risk appetite setting is also used by non-financial companies, although probably not in as comprehensive a way, and this is where lessons can perhaps be learnt from financial services. The important element is that the appetite statement should be an expression of the areas of critical importance for the firm, with some hard metrics, and then should be backed up by controls and incentive structures.

Peter Montagnon in the chapter on "The Investor Perspective on Risk Culture" underlines the importance of a clear risk appetite for all organisations given the interest from shareholders. Investors need to understand the company's tolerance for risk and how this could change as a result of changes to strategy.

Values and behaviours

As part of the search for a strong culture boards need to consider the firm's values and how to influence behaviour. There is often a muddling of values and culture, and Redmond, who seeks to distinguish between the two, argues that "values are the guiding principles by which we intend to work", while culture is the "way people behave". In the aftermath of the banking crisis and various conduct scandals, there have been various calls for a rethinking of values in banking, including from the Archbishop of Canterbury.[19] Banks are embracing the need for a change. For example, Deutsche Bank's Stefan Leithner said in an interview that cultural change is an "essential part of our Strategy 2015+. What we intend by that is to affect a renewal of our values and principles of conduct."[20]

Many organisations in different sectors are posting new value statements and one area they are trying to influence is people risk. Robert Potter and Miriam Earley in the chapter "Value Driven Performance Measurement" define people risk in terms of the risks people pose to their organisation, as well as the impact of the organisation on its people. They suggest that, in general, employees will behave in a way that they perceive the organisation expects. Potter and Earley believe that by promulgating the expected behaviours, the required values and culture will emerge. However, they also counsel against organisations setting expected behaviours or values that they believe they should espouse, rather than those that fit the business model.

One particular area where the industry is under pressure on behaviour is conduct with customers and in the market. Brendon Young in Chapter 8 looks at the goals of the Financial Conduct Authority (FCA) in the UK, which is focused on how firms treat customers, how they behave to one another and how they behave in the wider market. In terms of dealing with customers and mis-selling risk, Young sees the main solution as greater awareness of customer requirements. He suggests that the regulatory focus on areas such as product suitability is leading to "a retreat towards a much smaller range of simple products", which could impede innovation. Instead, firms should "seek to understand customer needs and let these drive product design".

A common theme across several chapters in the book is that strong leadership is required to deliver a desired culture, and an essential part of this is the board and senior management living by the values and behaving accordingly. This is the acid test. If employees see that where a trade-off between profit and risk culture has to be made, the board and senior management always come down on the side of profit, this will send a very strong signal throughout the organisation.

Potter and Earley see the chief executive officer (CEO) and executive team as needing to deal with particular high-risk areas, including "focusing on those key groups or individuals who have the potential to create high value as well as deep-impact risks". There is anecdotal evidence that in at least one investment bank, the CEO sees annual bonuses as one of the most important sources of information on high-risk areas. Where he sees individuals who are not leading a function being awarded large bonuses, he explores what actions/decisions led to the high award, probing the business activity in that area.

Another theme is that the expected behaviour needs to be inculcated through communications and training. Redmond covers various communication strategies, and looks at different approaches to designing effective training. She concludes that interactive training is most effective in this area. This is supported by anecdotal evidence that some investment banks find case study-based training important; groups can discuss different circumstances and decisions that have to be taken, and the pros and cons of different trade-offs.

Incentives

Performance management and risk-based remuneration
Performance management plays a central role in culture because no amount of training and communication will embed the expected behaviours if the risk culture is not reactive. If individuals act in a way that cuts across cultural expectations and no action is taken, they will draw conclusions about the real expectations. To create a responsive culture, structures that make clear the consequences of particular actions need to be created. This is where the performance management system plays a central role.

Potter and Earley set out a roadmap developed by the City HR Association to help organisations link individual performance to corporate values and use it to manage behaviour. Transparency regarding what is expected of employees is core in terms of targets, skills to be mastered and behaviours. It is here that a risk management dimension can be included. In terms of assessment, equal value needs to be given to what was achieved and how it was achieved, which enables broader cultural elements to be considered.

Remuneration committees have an important role to play in this, and Alan Judes in the chapter "A view from the Remuneration Committee: Emerging Good Practice in the UK" looks at how they are trying to ensure that risk behaviour is taken into account when assessing performance. He sees financial services firms leading the way, but that other industries are following.

Remuneration is an area where in cultural terms it is crucial that senior management and the board "walk the walk". There is anecdotal evidence from some investment banks that remuneration committees may be struggling to lean against high awards for "stars", even when they have breached risk culture expectations. One difficulty is that cut and dried evidence may not be presented to remuneration committees. Also, human resources departments in some banks are seen as supporting the front office in their struggle to recruit and retain good staff, rather than aligning with the risk culture objectives. The red flag systems being introduced by some banks to give automaticity to remuneration reductions if there are serious or multiple smaller breaches of controls will help. These can impact the bonus pool allocated to a business unit as well as individual bonuses and promotions. This system gives clarity about expectations and penalties, and certainty that the penalties will be carried through.

To provide greater scope to ensure that high earners share the downside in positions they have created or from their activities, various mechanisms have been introduced to enable remuneration awarded already to be reduced. José Luis López del Olmo from the Bank of Spain in the chapter "Compensation and Risk: Regulation and Design of Incentive Schemes" sets out the degree to which the authorities are now dictating fundamental elements in the structure of compensation in banking. One area of focus has been that a substantial portion of remuneration should be deferred – the FSB suggests 40–60% should be deferred for a period of not less than three years. The deferred remuneration can then be withheld if problems come to light. Clauses are also used enabling sums already paid to be recovered if there have been significant breaches of rules, for example. Judes explains how these clauses work in practice, and reports that they are also being used by non-financial firms.

In addition, López del Olmo looks at the debate concerning the instruments used to pay bonuses. Regulators and firms are starting to look at instruments for at least part of the bonus that have no upside if profits are higher, just downside if the firm falls to certain trigger points.

Wider incentives
One factor that needs to be considered in the debate about risk-adjusted compensation is that rewards come in many forms. Status may be as important as remuneration, and here the role of Human Resources and line management in taking risk behaviour into

account when considering individuals for promotion is important. However, it goes much beyond this. Mark Paradies has argued[21] that individuals may be being rewarded in a variety of non-monetary ways. To apply his thinking to financial services, in a dealing room an individual who is seen as highly successful and high profile in a market may receive approbation from colleagues and management for making large profits despite controls having been breached. The benefit of this informal status may be enough to counteract fear of loss of bonus. There is anecdotal evidence that some firms see one of the greatest threats regarding rogue trading coming from individuals who are performing in a mediocre way and want to boost their success to improve the way they are viewed by peers. Paradies also suggests that simple drivers such as a desire to save time or effort may lead to an undermining of controls.

Penalties clearly play a role in deterring bad behaviour. However, Paradies suggests that if a penalty is uncertain and in any case delayed, that will reduce its weight, whereas rewards such approbation would be immediate. This reinforces the point made earlier about the importance of the culture being dynamic and reacting quickly to control breaches, and also the need for clarity regarding objectives and, penalties as well as willingness to follow through.

This dynamic of wider factors influencing behaviour makes it important that firms track whether there are clusters of control breaches (or other forms of poor behaviour such as not attending training) in certain business units, which then need to be explored more thoroughly. How are the leaders of the unit or the business line reacting to the control breaches when accompanied by profit-making? What status do the individuals committing the breaches have? A decision could then be taken on the remedy needed.

Lack of loyalty to the firm may increase the likelihood of behaviour breaches, and this may be generated by management actions. Joris Luyendijk at an LSE seminar said that, in 1,000 interviews with participants in the financial sector, "it was striking that almost everyone had a horror story about redundancy – they come back from the gym and the person next to them has gone". He suggested that under these circumstances and given the combination of huge rewards, minimal punishments and an opaque environment, it was rational to seek short-term gain and avoid reporting misdeeds by others.[22] One aspect here is that in the case of individuals being asked to leave financial firms often mutually agreed confidentiality arrangements make it difficult for the employer to explain the reason to other employees, which makes it difficult to counteract the view that sackings are "unreasonable" and also makes it harder to spread the message that bad behaviour has consequences.

Negative incentives can in general be very powerful. Arguably Nick Leeson in the Barings case was driven more by the risk to his position as a trader if he owned up to a loss making position than to concerns about financial rewards. His unauthorised trading was to cover up and give him time to rectify the losses.[23]

Goal alignment
The implications and incentive effects of different goals set for the business need to be carefully thought through in all organisations whatever the sector. Targets are, of course, important in running any business, but nonetheless the potential detrimental effects need to be considered and mitigated.

Boards and non-executive directors should also pay considerable attention to the profit targets being set for different business lines and operational units. If a business area is set a target that cannot be achieved without more risk being taken, the board and senior management should not be surprised if added risk is the result. There is a good example of this in the structured product debacle at the heart of the 2007–08 financial crisis. One of the surprising facts uncovered by the crisis was the extent to which bank Treasury operations had invested in very large holdings of illiquid structured products. These operations (or at least a significant part of them) were in effect the insurance policy of the bank, holding assets that could provide liquidity if funding was scarce; but they had become profit centres and had been given targets that could only be met by investing in higher-yielding structured products.

Accountability

For the approach of clarity in expectations, and direct link of breaches in expectations to pay (and other forms of reward such as promotions) to work, accountability for risk has to sit with those creating it. Ashby, Palermo and Power refer to cultural change being achieved through structural change, and this is one of the reasons. Some time ago a three lines of defence model was established in banking. The theory is that the first line takes the risk and carries out risk controls; the second line provides oversight of the risks and controls; and the third line carries out independent review. Unfortunately, the way it has been applied has largely relied on limits being set for the front office, and they see their accountability as meeting business targets while not breaching those limits. The difficulty is that the limits do not contain all the financial risks and none or very little of the non-financial risk – eg, customer conduct risk or bad behaviour such as Libor fixing and reputation damage from actions. To change this does require a fundamental rethinking of roles and responsibilities, and also attitudes. Boards should challenge themselves and senior management over who is held to account if there is a risk culture failing. Is it the head of compliance or risk (as is often the case), or is it the head of the business line?

The FSB has produced various requirements[24] that should start to rectify the position. They have made crystal clear that accountability for all risk (financial and non-financial) must sit with the front office that created it. Of course the risk function could also be responsible if they have failed to spot excessive risk build-up, or compliance could be held to account if rules have been breached, but the primary accountability would sit with the front office. This is a sea change for the industry because, although this front office accountability is notionally the case in many firms, the structures have not been in place to enable the front office to assess the risk and penalties for taking on excessive risk have not been made clear. Also without a clear risk appetite framework, establishing that risk was excessive (prior to large losses being made) was difficult.

Risk transparency

Risk transparency is an essential accompaniment and facilitator of a good risk culture; without it, the culture cannot be dynamic, reacting to excessive risk and dealing with it, holding individuals accountable and adjusting performance. There is both an internal and an external aspect of transparency – internally it enables management to react and keep risk within risk appetite, and external transparency enables external stakeholders to understand the risk culture and react appropriately. Montagnon (Chapter 6) makes clear that investors have expectations about both the quality of internal risk transparency to support good governance and also external disclosure.

Openness to information

A necessary part of risk transparency is that the organisation as a whole wants to see risks reported and uncovered, and actively encourages reporting of adverse news or discussion of dissenting opinions. The behavioural scientist Gilmore Crosby advocates a range of techniques to encourage the organisational openness necessary to ensure information does not stay underground, including fostering communication up and down the hierarchy and teams stopping periodically to assess whether they do have an open culture.[25] Sylvie Mathérat from the Banque de France in the chapter on "Risk Transparency and Risk Culture for Financial Institutions" argues for setting clear accountability for employees to ensure risk transparency, facilitated by mechanisms enabling staff to share information on risks.

Failure to have internal transparency as a priority will result in too little investment in core systems and processes, as Darren Smith and Andrew Cross make clear in the chapter "The Importance of Data and IT for a Strong Risk Culture". It will also result in too little acceptance of dissenting voices and concerns being raised. One of the depressing aspects of many cases of risk culture failure is that concerns had been raised within the organisation at an early stage, but had been ignored. Carol Sergeant in the chapter "The Role of Whistleblowing in risk Culture and Effective Governance" sets out a number of examples across many industries. Organisations need to ensure that performance frameworks encourage senior and middle management to listen to concerns from below but, as Sergeant makes clear, formal whistleblowing arrangements need to be put in place as a fall back and need to be carefully designed.

Smith and Cross look at how risk culture shapes demand for information within a bank, determining who asks for information and supply. They make the point that good IT and data require significant investment and risk has to compete for scarce resources with the front office. Here the support of the board behind investment in risk systems is important. But Smith and Cross also suggest that the risk function must engage with stakeholders across the business to increase awareness of the costs of not investing. They highlight the issues around risk data aggregation where manual processes slow down reporting. They set out the challenges posed by the multifaceted nature of risk and the breadth of risk types which all require data, measurement and reporting.

Exploring high-risk areas

Top management and boards must also be alert to signals that high risks are being run in particular parts of the organisation, or that there are potential risk culture breaches. In banking, a process of focusing on high-profit areas to assess if excessive risk or even unauthorised or fraudulent trading lie behind the apparent success has been known for a long time – right back to the Leeson trading that led to the failure of Barings. However, it was not a guiding light being followed in the run-up to the crisis or in many of the cases of widespread mis-selling of products. In hindsight, many of the high-profit areas were those that should have been subjected to more scrutiny. This is where pressure for higher profit at an organisation level may discourage looking too closely at "geese laying golden eggs".

Improved techniques for assessing risks

A theme that surfaces in a number of chapters in this book is that, in order for the processes supporting risk culture to work, there needs to be good management information enabling boards and senior management to see if risk appetite is being breached or excessive risks are building up in particular parts of the organisation. This does require the development of monitoring information that will really uncover issues. In banking, the years since the 1980s have seen huge strides in the measurement of traditional risk types (ie, credit and market) that, albeit not perfect, do enable changes in risk profile to be tracked. The lacuna is in the non-financial risk types (conduct, fraud, legal risk, IT risk, etc), where a myriad of different non-aggregatable metrics are used to consider if risks are rising.

In terms of aggregate measurement, these non-financial risk types have been swept up into an operational risk category that is based to a significant degree on analysis and modelling using past loss data (internal and external) supplemented by scenario analysis. However, it is not really grounded in the actual and changing risk profile of different areas – for example, conduct risks could be rising because business units are selling more complex products to less sophisticated investors. The operational risk approach does not therefore give senior management a gauge of whether risks are increasing because of the change in activities within the business. Different risk categories within it (conduct, legal, IT risk, fraud risk, etc) need to be broken out, and intrinsic risk in the actual business and strategy assessed. These non-financial risks then need to pursue the historic path that traditional risks such as credit followed – judgemental scoring according to the risk factors, followed later by more scientific measurement.

Some industries are well ahead of financial services in terms of scoring people risk. Young (chapter 8), for instance, examines the nuclear power industry, where poor behaviour could be catastrophic. Here, human reliability analysis has been developed to estimate the probability of human error.

Better approaches to assessing risk concentrations
One factor behind risk culture failures in the financial services industry has been a build-up of risk concentrations that have gone unidentified. This too requires better techniques to uncover the risk and more willingness to challenge business line beliefs that risks are implausible. Improved stress testing has an important role to play in this. Many models underperformed in the run up to the crisis because they could not contain all risks, and in the case of economic capital models too sanguine a view on correlations had been built into them – ie, that different events were unlikely to occur at the same time. Stress testing, taking a different and more disaggregated calculation approach to the effect of extreme scenarios, is an important counterbalance. Mathérat advocates greater use of internal stress testing in addition to internal models to strengthen risk analysis. However, this will require improvement of stress-testing methods to enable it to be used as a flexible management tool.

External transparency
All organisations need to consider how they can explain their risk culture and risk appetite to external stakeholders. Montagnon in Chapter 6 looks at the growing interest of shareholders in better understanding the risk profile of the organisations in which they invest, and in the effectiveness of risk governance. Boards need to consider carefully what information core shareholders are looking for and how best to provide it. This is not an area that has been a resounding success. Montagnon looks at a range of ways of improving risk reporting to make it more useful for investors. Mathérat also sets out the information requirements for external

stakeholders to enable them to react appropriately to signals about risk culture in Chapter 12. She points out that greater transparency can help to restore confidence when there are concerns about a firm. However, like Montagnon, she believes that improvements in risk information are needed, and argues that it would be useful for stakeholders to indicate in which areas they would find mandatory, harmonised disclosure helpful.

In narrower terms, improved transparency is also needed to reduce the likelihood of products being mis-sold. Part of ensuring a strong culture is ensuring that in the conduct arena customers are aware of what they are buying. In Chapter 8, Young looks at a range of cases being brought against banks in this area, while Mathérat makes a number of concrete suggestions regarding disclosure of information on structured products that have been bedevilled by legal cases.

CONCLUSION

There are a number of strong themes that emerge from the different chapters in the book. One is the wide range of elements that influence risk culture, and the resulting conclusion that programmes to change culture that are too narrowly focused are likely to be undermined. Changes in tone from the top and ethics will not alone be sufficient – they need to be accompanied by work on incentives, accountability, risk governance and risk transparency. Likewise, changes to risk governance will not alone be sufficient.

In terms of tone from the top and risk governance, a consistent strand across the chapters is the importance of a clear and embedded risk appetite for all organisations, whether financial or non-financial. Trade-offs have to be made to deal with cost or profit pressures, and without a clear stake in the ground, risk drift can occur, or strategic changes may be agreed that lead aggregate risk to reach unsustainable levels. This has been seen in industrial companies and public sector organisations, as well as banks.

Another consistent theme is that values need to be thought about as the setting of acceptable parameters for behaviour, and for the board this means being consistent in aligning its decisions with values and being willing to give the necessary priority and focus to risk. An accompanying part of this is ensuring accountability in the organisation, and alignment of goals and incentives.

Without knowledge of risks being taken, none of these elements work and therefore that too has to be a clear priority – from openness inside the organisation, and focus on ensuring that significant risks are identified and transmitted to senior levels, to clarity with external stakeholders. There is a huge push behind this from the regulators in the financial services sector, but all boards should be asking themselves whether they and their organisations have more to do.

1 FSB, (2014), "Guidance on Supervisory Interaction with Financial Institutions on Risk Culture".

2 Guttentag, Jack M.; Herring, Richard J. (1986), Disaster Myopia in International Banking.

3 Jackson, Patricia, (2013) 'Shadow banking and new lending channels – past and future' 50 years of money and finance: Lessons and challenges, Editors Balling and Gnan. (http://www.suerf.org/download/50ymf/50y_ch11.pdf).

4 European Commission (2013), 'Two years after Fukushima – nuclear safety in Europe' *http://europa.eu/rapid/press-release_MEMO-13–182_en.htm*

5 Department of Transport, (1997), 'Inquiry into the King's Cross Underground Fire' https://discovery.nationalarchives.gov.uk/SearchUI/details/C11190-inquiry-into-the-king-s-cross-underground-fire-details.

6 Executive Order 13543, (2010), National Commission on the BP Deepwater Horizon Oil, Spill and Offshore Drilling *http://www.eoearth.org/topics/view/51cbfc8df702fc2ba812cf49/*

7 Hopkins, A. (2009) Preface. In A. Hopkins (Ed). Learning from high reliability organizations (p xi). Sydney: CCH Australia.

8 Sumwalt, Robert, (2013) 'The Role of Organizational Culture, Safety Culture, and Safety Climate in Aviation and Aerospace Safety' http://www.ntsb.gov/doclib/speeches/sumwalt/Sumwalt_121007b.pdf

9 MarketWatch, (2007), 'HSBC's bailout puts pressure on Citi, 'superfund' http://www.marketwatch.com/news/story/hsbcs-35-bln-siv-bailout/story.aspx?guid=%7b6E72 947D-F516–405A-A4FF3BA0A679DD7A%7d&siteid=yahoomy&print=true&dist=printTop

10 Hatfield Derailment Investigation (2002), http://www.railwaysarchive.co.uk/documents/HSE_Hatf_IntRep003.pdf

11 Columbia Accident Investigation Board, Report (Washington, DC: NASA and GP0, August 2003), Chapter 8.

12 Thanks to the Introduction to Section V, in *Critical Issues in the History of Spaceflight*, edited by Stephen J. Dick and Roger D. Launius, NASA History Division, 2006.

13 Zohar, D. (2010). Thirty years of safety climate research: reflections and future directions. *Accident analysis and prevention*. 42(5), 1517–1522.

14 NTSB report of WMATA accident (2009) http://www.ntsb.gov/doclib/reports/2010/RAR1002.pdf

15 Sumwalt, Robert, (2013) 'The Role of Organizational Culture, Safety Culture, and Safety Climate in Aviation and Aerospace Safety' http://www.ntsb.gov/doclib/speeches/sumwalt/Sumwalt_121007b.pdf

16 FSA, (2013) Final Guidance: Risks to customers from financial incentives, http://www.fca.org.uk/static/fca/documents/finalised-guidance/fsa-fg13–01.pdf

17 FSB, (2013) 'Thematic Review on Risk Governance', http://www.financialstability board.org/publications/r_120404.pdf

18 FSB, (2013) Principles for an effective risk appetite framework, http://www.financialstabilityboard.org/publications/r_131118.pdf

19 Archbishop urges banks to seek "justice" to change culture, http://www.telegraph.co.uk/finance/newsbysector/banksandfinance/10543784/Archbishop-urges-banks-to-seek-justice-to-change-culture.html

20 The importance of the cultural change for Deutsche Bank, Interview found here; https://www.db.com/cr/en/concrete-The-importance-of-the-cultural-change-for-Deutsche-Bank.htm

21 Positive vs. negative enforcement: which promotes high reliability human performance, http://www.researchgate.net/publication/4303602_Positive_vs._negative_enforcement_which_promotes_high_reliability_human_performance

22 See Campbell, Alexander "Zero-loyalty environment' blamed for financial malpractice": http://www.risk.net/operational-risk-and-regulation/news/2308819/zero-loyalty-environment-blamed-for-financial-malpractice

23 The original rogue trader: interview with Nick Leeson, (2011), http://www.hrmagazine.co.uk/hr/features/1019561/likeable-gbp827-million-rogue-interview-nick-leeson

24 FSB, (2014) "Guidance on Supervisory Interaction with Financial Institutions on Risk Culture", and FSB, (2013), "Principles for an Effective Risk Appetite Framework".

25 Crosby, Gilmore, (2007), *Culture Can Be Built: Lessons from the PECO Nuclear Turnaround"* Joint 8th IEEE HFPP/13th HPRCT.

2

Risk Culture: Definitions, Change Practices and Challenges for Chief Risk Officers

Simon Ashby; Tommaso Palermo and Mike Power

Plymouth Business School; London School of Economics

There can be no doubting the rise in interest in the risk culture of financial organisations since the financial crisis. Successive reports on the problems experienced at many organisations have identified defects in culture that permitted excessive and uncontrolled risk-taking.[1] In the US, an investigation into the so-called London Whale trade concluded that:

> In contrast to JP Morgan Chase's reputation for best-in-class risk management, the Whale trade exposed a bank culture in which risk limit breaches were routinely disregarded.[2]

Regulators in the UK are focusing increasingly on risk culture and, together with an industry of advisers, are searching for smart ways to define, operationalise, manage and supervise "good" risk culture.[3] In short, the financial industry is undergoing something of a "cultural revolution".[4]

However, we should remind ourselves that these preoccupations with culture are by no means new[5] or confined to the financial services industry.[6] Indeed, issues around culture are often invoked in the aftermath of failure and disaster when explanations based on technological or individual error are regarded as inadequate. Analysis of the *Challenger* launch decision in 1985 suggested that the explanation of the disaster was not to be found in the immediate cause of failing "O-rings" at low temperatures, but in the managerial culture of NASA itself and its engineering-based commitment to "flying with flaws".[7] This was famously described as a case of "normalised deviance", a concept that also characterised financial services prior to the crisis. In the UK, the 1988 Piper Alpha disaster, when 167 workers died on an oil rig platform, led to wide-ranging changes in the offshore industry and a heightened focus on something called "safety culture".[8]

Indeed, most of the precedents for thinking about risk culture in financial organisations can be found in developments in safety culture thinking in the offshore industries, which took yet another turn following the Gulf of Mexico oil spill.[9] While the BP/Deepwater Horizon case is distinctive, there are striking parallels between investigations of this event and the reports produced following the Barclays Libor scandal (Salz, 2013) and the London Whale case noted above. These parallels extend to the field of health care: the Francis Report (2013) into the problems of the Mid Staffordshire National Health Service Trust in the UK attributed many of them to a pathological culture characterised by a climate of fear and an excessive concern with targets at the expense of patients.

Against this background, this chapter explores some of the results and implications of our research into risk culture in financial organisations during 2012–13 (see Power et al., 2013). First, we discuss some of the challenges involved in defining risk culture as an object for managerial and regulatory attention, not least the confusion about the difference between culture and risk culture. Second, we review some of the practices adopted by financial organisations in order to think about their risk cultures more effectively: the key message here is that there is considerable variety. Third, we examine our findings about the role and authority of the chief risk officer (CRO) and the risk function in a "three lines of defence" (TLD) structure. Clearly, risk culture is a front-line business issue regarding the extent to which the right behaviours are embedded, but our research focused for various practical reasons on the cultural position of the CRO in relation to the front line. We suggest that this can be regarded as an indirect indicator of the quality of risk culture for the business as a whole.

WHAT IS RISK CULTURE?

Many definitions of risk culture exist. We provide a selection of these definitions in Table 2.1, but there are many others. In our research, we wanted to avoid defining risk culture prematurely, preferring to listen to how organisations were dealing with the concept. However, at some point the need for definition and clarity becomes important.

Table 2.1 Selected definitions of risk culture

	Selected definitions	Source
	While various of definitions of culture exist, supervisors are focusing on the institution's norms, attitudes and behaviours related to risk awareness, risk taking and risk management.	FSB (2014)
Practice literature	...the norms of behaviour for individuals and groups within an organisation that determine the collective ability to identify and understand, openly discuss and act on the organisations current and future risk ... A financial institution's risk culture plays an important role in influencing the actions and decisions taken by individuals within the institution and in shaping the institution's attitude toward its stakeholders, including its supervisors.	FSB (2013)
	...the general awareness, attitude and behaviour of its employees and appointed representatives to risk and the management of risk within the organisation.	FSA (2006)
	...the norms and traditions of behaviour of individuals and of groups within an organisation that determine the way in which they identify, understand, discuss, and act on the risks the organisation confronts and the risks it takes.	IIF (2009)
	...the values, beliefs, knowledge and understanding about risk shared by a group of people with a common purpose, in particular the employees of an organisation or of teams or groups within an organisation.	IRM (2012)
	...the system of values and behaviours present throughout an organisation that shape risk decisions. Risk culture influences the decisions of management and employees, even if they are not consciously weighing risks and benefits.	KPMG (2010)
	...the norms of behaviour for individuals and groups within an organisation that determine the collective ability to identify, understand, openly discuss, and act on the organisation's current and future risks. It is the last line of defence in grave situations.	McKinsey (Levy et al., 2010)
	...organisational behaviours and processes that enable the identification, assessment and management of risks relative to objectives ranging from compliance to operational, financial and strategic.	PWC (2012)
	...the norms and traditions of behaviour of individuals and groups within an organisation that determine the way in which they identify, understand, discuss and act on the risks the organisation confronts and takes.	Towers Watson (2011)
Academic literature	The organisation's propensity to take risks as perceived by the managers in the organisation.	Bozeman and Kingsley (1998)
	A risk culture is based on particular beliefs and assumptions. These can be clustered according to specific cultural tenets, namely risk, integrity, governance and leadership, decision-making, empowerment, teamwork, responsibility and adaptability ... These tools are expressed in everyday workplace practices via attitudes and behaviours and, when they are expressed by leaders, they serve as powerful (human) culture embedding mechanisms.	O'Donovan (2011)

Each of these definitions are different on the surface but, with the exception of IRM (2012), refer to the behaviour of individuals within an organisation in relation to risk taking and control, and the effectiveness of risk management processes. Ethics and values are also prominent (see Welby, 2013). Most of the practice-orientated documents that we reviewed make more or less explicit references to academic work on organisational culture – a topic that has been popular particularly in management and organisational studies since the 1980s. Specifically, the following much-cited definition of organisational culture is often used in practitioner documents to frame the concept of risk culture:

> ... a pattern of shared basic assumptions learned by a group as it solved its problems of external adaptation and internal integration, which has worked well enough to be considered valid and, therefore, taught to new members as the correct way to perceive, think and feel in relation to those problems.[10]

This idea of culture raises an important question about the relationship between culture and risk culture. Are they different things, the same thing or what is the point of overlap? It has to be admitted that, despite the considerable interest in risk culture and the definitions offered above, the concept is a fuzzy one and is inherently difficult to pin down. Indeed, we have argued that it is a "symptomising" concept, meaning that it is a provisional label for things we do not fully understand yet represents a recognition that the root cause of the financial crisis was more a failure of values and behaviour than of technology or process.

We maintain that culture and risk culture are not two separate things, but rather aspects of one another. Accordingly, the focus on "risk culture" is a way of framing, and directing attention to, organisational culture issues from a risk point of view. This perspective places the quality of decision-making about risk taking and avoidance at its very centre. Another conclusion from our research is that risk culture understood in this way is heterogeneous and not amenable to standardisation. Not only do organisations have different subcultures, but we found evidence of a financial services risk culture that is trans-organisational. Therefore, in thinking about risk culture we should be careful to remember that the cultural unit of analysis is not necessarily the organisation as an entity.

Drawing on previous work on safety culture (Reason, 1997), we decided to approach "risk culture" as a range (or several ranges) within which different qualities might vary. This multi-dimensional "bandwidth" model of risk culture suggests that there is no ideal optimal risk culture, and is based on a fundamental trade-off between risk control and risk-taking activities. This overarching trade-off is the basis of our simple visual conceptual model of risk culture shown in Figure 2.1. In a similar way to the tension between production and protection (as highlighted in the safety literature, see Reason, 1997), the basic idea of our conceptualisation is that too much control or too little control can lead to mediocrity or lost opportunity (risk of bankruptcy) and catastrophe or value destruction (risk of catastrophe), respectively. However, any specific trade-off is a matter of organisational choice. This is a bandwidth model of risk culture, meaning the norms and habits that populate the operational space between organisationally specified levels of control and risk-taking.

Reckless organisations are not necessarily high risk-taking organisations as such. They are those that violate their own authorised bandwidth limits and norms. In a similar vein, precautionary organisations may in fact operate beyond their authorised control propensity (ie, high levels of control – potentially leading to the "gold-plating" of the required level of control – may hinder the achievement of business objectives. This is the so-called "bureaucracy problem"). While the risk culture debate is primarily motivated by the spectre of reckless risk-taking, the bandwidth model is more neutral and symmetrical since it applies equally to the organisational violation of risk-taking and control norms and boundaries.

Figure 2.1 shows two organisations, A and B, which have different bandwidth profiles and different sub-units driving that profile. Organisation B is more internally complex and heterogeneous with a unit that is pushing the limits of the targeted profile. The model suggests that specific areas and hot spots may drive a business outside its prescribed "safe" zone (eg, unit B is leading organisation B beyond its target bandwidth). It also tries to capture directionality (through the use of the arrows), suggesting that a given position is never fixed but subject to continuous pressures for change, potentially leading an organisation (or any of its organisational sub-units)

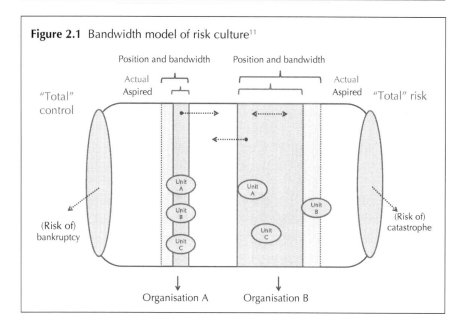

Figure 2.1 Bandwidth model of risk culture[11]

to get closer or more distant to an initial risk-taking and controlling benchmark (within or outside the initial desired/actual bandwidth).

The bandwidth profile will be highly contingent on organisational features such as strategy, and will involve many different trade-offs within the master trade-off between risk and control. We think this is a useful way to visualise risk culture, at least initially, because it avoids getting lured into pre-judgements about whether a particular risk culture is good or bad. We wanted to understand risk culture as the outcome or manifestation of a series of trade-offs before passing judgement on them. This neutral stance was quite challenging to maintain since we encountered many strong views about what good and bad look like, and about the necessity of fixing the bad bits.

Normatively, we argue that it is important for leaders in firms to understand their trade-off space and how trade-offs are made. Deviant risk cultures can be defined as those that allow trade-offs to "drift", leading for example to excessive (outside bandwidth) risk taking (in terms of Figure 2.1, does organisation B know that its unit B is outside targeted bandwidth? Does it have clarity about the limit itself?). The bandwidth model has obvious affinities with the concept of risk appetite, and just as there are different currencies of risk appetite (trading limits, capital and target credit rating, ethical boundaries, strategic choices about markets to be in or out of, etc) so too is this bandwidth defined by a number of different trade-offs, as we found in our study. We discuss some of these further below in the context of CROs and risk culture.

Finally, one of the most interesting issues in defining risk culture is how different definitions and emphases are more or less aligned with specific change programmes in organisations. For example, if the ethical dimension of culture is emphasised in an organisation (eg, Salz, 2013), changes are likely to take a specific path in response to that, such as workshops, restatement of mission, etc. If the cultural problem is defined predominantly in terms of wrong incentives, then cultural change will be envisaged in terms of new forms of performance management (FSA, 2012; Wheatley, 2012). Of course, both kinds of change often occur at the same time; they are not necessarily polar opposites. However, the point is that risk culture is something that firms and regulators diagnose, define and seek to manage and reform in different ways, as we discuss in the next section.

CHANGING RISK CULTURE: INDUSTRY INITIATIVES

This section builds on the last point above and provides an overview of the different management approaches to changing culture that we observed in our research. What is striking in all this is the sheer variety of initiatives in play, not all of which look at first sight as if they have anything to do directly with culture or risk culture. For example, we were struck by the amount of "structural change" in financial organisations in the period 2010–12, specifically to create new central risk units with a mandate to draw together (aggregate) different information sets, perform root cause analysis of losses and incidents and, within this, to find the cultural drivers of errors. We were surprised to learn that risk functions, and even more importantly their data feeds, were often fragmented in the period prior to the financial crisis, but that all our participant organisations – a mix of insurers and banks – were engaged, to varying degrees, in strengthening the central risk function capacity in many ways. One bank went so far as to create a second CRO with oversight responsibilities, including reporting to the board. However, the changes were not only structural. They had much to do with the personal authority and capability of the incumbents as potential "cultural carriers" or ambassadors of the organisation at the grass roots level, as well as being able to operate with boards and executive committees. The role of these individuals in brokering key relationships within the organisation was more important than their formal job description.

At the more formal level, many organisations explored their risk cultures by using some kind of survey instrument (eg, Farrell and Hoon, 2009), a practice with a considerable history (Ashkanzy *et al.*, 2000). In some cases, the annual employee survey was adapted to include key questions about attitudes to risk and control, such as how easy it is to raise concerns about risk within the organisation; in others, specialist culture surveys were used with the help of advisers (eg, Deloitte, 2012; PWC, 2012). In all these cases, the aim was to produce a snapshot "score" of risk culture against different dimensions, the factor categories in Table 2.2, which can be compared to some kind of benchmark. The resulting "gap" between actual and the benchmark or ideal provides the motivation for change.[12]

In our research, we documented a wide variety of such survey instruments (see Power *et al.*, 2013, Appendix C), but we know that they are constantly evolving. At the time of our research in 2012–13, the different approaches seemed to emphasise different key factors in thinking about risk management (see Table 2.2), although we would expect some convergence over time. One example of the evolution of the approaches can be seen in the difference between the EY model presented by Stephen Gregory in Chapter 12 of this book and the 2012 version used in our comparison. The newer areas of focus are aspects of risk transparency, accountability and risk governance.

What we see in this snapshot of the different approaches is a common attempt to reduce risk culture to a few attributes that can be measured and tracked in some way. We have no doubt that all the advisers recognise the complexity and richness of cultural issues in organisations, but without some kind of reduction of this complexity it is very hard to create something that is actionable. In addition, we admit that the perfect can be the enemy of the good. In place of a comprehensive account of all aspects of an organisation's risk culture, it is more practical to focus on a small number of drivers of perceived good practice. In this respect, there are many parallels between approaches to risk culture and philosophies of total quality

Table 2.2 Summary of risk culture model factors by organisation

Factor categories	Deloitte	Ernst & Young	IRM*	KPMG	McKinsey	PWC	Towers Watson
Acknowledgement of risk (potential for over confidence, level of challenge)					✓		
Communication (regular risk reporting and escalation of risk issues)		✓	✓		✓	✓	✓
Compensation and performance management (incentives)	✓	✓	✓			✓	
IT systems							✓
Leadership ("tone from the top")		✓	✓	✓		✓	✓
Relationships (between employees)	✓						
Respect for risk (potential for gaming the system)					✓		
Responsiveness to risk (ability to react to risk issues)					✓		
Risk competencies (of employees)	✓		✓			✓	
Risk facilitation (status of risk function and ability to support business)			✓	✓			
Risk management processes and procedures						✓	✓
Risk ownership (clear accountabilities)			✓	✓		✓	
Structure of organisation and governance	✓	✓	✓				✓

* The IRM's 4 categories of "tone at the top", "decisions", "governance" and "competency" are quite broad and cover more than four of the factors listed here; the same is also the case for PWC and Towers Watson.

management and continuous improvement. Many enablers of good practice are similar (eg, leadership commitment). There are also overlaps with corporate governance advice more generally in terms of an open culture and effective escalation where employees feel able to raise concerns, and a commitment to the enforcement of breaches of whatever kind. Common examples of good risk management therefore tend to have a strong governance flavour, such as the clear and consistent communication of an organisation's values and ethical code of conduct by senior management, together with incentives to "do the right thing" and greater attention to recruiting the staff who are compatible with the prevailing culture (Salz, 2013).

All these initiatives, which are different yet overlap, present financial regulators with a challenge. While a good risk culture may be demanded, and there is agreement at a general level about some of the things that this implies, detailed execution is difficult to operationalize, and the evidence base at the grass-roots level is likely to be idiosyncratic and partly visible. Risk culture is not amenable necessarily to management and oversight by standardised templates or a limited range of metrics that serve as risk culture proxies, and it is for this reason that the Financial Conduct Authority (FCA) in the UK has articulated what it calls a "joining the dots" approach to risk culture templates:

> Our approach today is to draw conclusions about culture from what we observe about a firm – in other words, joining the dots rather than assessing culture directly. This can be through a range of different measures such as how a firm responds to, and deals with, regulatory issues; what customers are actually experiencing when they buy a product or service from front-line staff; how a firm runs its product approval process and the considerations around these; the manner in which decisions are made or escalated; the behaviour of that firm on certain markets; and even the remuneration structures.[13]

In essence, the "joining the dots" approach is a kind of meta-analysis of existing data and findings, a reflection on what they mean and the triangulation of different sources. It would mean standing back from existing key risk indicators and compliance data, and relating them to a wider range of observations in the course of supervision. For example, it would mean looking at practices, such as stress testing, through a cultural lens. Technically, a stress test might seem very well executed with the right expertise, but culturally it may be disconnected from senior executive thinking and ownership or be an exercise to please the regulator only. What difference does stress testing make to the business? A regulator may be content that the organisation is well capitalised, but the nature of the engagement with the stress-testing process may tell them something important about the culture; revealed attitudes to stress testing may reflect attitudes to risk management more generally.

From this small example, it is clear that "joining the dots" may not be an easy thing, and would require a different kind of supervisory capacity and sensitivity (to help detect the "hidden" clues about risk culture). For example, we have recommended to UK supervisors that such an approach might require a disciplined approach to the gathering of field notes during the supervision process, drawing on ethnographic skills. In our own activity as researchers, we reflected on how we were received and treated in the 14 different organisations where we were able to conduct interviews (whether we were offered refreshments, whether we were allowed to record interviews, the level of "small talk", etc). These and other dimensions of the way organisations are open to, and engage with, outsiders are potential indicators of their internal culture.

There are no definitive answers to the risk culture question in a "joining the dots" approach, only more questions and more points of enquiry for regulators and more necessity for conversations. This will frustrate practitioners and regulators looking for clarity and points of intervention with strong organisational and behavioural leverage. Indeed, our work runs somewhat counter to the interest in behavioural economics seen in the financial sector. It suggests that risk culture is more likely understood as a form of "continuing conversation", both inside organisations and between organisations and their regulators. The remainder of this section highlights some of the elements we discovered that can influence the nature and topics of these conversations.

Risk appetite and risk culture

This "conversation" concept of risk culture applies very directly to the way risk appetite operates within organisations.[14] Indeed, we think of risk culture and risk appetite as two sides of the same coin; risk appetite is in many respects the material manifestation of the risk culture. In our research, we detected some differences in the way organisations operationalised risk appetite. On the one hand, there were those we called the "sandbox guardians" (a term heard during our investigations). From this point of view, the culture of limits is very strong coupled to considerable freedom to operate within them. On the other, we encountered so-called "gold platers" (again a term heard often), suggesting that risk appetite policies and procedures were framed as a form of compliance practice. The differences between these two examples may be subtle, but they show that the way risk appetite is made real in organisations says a great deal about culture and, indeed, attitude to risk. In the former case, risk appetite operates to encourage risk taking within limits; in the latter, it has a more precautionary flavour in which, at the extreme, compliance becomes an end in itself and is "gold-plated". The acid test is how risk appetite evolves and changes, and who is involved in this change process. Does the risk appetite policy simply drift along behind the business or does it lead, and does the risk function play a part in this? We think that the mark of a good risk culture is that there is a discipline for triggering conversations around such changes. The following excerpt taken from our discussion with a senior risk manager provides a practical example of how organisations can have ongoing conversations around risk appetite constraints:

> If you look at the housing market at the moment, there's clearly a greater demand for buy-to-let mortgages than you might have expected because less people are able to afford deposits, more people are renting so there's more demand for buy to let. Therefore, given that change in the marketplace it's right to look at your risk appetite where you'd severely constrained your buy-to-let within your overall mortgage portfolio. So it's right to have that debate to look at the risks and decide okay can we move our risk appetite to allow more buy-to-let given the changes that have taken place out there? You lay down some constraints, you lay down some criteria. You have a sensible discussion and you reach an agreement that allows the business to grow and accommodate some of that demand for buy-to-let while still maintaining the overall risk appetite for the group.

Risk appetite policies live and breathe in an organisation via risk indicators that can determine for a specific risk whether the likelihood of crystallisation is changing in terms of exceeding predefined limits. Therefore, an important feature of risk culture and the conversations about it is the extent to which such indicators are designed, owned and actioned by businesses themselves, rather than existing purely for the oversight function. There can be considerable organisational politics involved in aligning risk indicators and performance metrics at the business level. One need only recall various banks' efforts to exert divisional control via risk-adjusted rates of return in the 1990s to be persuaded of this (Power, 2005). New indicators or metrics can be initially disruptive, and risk functions have to learn to cut with the grain of business operations.

Appetite for knowledge about risk

During investigations at an airline for comparative purposes, we were struck by the scale and complexity of their safety management reporting system. The airline had a considerable appetite to know about safety-relevant issues and events in minute detail, and had created a reporting culture for staff in which any small fact could be considered important. This example, although perhaps an extreme case, shows that there is a further dimension to the conversations that financial organisations have about risk appetite and risk culture, namely their appetite for knowledge about risk. For organisations who are serious about knowing and tracking their risk culture, they will need to decide on the extent to which they can do this using existing performance and risk metrics to "join the dots" as described above, or whether new ones with new and incrementally costly data requirements need to be created. A "big data" management system of the kind used by airlines may not be appropriate, but nevertheless organisations will need to make decisions about how much they invest in acquiring knowledge about employee behaviour, and the extent to which such monitoring is even desirable. Furthermore, relevant data may exist in parts of the organisation not conventionally associated with risk management.

Human-resource management and risk culture

Conversations about risk culture involve a range of actors and may link functions that have not had close relationships in the past. Notably, during the research we observed that human resource functions and risk functions were working increasingly in cooperation, and that advisors were creating hybrid teams of risk and human resources (HR) specialists. This increasing alignment of HR with risk is interesting in the light of earlier criticisms of its role. For example, the Salz review reported that:

The HR function was accorded insufficient status to stand up to the business units on a variety of people issues, including pay. This undermined any efforts to promote correlation of pay to broader behaviours than those driving individual financial performance. This mattered, because pay was seen as the primary tool to shape behaviour.[15]

A major dimension of organisational culture concerns the processes for admitting new organisational members, their vetting, selection and induction. These processes come under considerable pressure at times of growth and expansion, but may not be sufficiently visible to senior executives. One of our interviewees gave a practical example related to acquisition strategies. The argument was that acquisition strategies can give rise to problems of "cultural digestion". A quick way to expand in new businesses is to acquire entire teams, but then it is hard to know what you are bringing in (ie, a potentially destructive risk subculture). New people may bring new clients with them, which is positive, but their motivations are also important. Often people are hired on a probation period to find as many clients as possible in one year – which could promote a short-termist attitude and reckless risk taking. This suggests that an important aspect of risk culture, and one of the so-called "moments that matter" is the point at which new entrants join an organisation and how and whether organisations really understand what this does to the risk profile of the organisation.

Overall, in this section we have given some flavour of the variety of conversations and approaches to risk culture that are in play in different financial services organisations. We show how risk culture change programmes are related to a variety of processes, roles and instruments, such as structural changes, staff surveys, risk appetite policies, selection and induction processes. We make no judgement about which of these is somehow superior – the variety is to a large extent contingent on specific organisational histories and characteristics. For example, the banks and insurers in our sample were clearly very different in many respects, but there was also variety within the set of banks and within the set of insurers. Nevertheless, there is one general challenge that all these organisations face, namely the necessity of reducing risk culture to observable and manageable properties of some kind. This involves shaping risk culture as a management object in very distinctive ways and changing organisational realities (Dent, 1991). More crucially, it may even mean changing risk culture via the process of measuring it, in both intended and unintended ways. It is for this reason that our research concludes with a degree of measurement scepticism regarding risk culture. Or, rather, we think that in addition to metrics and changes in performance recognition systems is a need for cultural transmission of values via new organisational narratives about values and risk embedded in everyday operational conversations. This is not something that can be easily engineered, and requires concerted leadership and internal network building. An important figure in that leadership is the CRO, as will be discussed in the next section.

THE CRO AND THE ORGANISATIONAL FOOTPRINT OF THE RISK FUNCTION

We decided at an early point in the research process that the organisational footprint of the risk function was central to understanding risk culture. Therefore, we used CROs and risk functions as our first point of access to financial organisations. We recognise the limitations of such approach, as without doubt real action within risk culture and risk management also takes place in the business units themselves, and this is an area for future investigation. However, we considered CROs to be a valuable starting point to investigate such a complex phenomenon as risk culture. The reason is that the position of the risk function that CROs lead in a financial organisation – and their status and authority – can be considered to be a strong indicator of the quality of risk culture, particularly in relation to the number and quality of the touch points between risk, other parts of an organisation and external stakeholders (eg, chief executive officers (CEOs), line managers, staff functions such as internal audit and HR, regulators and consultants). The status of the risk function has been explored in other academic studies. Kashyap (2010) suggests that the ratio of CRO to CEO pay is a proxy measure of status of the CRO, and also can be related to the amount of risk taken. Similarly, Ellul and Yerramilli (2013) construct a risk management index from seven proxies for the "strength" and independence of the risk management function and find that, across a large sample of banks, holdings of risky assets were higher for banks with lower-status CROs. Our own approach to the status of the CRO is somewhat different from these studies, focusing on the many delicate balances and permanent tensions involved in the role.[16]

CROs must manage a number of dilemmas or trade-offs on a daily basis (Walker, 2009). The CRO and the risk function have become understood to be part of the second line of defence, in a position of oversight and advice. However, the reality is that the CRO is also a lightning rod for blame, and may often find themself in governance committees forced to speak on behalf of a first-line business function that should be speaking for itself.

In our research, these dilemmas and tensions were also manifest. As one CRO commented:

> The second line, it's very difficult to necessarily define exactly what that role should be. So what am I? Am I the policeman, am I the friend, am I a critique? And it's ... and because the second line has tentacles all over the business and has a good understanding of what's going on, it's a very, very difficult role to actually describe to say well I'm your friend but actually I'm going to do other things to you if you don't do X, Y and Z. And how do you do that is difficult. And I imagine most risk functions are in that sort of middle ground where they're trying to ... they've got to work with the audit, the independent and they've got to work with the business and it's facilitating and understanding what's going on.

Balancing the role of police versus friend can create significant challenges, which were well understood by the CROs and other senior risk professionals that we interviewed. On the one hand, a police-type approach can preserve the independence of the CRO/risk function and facilitate robust challenge. On the other, it can drive a wedge between risk and the business, hindering the development of trust that can come from a more flexible approach. In reality, none of these individuals were comfortable with either extreme, although we still observed differences in approach.

How exactly this "middle ground" between police and friend works, and the stability of the *modus operandi* of the CRO, is a strong indicator of risk culture. We encountered two different "voices" of the CRO that suggest how difficult it is to operationalise the role. On the one hand, we came across what we described as "partnership builders" who aimed in a very pragmatic fashion to increase the level of contact between risk staff and key business line actors, while not being excessive and wasting their time. This increased level of contact would include both relationship building and formal representation on key decision-making and governance committees. In turn, such a partnership-building strategy gives the CRO a feel for the risk culture in the wider organisation, enabling a "joining of dots" between different pieces of operational data and their own points of contact.

In contrast to "partnership builders", we identified a second CRO style in the form of "partnering overseers" whose aim is less to move closer to business functions and more to move business functions closer to risk, and to have an overview of risk capability in the organisation as a whole. This places the CRO in an educational space, and we encountered a number of formal development programmes in both insurers and banks that sought to train people and thereby expand the experience of risk ownership in the organisation. In one bank, the experience of risk training had been to reinforce silos and this was something the CRO wanted to change. Within insurers, such initiatives tended to be necessarily absorbed into Solvency II development programmes.

These two approaches to partnering the business are not polar opposites and reflect degrees of emphasis in the work of CROs. This was closely paralleled by another contrast between risk actors who engaged extensively in intra-organisational networking and those who relied more on formal metrics for oversight purposes. We encountered what we called "touch point enthusiasts" who actively built interactive networks involving key actors in the business and other support functions, such as HR (as noted in the previous section). Prior work on safety cultures emphasised the significance of interaction for risk management, especially in stressed or crisis environments. It is well known that communication among key actors must increase in crises, so the existence of pre-existing networks cutting across the lines of defence would be an indicator of a healthy risk culture.

However, interaction may not be valuable *per se* and trade-offs are at stake. Two specific examples can be made. First, interviews in several organisations suggested that healthy interaction is not one-sided. Interaction should not be instigated only by the risk function, but business units should also be able and willing to contact the risk function for help and advice. From this we concluded that it is important to understand and keep track of who instigates the interaction. A provocative indicator of risk culture might be the number of times that the first-line business function seeks advice from the CRO and their colleagues. Second, in one insurer that valued underwriter/risk function interaction, it was argued that interaction was not intrinsically valuable. Too much interaction may result from a culture that is over-consultative and too democratic. In enquiring further, we learned that the democratic model had its roots in a fear of individual responsibility for decision-making because of an event in the recent history of the company.

The status and interactive style of CROs and the risk function is clearly related to the scope and nature of their work. The creation of the new risk oversight units noted earlier suggests that risk experts had been too narrowly and technically focused prior to the crisis. Indeed, surveys from organisations such as Ernst and Young (2013) reveal that, prior to and sometimes even post-crisis, CROs and their risk functions can find it difficult to find a voice in more strategic-level decision-making, such as for mergers and acquisitions or new product development. This is despite a widespread consensus that CROs and their risk functions should be so involved in strategic decisions (IIF, 2008). Our own survey work[17] highlighted similar issues although, contrary to the recommendations of the IIF, we found that the TLD approach, and the "second-line" positioning of the risk function, may be an impediment to the development of a more strategic role and to higher organisational status. In the course of our interviews, we were told that restricting the CRO/risk function to this kind of oversight role may reinforce the perception that they are compliance functions. It was also shown that segregation from the business can prevent "real-time" challenges and bar risk professionals from active involvement in first-line committees.

All this means that there is no easy solution to the role complexity of CROs. Indeed, an indirect indicator of risk culture might be the extent to which other executives, such as the CEO, understand and appreciate this role complexity, and seek to work with it and make it easier for the CRO. A significant finding is that the mixed roles of the CRO, and their strategic aspirations, sit uneasily with the regulatory preference for TLD clarity, although there also is evidence of some scepticism among regulators about TLD as a "structural risk culture fix". Our research suggests that effective CROs and their teams operate in the fuzzy territory between the first and second lines of defence.

CONCLUSION

This chapter has sought to do three things based on research conducted by the authors. First, we have discussed the very idea of risk culture, reminding readers that it is neither new nor confined to financial services. Second, we have explored some of the variety of approaches to understanding and changing risk culture that are in play in the marketplace. These different approaches suggest that standardisation in the area of risk culture, even if it were desirable, is a long way off. Finally, we focused on the role of the CRO as a transmitter of risk culture and some of the issues that risk functions face as they navigate TLD structures.

We suggest, in conclusion, that much can be learned by banks and insurers from other industries, such as airlines, and from the challenges of the "safety culture" movement of the 1980s. Our research also suggests that risk culture may be strongly associated with increased precaution and risk aversion in industry, and that the interest in risk culture may be cyclical. Time will tell on this point, but the lingering challenge for regulators and financial organisations is to operationalise risk culture in an "all-weather" fashion. Our research in a number of financial organisations has convinced us that the quality of risk culture should not be inferred from the level of risk taking as such, although when things go wrong this is how the media and others will judge it in hindsight. Rather, we think it is something fundamentally to do with the self-transparency of risk taking and control investments within an organisation. In short, we think that risk culture is fundamentally about organisational self-knowledge.

1 See Treasury Select Committee (2009a; 2009b); Group of 30 (2012); Parliamentary Committee on Banking Standards (2013a; 2013b).
2 Permanent Subcommittee on Investigations, US Senate, March 2013.
3 See Sants (2010a; 2010b); Adamson (2013); Ashby (2011).
4 DeJonghe et al. (2013).
5 Bozeman and Kingsley (1998).
6 Atkins et al. (2012).
7 Vaughan (1995).
8 For example, Reason (1997).
9 Hopkins (2009); National Commission on the Deepwater Horizon Oil Spill and Offshore Drilling (2011).
10 Schein (2010), p 18.
11 From Power et al. (2013), p 24.
12 A debate on the viability of effective culture measurement using quantifiable metrics has long been underway in the academic literature on safety culture (see, for example, Haukelid, 2008).

13 Adamson (2013); in contrast, international regulators (FSB, 2013b) appear to be taking a more prescriptive and metric-driven approach.
14 Anderson (2011); Ashby and Diacon (2012); FSB (2013a).
15 Salz (2013), p 9.
16 Power (2007); Mikes *et al.* (2013).
17 See Ashby, Palermo and Power (2013).

REFERENCES

Adamson, C., 2013, "The Importance of Culture in Driving Behaviours of Firms and How the FCA will Assess This", Financial Conduct Authority Speech at the CFA Society, April (available at http://www.fca.org.uk/news/regulation-professionalism).

Anderson, R., 2011, "Risk Appetite and Tolerance", Institute of Risk Management, London.

Ashby, S., 2011, "Picking up the Pieces: Risk Management in a Post Crisis World", Financial Services Knowledge Transfer Network, London.

Ashby, S. and S. Diacon, 2012, "Understanding Enterprise Risk Appetite", Insurance ERM, August 3.

Ashby, S., T. Palermo and M. Power, 2013, "Supporting Strategic Objectives or Another Compliance Exercise? Understanding Corporate Risk Culture in Insurance", CII Thinkpiece No. 95, May, pp 1–5.

Ashkanasy, N. M., L. E. Broadfoot and S. Falkus, 2000, "Questionnaire Measures of Organisational Culture", in N. Ashkanasy, C. Wilderom and M. F. Peterson, 2000, *Handbook of Organisational Culture and Climate* (Thousand Oaks, CA: Sage Publications), pp 131–46.

Atkins, D., A. Fitzsimmons, C. Parsons and A. Punter, 2012, "Roads to Ruin: A Study of Major Risk Events: Their Origins, Impact and Implications", AIRMIC, London.

Bozeman, B. and G. Kingsley, 1998, "Risk Culture in Public and Private Organisations", *Public Administration Review*, 58(2), pp 109–18.

Davidson, O., P. MacKenzie, M. Wilkinson and R. Asselin-Miller, 2012, "The Need to Build a Strong Risk Culture is Growing: Effective Diagnostics Support a Positive Culture", Towers Watson, UK.

DeJonghe, F., M. Edelsten and I. Xavier, 2013, "The Cultural Revolution in Risk Management", *Journal of Financial Perspectives*, 1(1), pp 1–9.

Deloitte Touche Tohmatsu, 2012, "Cultivating a Risk Intelligent Culture: Understand, Measure, Strengthen and Report", London.

Dent, J. F., 1991, "Accounting and Organisational Cultures: A Field Study of the Emergence of a New Organisational Reality", *Accounting, Organisations and Society*, 16(8), pp 705–32.

Ellul, A. and V. Yerramilli, 2013, "Stronger Risk Controls, Lower Risk: Evidence from U.S. Bank Holding Companies", *The Journal of Finance*, 68(5), pp 1,757–803.

Ernst and Young, 2013, "Remaking Financial Services: Risk Management Five Years After the Crisis", New York.

Farrell, J. and A. Hoon, 2009, "What is Your Company's Risk Culture?", Directorship.com (available at http://www.kpmg.com/MT/en/IssuesAndInsights/ArticlesPublications/Documents/Risk-culture.pdf).

Francis Report, 2013, "Report on the Mid Staffordshire NHS Foundation Trust: Public Enquiry", The Stationary Office, London.

FSA, 2012, "Guidance Consultation: Risks to Customers from Financial Incentives" (available at http://www.fsa.gov.uk/static/pubs/guidance/gc12–11.pdf).

FSB, 2013a, "Principles for an Effective Risk Appetite Framework", Bank for International Settlements, Basel, Switzerland.

FSB, 2013b, "Guidance on Supervisory Interaction with Financial Institutions on Risk Culture", Bank for International Settlements, Basel, Switzerland.

FSB, 2014, "Guidance on Supervisory Interaction with Financial Institutions on Risk Culture: A Framework for Assessing Risk Culture", Bank for International Settlements, Basel, Switzerland.

Group of 30, 2012, "Toward Effective Governance of Financial Institutions", Washington DC.

Haukelid, K., 2008, "Theories of Safety Culture Revisited: An Anthropological Approach", *Safety Science*, 46(3), pp 413–26.

Hopkins, A., 2009, *Failure to Learn: The BP Texas City Refinery Disaster* (Sydney: CCH Australia).

IIF, 2008, "Final Report of the IIF Committee on Market Best Practices: Principles of Conduct and Best Practice Recommendations", Washington DC.

IIF, 2009, "Risk Culture", Washington DC.

IRM, 2012, "Risk Culture: Guidance from the Institute of Risk Management", London.

Kashyap, A., 2010, "Lessons from the Financial Crisis for Risk Management", paper prepared for Financial Crisis Inquiry Commission, February 27.

KPMG, 2010, "Risk Management a Driver of Enterprise Value in the Emerging Environment" (available at http://www.kpmg.com/IN/en/IssuesAndInsights/Thought Leadership/KPMG_Risk_Management_Survey_2011_1.pdf).

Levy, C., E. Lamarre and J. Twining, 2010, "Taking Control of Organisational Risk Culture", McKinsey Working Papers on Risk, 16, February, pp 1–11.

Mikes, A., M. Hall and Y. Millo, 2013, "How Experts Gain Influence", *Harvard Business Review*, 91, July/August, pp. 1–6.

National Commission on the BP Deepwater Horizon Oil Spill and Offshore Drilling, 2011, "Deep Water: The Gulf Oil Disaster and the Future of Offshore Drilling", US Government Presidential Report, The Government Printing Office, Washington DC.

O'Donovan, G, 2011, *Solvency II: Stakeholder Communications and Change* (Surrey, UK: Gower Publishing).

O'Reilly, C. A. and J. Chatman, 1986, "Organisational Commitment and Psychological Attachment: The Effects of Compliance, Identification, and Internalization on Pro-social Behavior", *Journal of Applied Psychology*, 71(3), pp 492–99.

Parliamentary Commission on Banking Standards, 2013a, "An Accident Waiting to Happen: The Failure of HBOS", House of Commons Paper 705, The Stationary Office, London.

Parliamentary Commission on Banking Standards, 2013b, "Changing Banking for Good: First Report of Session 2013–14", House of Commons Paper 175–1, The Stationary Office, London.

Parliamentary Commission on Banking Standards, 2013c, "Changing Banking for Good: Volume II", HL Paper 27-II, HC 175-II, The Stationary Office, London.

Permanent Subcommittee on Investigations, 2013, JP Morgan Chase Whale Trades: A Case History of Derivatives Risks and Abuses", US Senate (available at http://www.hsgac.senate.gov/subcommittees/investigations/hearings/chase-whale-trades-a-case-history-of-derivatives-risks-and-abuses).

Power, M., 2005, "The Invention of Operational Risk", *Review of International Political Economy,* 12(4), pp 577–99

Power, M., 2007, *Organised Uncertainty: Designing a World of Risk Management* (Oxford: Oxford University Press).

Power, M., S. Ashby and T. Palermo, 2013, "Risk Culture in Financial Organisations", Centre for Analysis of Risk and Regulation, LSE, London.

PwC, 2012, "The Risk Culture Survey", Delaware US (available at http://www.pwc.com/us/en/risk-culture/index.jhtml).

Reason, J., 1997, *Managing the Risks of Organisational Accidents* (Surrey, UK: Ashgate Publishing).

Salz, A., 2013, "Salz Review: An Independent Review of Barclays Business Practices", Barclays, London.

Sants, H., 2010a, "Do Regulators Have a Role to Play in Judging Culture and Ethics?", speech to Chartered Institute of Securities and Investments Conference, London.

Sants, H., 2010b, "Can Culture be Regulated?", speech to Mansion House Conference on Values and Trust, London.

Schein, E., 2010, *Organisational Culture and Leadership* (San Francisco, CA: John Wiley).

Towers Watson, 2011, "Measuring Risk Culture Under Solvency II: A Powerful Approach to Demonstrate Embedding of Risk Management Within an Organisation", London.

Treasury Select Committee, 2009a, "Banking Crisis: Dealing with the Failure of the UK Banks", House of Commons, London.

Treasury Select Committee, 2009b, "Banking Crisis: Reforming Corporate Governance and Pay in the City", House of Commons, London.

Vaughan, D., 1995, *The Challenger Launch Decision* (Chicago, IL: University of Chicago Press).

Walker, D., 2009, "A Review of Corporate Governance in UK Banks and other Financial Entities: Final Recommendations", HM Treasury, London.

Welby, J., 2013, "What Kind of City Do We Want?", keynote speech, St Paul's Cathedral, London, June (available at http://www.archbishopofcanterbury.org/articles.php/5075/listen-archbishop-justin-on-good-banks).

Wheatley, M., 2012, "The Incentivisation of Sales Staff – Are Consumers Getting a Fair Deal?", FSA speech, London, September 5.

3

Risk Culture: A View from the Board

Louise Redmond

Risk Culture Insights

This chapter examines the role of the board in creating the culture needed by organisations for sustainable success. The board's role in risk management is the starting point for this exploration, with boards from organisations across a wide range of sectors and public services being reviewed. The chapter will also look at corporate culture in the context of risk, and what the board can do both to shape the appropriate risk culture and to assure itself that major policies and processes are working to deliver the desired culture.

The cultural challenges for the board itself are then reviewed, since the board is the ultimate role model for the whole organisation. Boards, as for any organisation or group, are subject to their own challenges in creating the right culture. Many organisational failures have been traced back to ineffectiveness at board level, particularly with their ability to set the right culture. Examples commonly discussed include the UK National Health Service (NHS), where a few extreme failures (such as at Mid Staffordshire Hospital) highlighted widespread weaknesses in the culture, and where caring for patients became sidelined. Other examples of board weaknesses emerged from the financial crisis and affected many global banks, with fixing benchmark and exchange rates appearing to have been the norm to the detriment of banking customers (Barclays was the first bank to be fined for Libor rate fixing, for example).

Why did the boards of these organisations fail to set the right culture? What can be done by boards to avoid such problems? The simple answer is that boards can be more aware of their own impact on organisational culture, and more in control of their own board culture. The ways and means for doing this are becoming more sophisticated.

THE BOARD AND ITS ROLE IN RISK CULTURE
The role of the board

The classical view of the role of the company board is that it should solve the problem paid managers running the company for their own benefit, not those of the shareholders who have provided investment funds; this is a principal agency problem in economic terms. It is also a relatively narrow view of the board, as boards' agendas clearly cover many topics (such as market needs, employee issues, regulator requirements and reputational challenges) that also concern the interests of other stakeholders in the work of the company. Typically, boards are seen as both overseers – to ensure managers do not run organisations for their own gain – and as supporters – to provide additional expertise, insight and contacts for the long-term benefit of the company. For some organisations, the supportive work of the board would seem to dominate the over-seeing role – eg, new private start-ups, smaller public-listed companies and non-commercial organisations, foundations and trusts. In many of these cases, managers need the specific skills and contacts of their independent board member colleagues to run their organisations.

The main function of a board is enshrined in corporate governance codes applicable in many jurisdictions. The UK, for example, has operated a code of corporate governance practice since 1992, now simply referred to as the Corporate Governance Code (FRC, 2013). This code is intended to enforce good practice for the boards of publicly listed companies. Boards should comply with the general principles of the code and, with regard to the more detailed specific provisions, need to explain if they have not complied, giving reasons and any plans to comply in future. This "comply or explain" approach is considered central to the UK regulatory approach to company boards and, following the 20th anniversary of the code in 2012, significant commitment to retain this approach was made by regulators as well as industry groups (FRC, 2012). The operation of a code, rather than hard and fast laws, is often described as "soft" law. It is closer to a system of self-regulation, in that the board ensures that it complies or explains with a dose of market regulation, in that shareholders can vote against the re-election of the board or disinvest if truly dissatisfied.

Much of the UK Corporate Governance Code, as with codes in some other countries, concerns good practice for the structure of the board, its membership and independence; in other words, it deals with "how" the board should operate. However, the code also reveals the main functions of the board, or "what" should be done by the board. These can be summarised briefly as:

❏ providing entrepreneurial leadership, setting strategic direction, ensuring resources are available and setting values and standards;
❏ presenting a fair, balanced and understandable assessment of the company's position and prospects;
❏ determining the nature and extent of the significant risks the board is willing to take in achieving the strategic objectives;
❏ ensuring that a significant proportion of executive directors' remuneration is structured so as to link rewards to corporate and individual performance; and
❏ ensuring effective dialogue with shareholders, including making good use of the company's AGM for communication to shareholders.

This Financial Reporting Council (FRC) list highlights two important elements of relevance to a consideration of risk culture. First, the board must set values and standards for the company; this impinges directly on culture. Second, the board must determine the nature and extent of the significant risks; this implies an effective risk management approach, including how risk is viewed throughout the culture. Hence, the conclusion is clear that the board has a key role in risk culture in the eyes of the FRC. In its 2011 "Guide to Board Effectiveness", the FRC stated that "an effective board develops and promotes its collective vision of the company's ... culture, its values and the behaviours it wishes to promote in conducting its business". Hence the board's role in setting culture is placed at the centre of board good practice.

There are many dichotomies faced by board directors, including the need to find an effective balance between entrepreneurialism and risk management. Adams (2013) provides a useful model of risk that demonstrates the equally important need to manage the potential upside of taking risks, as well as the potential downsides of failures and errors. The exact balance for any one organisation between the board encouraging entrepreneurialism and the board prioritising risk management is difficult to achieve. There is some evidence that, at different times, boards have tended to emphasise one rather than the other. One view is that during boom economic times boards tend to focus on growth and other entrepreneurial aspects. In contrast, during a recession boards focus more clearly on risk management (Clarke, 2004). It may seem paradoxical to both encourage risk and seek to manage risks thoroughly. This is because, in everyday language, risks are usually seen as bad things: threats not opportunities. However, this balance of managing both the upside and the downside of any venture is critical to organisational success.

The board's role in risk culture

Risk culture requires careful definition and depends substantially on our views on culture as it applies to organisations. The culture of organisations cannot be expected to be as enduring as national, regional or tribal cultures, but nevertheless can be relatively stable. Organisational culture refers to the norms of behaviour that enable employees to know, intuitively, how to behave with each other and with outsiders on a routine basis. Hence, when boards consider the culture of their organisation they are dealing with an intangible phenomenon that somehow they will have to make more tangible if they are to ensure the culture is as desired. When boards focus specifically on risk culture, they consider how the culture operates with regard to managing the risks the organisation faces.

Alvesson (2002), in a major review of organisation culture, says that he considers the symbolism of rituals, myths, stories and legends as well as the interpretation of events, ideas and experiences from the people within the setting. He writes: "I will also, however, take organizational culture to include values and assumptions about social reality, but for me values are less central and less useful than meanings and symbolism." Definitions of culture in the academic world have become looser. As one organisational ethnographic expert has put it (van Maanen, 2011, p 221), "Culture simply refers to the meanings and practices produced, sustained, and altered through interaction ... Perhaps more important these days than in times past, culture should be understood to reside largely within a sphere of social relationships and only indirectly tied to places (or organizations)." Taking this viewpoint, we would argue that a culture is a product of social interactions, particularly where these can be sustained and developed through relationships that last over a reasonable period of time, such as in a work setting. It is based on how people behave, together, to meet their understanding of what work should be done and how.

One definition for culture in organisations is: "the way we do things around here". This definition, attributed to the management consulting firm McKinsey, often provides a workable definition for board members. In Deal and Kennedy (1982), a book that was one of the earliest on this subject for general publication, the authors recognise their debt to McKinsey colleagues. Some have seen culture as a static condition and as something that an organisation possesses, like property or assets, and which leaders are in a strong position to control or change. For others, it is more of a dynamic process between groups that can be highly fragmented and developed differentially in different parts of the business. Schein (1996), for example, describes the culture of an organisation as constantly recreated in different ways in different areas, as employees and managers make sense of what is required of them, what is impacting them from the outside and how to integrate their activities with colleagues. With this view, it is clearly much more difficult for anyone, including the board and the leadership team, to direct culture. Expecting a few straightforward changes – such as a new list of organisational values, some adaptations to human resource systems or a newly empowered risk management department – may not in themselves achieve much in the way of culture change. The organisation is not like a machine where you can pull a few levers to get it moving in a new direction. Frances Hesselbein, whose leadership achievements include revolutionising the Girl Scout movement in the US in the 1980s, said: "Culture doesn't change because we desire to change it. Culture changes when the organisation is transformed" (Hesselbein, 2011). Board members must therefore expect to make more than just a few changes to achieve a desired culture shift as many pockets and subcultures within the organisation have vested interests in maintaining their existing mini-cultures.

Poor or inappropriate cultures were considered to be key factors behind the 2007–08 financial crisis, particularly with reference to the lack of oversight executed by boards of directors of several significant banks, mortgage lenders and insurance companies. In the UK, for example, Sir David Walker was asked by the government of the time to review the governance failures of UK financial institutions. His 2009 report made it clear that culture failings were exacerbated by insufficiently skilled non-executive directors and weaknesses in the status and resourcing of internal risk departments.

The term "risk culture" could apply equally well to aspects of the organisation culture in other sectors. In some cases, the risk culture may focus on the safety of employees, such as in the mining and extraction industries. As the incoming chief executive officer (CEO) of AngloAmerican, Cynthia Carroll was determined to change the company's assumption that employees would die because mining was a dangerous business. Following a fatality at their Rustenburg platinum mine in South Africa, Carroll ordered a closure to change things thoroughly. She wrote: "I wanted an indefinite shutdown, during which we would fundamentally overhaul our safety procedures with a top-to-bottom audit of our processes and infrastructure followed by a complete retraining of the Rustenburg workforce" (Carroll, 2012).

Equally, for industries that involve safety risk to their customers, such as the airline industry, risk culture is important; Thomas Kochan was quoted, for example in Wee (2013) on the Asiana airline crash at San Francisco airport: "The Korean culture has two features – respect for seniority and age, and quite an authoritarian style. You put those two together, and you may get more one-way communication – and not a lot of it upward".

Clearly a board will wish to establish its own views on the effectiveness of risk culture in the organisation before its regulator does. This will involve reviewing both the culture of the whole organisation and also its own board culture.

SETTING THE CULTURE: WHAT THE BOARD CAN DO

It is one of the board's key duties to ensure that the culture of the organisation is appropriate for the activities it intends to carry out. As a board agenda item, culture may not come up too often as a single, focused topic. However, an effective board will consider matters of culture for each agenda item, whatever its purpose.

Culture, values and behaviours should be disentangled, as they are often used interchangeably or loosely by business leaders. The values of the organisation are the guiding principles by which they intend to work; they are important expressions of how things should be done. Culture, on the other hand, is the actual way people behave, which could be different in different parts of the organisation. The culture represents the actual ways in which employees make sense of the behaviours of managers and the rules they work by, and how they deal with customers and colleagues in practice. It is therefore possible to distinguish between values as intent and the culture as actual experience, resulting in observable behaviours.

Although boards will establish a set of values for the organisation to develop the culture accordingly, they may not result in the desired culture and behaviours. There may be significant gaps or variations, even distortions that may arise accidentally or deliberately – for example, by turning a blind eye to certain practices because they are so profitable.

Will effective values drive company success? This is hard to demonstrate. Guiso *et al.* (2013) found no correlation between published values (on the Internet) and company short- or long-term performance measures, using data relating to 1,000 US companies. This may not be surprising as many other factors determine corporate performance. The only correlation that the authors found with business performance was for those companies where employees believed managers to have high integrity. The researchers acknowledged that correlation does not indicate causality, let alone the direction of that causality; does good business performance result in workers believing their management have higher integrity, or the other way round? However, the study does show that some fundamental behaviours may encourage better performance.

Setting values

As the board sets the espoused values for the organisation, they will want to ensure that the values are expressed in such a way that they will really mean something to employees, and that they will be able to guide day-to-day behaviour in a practical way. A review of the values selected by organisations may well reveal that a relatively small number exist, and that these tend to recur in organisation after organisation; what is important is that they make sense for that particular organisation. For instance, Lloyds Banking Group has adopted three values – one of which is "Keeping it Simple". This seems appropriate following a mis-selling scandal costing the bank billions of pounds; keeping products and services simple for the customer may help prevent another such scandal.

Other companies list their preferred behaviours instead of values, although the end-result – to guide employee behaviour – is the same. For example, GlaxoSmithKline includes "Flexible Thinking" and "Enabling and Driving Change" among their preferred behaviours. It could be argued that these could apply to organisations in any industry. However, it is particularly important for GSK, in an industry struggling to produce new drugs to replace those going off-patent, to encourage flexible thinking in its employees as this could lead researchers to find new medicines or to find ways to extend the life of existing products. As an industry experiencing dramatic pressures in healthcare budgets, the company must encourage the ability to change the way business is done.

What matters is that the set of values selected by the board will be able to achieve what the business needs, not whether someone else has thought of it before. The values do not necessarily reflect the current culture or a short-term change, as any substantial shift in culture must necessarily take time. Espoused values will make tangible recognition for good behaviours and the application of sanctions for breaches much easier for management.

Obstacles to creating the desired culture

From time to time, boards may become convinced that the organisational culture is not working to the best effect. This will usually prompt a change of leadership and revisiting the requirements for new senior executives. Rumelt (2011) looks at how a culture may inhibit the adoption of new strategic positions in a company, particularly from his work at AT&T in the 1980s. He found a massive inertia in the culture, which meant that innovation crept forward at a speed more suited to the 1960s. From this experience, Rumelt proposed cultural change as several steps, starting with simplification: stripping out excess layers, disbanding committees, initiatives and duplicative teams. Businesses or product lines should be sold or eliminated to release value. Following simplification comes fragmentation, in which remaining units are split for greater scrutiny by the leadership. A treatment stage then ensues, during which operations are changed to improve performance. Units with long-term potential are checked to ensure their culture is optimal so that if retained they do not infect other units. Once the units are working well with the right culture, it may be appropriate to reunite or to set up new overarching committees. Whether or not Rumelt's model is taken in this exact form, changing culture is clearly a substantial and dramatic task; it is even quite brutal and cathartic. This is essential, as cultures tend to be self-reinforcing in order to create a stability and certainty for large numbers of people who need this structure for their day-to-day tasks.

Developing culture through communication and training

There is common agreement that involving employees in the definition of a new risk culture will improve understanding and implementation. Hence, communication plans will need to take into account the opportunity for employees to engage with the cultural changes required within the context of their own work. An active participation will increase commitment to the new culture and give it a better chance to succeed.

Initial reactions to the roll out of new cultures or values often trigger cynicism or lethargy among employees or, at best, a desire to comply rather than to take personal responsibility for implementing the new culture. This is partly just a defence mechanism against change, which can be unsettling and even frightening. A natural healthy scepticism may be no bad thing in an organisation as it is possible that the board is just appeasing regulators or shareholders. It takes time to develop a new culture, as it needs to be negotiated and accepted by all involved. It is likely there will be many challenges and much interference in the process of adopting new behaviours. Everyone will be paying attention to the specific incentives and risks that apply to them in their new situation.

Communications principles

Some practical and thoughtful approaches to developing organisation culture are provided by Stanford (2010). However, some common principles of effective communication for culture change are also detailed below.

❏ Start at the top: This usually requires the CEO or business leader to demonstrate their own personal belief in the espoused values and to offer practical examples of how they will change their own behaviour. This has to be delivered by the most senior executive as a functional head rarely succeeds and will not have the same impact, however senior. Therefore, a chief operating officer (COO), a head of risk or a head of HR will not be as effective.

❏ Regular reminders are needed: Local team meetings are critical to making this a regular item and a real approach to work. Hence, it is important that managers at all levels are supportive of the change. Change is often dissipated or misinterpreted by managers in the middle and junior ranks, and dramatic gaps emerge in the understanding of the new culture as often witnessed when junior employees subsequently hear directly from the CEO.

❏ Make sensible use of various media: Multiple methods can help to reinforce the cultural message. If "Keeping it Simple" is a value, methods will reflect this as well as messages. Select media that can be interactive wherever possible. CEO blogs that enable comments from employees are better than ones that do not.

❏ Senior leaders should live and breathe the values: This will be demonstrated by senior leaders' behaviour, including those of all board members. Small lapses can be forgiven, but the best leaders ensure they have genuine feedback methods and so are aware of their own lapses and can then acknowledge, respond and apologise.

Training programmes to develop a risk culture

The dividing line between communication and training is often blurred. However, a training programme will usually also include an introduction to new policies and procedures, particularly when related to new risk management practices. A mix of training methods may be needed to ensure employees understand new approaches and have the relevant knowledge and skills to operate the risk management processes in their own function. It cannot be assumed that employees will place the same degree of importance and attention on new risk management requirements, so a training strategy is essential. Boards will also want to see evidence of how management intend to roll out changes and new developments.

Some of the key features of a comprehensive training strategy will now be assessed.

❑ Training for senior leaders: Senior leaders have a key role in role modelling and developing the new risk management framework. They may also need to understand the new aspects of decision-making, reporting and establishing controls that they have personal responsibility for. For senior leaders, shorter sessions, potentially during or around committee meeting time, will be the most useful approach. At these, they can discuss the organisational challenges to new frameworks. The individual should sign to show that they have completed the training and feel equipped to lead in the new environment.

❑ A comprehensive offering for all relevant employees: A comprehensive offering with programmes matched to role and involvement in the framework will be needed. A key question regards standardisation of the programme – does it apply to all departments and business units, or should it be tailored to meet their different work and roles? Organisations should make it clear what elements are mandatory and which are role-dependent or optional. Some business leaders may prefer to have their departments opt out of training if they do not see it as a priority. However, both the organisation and the individual could be exposed if there is no evidence that they have completed at least some fundamental risk management training. Record keeping on central training systems is critical to tracking progress and complying with organisational, and indeed regulatory, requirements. Many leading organisations have found that it is better to reinforce mandatory requirements through their performance management and reward systems – eg, employees who do not comply are penalised through reduced bonuses.

❑ A variety of interactive training methods: Training regarding risk management and risk culture can take a number of forms and is best delivered in an informative, interactive and lively style. Many organisations seek to add to standard training room delivery with online community learning groups, desktop or mobile training applications that can include dynamic graphics and simulations. Most people have some downtime in their work (for example, when travelling), or can be given short bursts of time when they can engage with a computerised simulation or game. New methods will increase uptake and speed up the training process so that new frameworks can be introduced quickly across the organisation, including multiple locations and business units.

❏ Evaluation and follow-up: All training should be evaluated quickly and promptly to improve delivery for the next phase of participants, but also for the impact it has had on work operations. Are new practices fully adopted? Have control breaches reduced? Are more incidents and near misses reported? Are lessons learnt being implemented quickly and effectively? Each organisation will need to determine what business and operational changes are expected as a result of training. These should be as practical, tangible and specific as possible. It is the day-to-day actions that reflect the new culture. Boards should expect to see evidence of improvements following a reasonable implementation timespan.

POLICIES AND PROCESSES THAT REINFORCE CULTURE

There are a significant number of policies and processes in an organisation that can develop and reinforce the desired culture if they are appropriately designed and used. Equally, they can get in the way of developing the right culture if not adequately thought through, thereby resulting in conduct and regulatory risk. The following subsections pick up on some key points on a few of the most critical policies and processes. Each is a key risk mitigation process in its own right; ensure the policy is operating at its most effective with robust control indicators and the policy will offer strong mitigation against many conduct breaches.

Codes of conduct

Many organisations select to write their own code of conduct. This might be referred to as a "code of business conduct" or a "code of ethics and business conduct" or similar name. The Group of Thirty, a top-level global financial services industry thinktank, advocates embedding the organisation's values in the form of a code, with the purpose of guiding employee behaviour in the most challenging situations – as they put it, "so that directors, senior executives and all other employees in an entity are fully aware of the standards of behaviour that are expected of them".

A conduct code is most useful if it demonstrates the kind of behaviour the organisation would like to see in all areas of the way it conducts its business. Constructive examples of how to behave are likely to be better received than many legalistic warnings. However, ultimately the code of conduct is based on what could be a legal defence, for both the organisation and the employee, should some aspect of the operation be challenged in a legal context.

Some key points to note regarding codes of conduct are:

❏ the document should be written to engage and inform all employees at all levels and all parts of the organisation;
❏ the areas covered should be the main areas of conduct risk for the organisation, such as all dealings with customers, suppliers and counterparties, all financial dealings and probity, and the impact of relationships between employees;
❏ the input of functional representatives from risk, internal audit, compliance, human resources and legal is critical to ensure good coverage; communications experts will help ensure the document remains simple and straightforward;
❏ practical examples should be used to illustrate potential situation or scenarios where employees might be put in difficult situations; and
❏ contact details for further advice and guidance should be provided; a confidential hotline phone number and email address to report concerns should also be provided.

Examples of codes of conduct are easy to find, as they apply to professions, trade bodies, students, trustees and many other roles where there is a degree of responsibility. It is not difficult therefore to prepare a draft. However, it is more challenging to make the document truly relevant to employees of the organisation, and to include genuine examples of how to behave in the most difficult and yet plausible situations. Organisations will make their own code of conduct tie in with their business model and top key behavioural risks. For example, Shell, the global oil giant, has split its code of conduct into five pertinent sections: people and safety; national and international trade; safeguarding information and events; fighting corrupt practices; and communications. While some of these aspects may be common to many organisations, the detail within should be closely related to specific business challenges.

Raising concerns, speaking up and whistleblowing

It is important that an organisation offers a number of ways in which employees can report incidents, raise concerns and suggest improvements to risk management systems. The usual route would be the regular or *ad hoc* discussions held with line managers. Organisations will prefer to provide a number of alternative avenues should the line management one be inappropriate – eg, internal audit, human resources, company secretariat and risk management. The more avenues provided and the more that the organisation is receptive and listens to employee feedback, the less likely an employee will be to take a more formal or external route.

The performance management framework

The performance management framework in an organisation is one of the most powerful tools in setting and reinforcing a desired risk culture. Its design and usage will therefore be of interest to the board, even although the operational details will be left to the executive.

Most organisations operate some kind of performance framework by which corporate objectives are set with specific targets to be achieved. A review cycle and process is established whereby each employee is reviewed against their own objectives, and performance feedback may be given, development or training actions can be agreed and, possibly, performance-related awards calculated.

Effective human resources practices have been shown to improve organisation performance. For example, Combs *et al.* (2006) carried out a review of many research studies into human resource management and organisation performance. They reported that "a key task … has been to understand how human resources can be managed to maximize productivity and enhance creativity while controlling costs". Human resource practices that impact performance are known as high-performance work practices. These practices include, for example, incentive compensation, training, employee participation, selectivity and flexible work arrangements. Theory asserts that these practices increase employees' knowledge, skills and abilities, empower employees and increase their motivation. The result is greater job satisfaction, lower employee turnover, higher productivity and better decision-making, all of which help improve organisational performance. Although performance management processes *per se* do not always feature in these lists of high-performance work practices, their impact can be on ensuring effective incentive compensation and on focusing training.

Bloom *et al.* (2012) summarised a decade of work covering thousands of companies, but also schools and hospitals, in several countries to show that "good" management practices do work to enhance organisational performance. Lawler (2006) argued that performance management is particularly important, claiming that "the ability to manage performance is often the major differentiator between organisations that produce adequate results and those that excel". He noted 13 design features that are fundamental to a performance management system for organisations that wish to achieve competitive advantage through their people. These features make a useful checklist for board directors wanting to complete a quick review of what is happening in their organisation (see Table 3.1).

Table 3.1 Design features for a performance management system

1	Appraisals are conducted from top to bottom
2	Appraisal delivery is evaluated for effectiveness
3	Goals are set in advance
4	Goals are updated when the business environment changes
5	How goals are accomplished is part of the assessment
6	Individuals should be able to provide their own performance self-assessment
7	Objective performance measures are used for assessment
8	Measures should relate to the expected performance of the organisation
9	Rating systems should be meaningful, justifiable and avoid forced distributions
10	Pay discussions should be separate to development discussions
11	There should be a skills recording system where individuals' skills are noted
12	Ongoing feedback is the norm
13	Team performance is managed and measured

Source: Adapted from Lawler (2006)

Ensuring the performance framework supports the desired culture

All performance management approaches, whatever the specifics of their design, communicate and reinforce two aspects of performance: "what" should be achieved and "how" it should be achieved. Clearly, the "how" aspects are directly related to behaviour and how people interpret the culture of their organisation. Therefore, attention should be paid in all performance management approaches to ensure there is some opportunity to discuss "how" the job is carried out and whether staff behaves according to espoused values. This is one of the most important ways to set and reinforce the desired culture in an organisation.

A practical guide to linking performance management to values was created by a joint project between the City Values Forum and the City HR Association (2013) to respond to the weak cultural issues among certain UK financial services firms. This guide provides a useful checklist for building cultural aspects into common human resource procedures.

Monitoring the use of the performance framework

At board level, an annual review of performance management and its operation is likely to be sufficient for assurance that managers are inculcating the values as well as directing work activities. Key questions for board directors could include:

❏ how effectively has the performance management framework been used throughout the organisation?
❏ to what extent have the published values and the risk culture been reinforced by the use of the performance management framework this year?
❏ where values have clearly not been upheld, has this been taken into account in performance feedback and compensation decisions?
❏ what improvements will be made to the performance management framework to increase its effectiveness for the new performance year?

Although, in theory, performance management frameworks can be quite straightforward to operate, there are some common difficulties that will impact the risk culture that boards should consider. A key issue will be the extent to which the use of the values in the framework gets "drowned out" by the achievement of specific business objectives. For example, a salesperson may have achieved extremely high sales in the period but has left things such that the customer service team cannot achieve their delivery standards; thus, a customer service value is jeopardised. Has "how" they achieved their objectives impacted on one of the values? Employees who routinely achieve high results often develop a star status in the organisation; this becomes self-perpetuating and the business can become heavily reliant on them. They are then often forgiven by managers for slippages in the way they operate. Managers may choose not to correct or change this. Star performers are common in many industries: fund managers, traders, salespeople, professors, surgeons, etc. These people are critical to organisational performance, to attracting and training talented junior staff and to overall success. However, the tendency to allow "star" performers to behave outside the values can have unfortunate long-term consequences. The board will wish to achieve an understanding of how the organisation deals with such individuals, and to weigh up the risks associated with excessive tolerance. Research on some investment banks shows that there can be a clear conflict between the actions that support the reputations of "star" performers and the actions that impact the institution's reputation (Chen 2013).

Sanctions

Sanctions must be applied when aspects of the risk culture are seriously breached. If not, other employees will cease to comply, especially with the more tedious or less obviously critical requirements of their organisation. Whereas good leadership will encourage compliance with positive feedback and rewards, it will still be necessary to operate sanctions of some type.

Employees and managers should expect to be able to find all relevant materials on values, culture, codes of conduct and disciplinary policies and procedures in easy to find places on organisation Intranets. They should also expect to be offered comprehensive training and easy to access advice lines and guidance documents. There is clearly no excuse for not knowing if information and help is readily available.

However, employees can still be placed in difficult situations.

Sometimes, transgressions may seem minor and inoffensive; perhaps no one has appeared to have suffered due to the transgression. Equally, employees may occasionally be asked by managers to do something that may not appear quite right but could be considered to be within the acceptable range of the manager's discretion and company policy. Clearly, the risk is that some transgressions become more common, part of the local culture and then accelerate and extend. This is how cultures evolve and is to be expected. If a department operates with clear transparency and reporting to the rest of the organisation, problem areas can be resolved with the help of specialist departments such as finance, risk or compliance. Equally important, the likelihood that sanctions would be applied if necessary can act to moderate behaviour. Will I be found out? If I am found out, would anyone punish me, and if so, would it be so bad?

Although organisations will prefer to focus on preventative measures such as communication and training, and positive steps such as recognising and reward effective behaviours and achievements, the sanctions or disciplinary processes need to be robust, consistently applied and patently fair. Clearly, individual cases will not be publicised and details disclosed but informal, internal (and sometimes external) grapevines exist, and it is important for other employees to see that actions are taken quickly and consistently by their own organisation and not just by the external regulators.

Recruitment and clearance policies

Arguably the recruitment process is the most important of all organisational processes in ensuring that the culture is defined clearly and adhered to. As new people enter the organisation, it is critical that their past behaviours and current attitudes will fit with the espoused culture of the organisation. Recruitment materials must be judged as for their reflection of the espoused culture; for example, one long-standing organisation dropped many photographs of its historic buildings in favour of photographs of the people and technology inside to demonstrate how forward-looking it was.

Some businesses, particularly in service industries such as professional partnerships and high-margin retailers, set extensive processes to assess attitudes and behaviours as well as specific job skills. These processes can include internal assessments, including interviews, tests and assessment centres, but also external assessments such as references, immigration and security checks, Internet checks, *curriculum vitae* and qualification checks. Once recruited, induction processes and training are intended to introduce new employees to the most significant policies and practices, and to remind them of their obligations. Hence, all materials at induction should refer closely to the values and code of conduct. Probation policies then follow to enable quick reversal of decisions that do not work out.

Succession and key person risk

Talent management and succession planning are risk mitigation processes in their own right. Boards need to address the top levels of the organisation in detail and have a strong degree of comfort that management is conducting these processes fully throughout the organisation.

Key roles and their impact on culture

Some roles are more critical to the creation of the culture and risk governance practices. Other than the CEO and the chief financial officer (CFO), other senior leaders are important – such as the chief risk officer (CRO), and heads of HR, compliance and internal audit. Therefore, the performance of these individuals in relation to the development of the risk management framework is critical.

Succession planning mitigates the risk that an appointment will go wrong, not only on a competence basis but also on a behavioural one. An appointment, particularly a senior, high-profile role, could signal a mixed message if the appointee has not or does not behave according to the espoused values.

Monitoring key talent

There are always roles in an organisation that have a high internal status through their critical business skills or essential roles in the value chain. Typically, revenue earners or traders have a higher status than operations staff as they bring in income. Of course, they might bring in income at the expense of profit, depending on the means by which they operate. The actions and behaviours of these groups of employees tend to communicate what might be seen as the "true" culture of the organisation, if they do not fit the espoused values. Hence, it is important that talent management processes identify those individuals who operate according to the espoused values and develop leadership behaviours accordingly.

Often, promotions or appointments to more senior roles offer a strong signal to colleagues on the type of behaviours desired. Therefore, if ambitious and aggressive individuals are promoted over collaborative and detail-oriented individuals, it will be interpreted that the former behaviours are worth more to the organisation, and others will then copy the behaviour.

As boards are responsible for the long-term sustainability of the organisation, they will naturally be interested in how talent is brought in, developed and deployed. The talent management approach is one of the key ways in which behaviours are encouraged and rewarded, and so is critical for a board to review in the context of the risk culture. Clearly, the talent management approach should ensure a good supply of functional skills for the business, which will include risk and compliance management, as well as entrepreneurial, front-line and operational capabilities. A good talent management approach will specify the organisation's expected demand for skills (at least as far as any forecasting method can specify the future) and also specify the most effective recruitment and development processes. However, beyond functional capabilities and skills, the board will seek evidence that the next couple of generations of leaders, and key functional heads, will also demonstrate the behaviours that will develop the culture of the future.

MONITORING CULTURE AT BOARD LEVEL

Most organisations prefer to monitor performance through specific indicators or ratios that can be reliably and readily calculated and tracked. At board level, simple measurement dashboards on key performance and risk indicators will enable rigorous discussion. It is up to the CEO and the senior team to ensure that quality information is shared with the board. However, when it comes to risk culture, boards have some difficult choices to make as it is harder to track developments in corporate culture than it is other aspects of performance.

Indicators of risk culture can effectively be of two kinds: metrics of structures and processes in place and their effective operation; and metrics of behaviours and actions taken. The first type can demonstrate that structures are in place and are operating effectively. For example, risk committees may be in place and meet regularly, roles may be clear with regard to risk management, reporting processes may be routinely used, internal audit recommendations may be speedily implemented. Conduct-related controls may also be well operated and adjusted as needed, including completion of mandatory training, compliance with administrative policies, adherence to recruitment checks, and so on. Surely, if indicators of this kind look satisfactory or even good, there is little for a board to worry about?

The second type of metric, concerning actual behaviours observed in the business, is more difficult to collect and report on, particularly at the same regularity as other indicators – quarterly, monthly, weekly, daily. However, the actual behaviours observed are important indicators of where something may spin out of control, contravene espoused culture or result in actions that contravene laws, regulatory requirements or general good practice. Some organisations have attempted to use employee surveys to track metrics of overall behaviours. Clearly, there is always a risk of extreme behavioural non-compliance, including fraud, in an organisation; this will never disappear completely. However, some employee surveys may seek to get to grips with behaviour shifts or pockets of cultural weakness.

Personal contact with key players and throughout the organisation

Many board members assess the culture of the organisation through contact with executives, employees, customers, suppliers and advisers. Collecting as much anecdotal information as feasible within the time constraints of non-executive, independent directors is perhaps the most typical approach. It is also reassuring to independent board members, as they often believe they can trust their own eyes and ears more than that of an intermediary.

Survey data on culture

Organisations have an abundance of formal information on how they operate and summaries of meetings and decisions that reflect their culture. Some of these reports may be useful to determine how the culture operates in practice. Many shy away from data such as this due to its "qualitative" nature – reports of actions, statements, discussions in meetings. However, it is this kind of data that can provide real insight into what happens in practice. There are continuing developments in software tools that aid the rudimentary analysis of such information.

What might be included? Employee opinion surveys are common practice in many organisations. Surveys may be "quantitative" in that employees are asked to rate their experience of the organisation on a given numerical scale, say from one to five. However, if space is provided for employees to write whatever is on their mind or to comment freely in response to other questions, a set of comments can be gathered and analysed in a qualitative manner. Quantitative and qualitative can be sorted and combined, or contrasted using common analytical practices. Organisations can seek qualitative data from other key documents, such as performance appraisals, recruitment and promotion reports, and comments from training programmes. There are many examples. Confidentiality can be maintained and data analysed from an aggregate perspective seeking to point out "themes" across the organisation or with sub-groups of individuals.

Some organisations will seek to assess risk culture more directly through tailored survey methods. Surveys can be designed to pursue what employees believe would happen in relevant situations that could pose behavioural challenges, perhaps where there are several options for what actions could be taken. These survey approaches are often referred to as "situational judgement tests", where someone is asked to rank or rate the steps they would take in a particular scenario. These can be very useful to judge what employees would actually do in hypothetical situations. Equally, they can be used to determine what employees would think their managers would do in hypothetical situations, thereby revealing real leadership behaviours. Descriptions of specific management behaviours can be tested to determine the relative frequency or likelihood of them occurring. Questions of this nature need to be carefully devised to match workplaces, and also to reduce the likelihood of employees falsifying their responses to reveal how they think they should behave rather than how they actually behave. However, all assessments are subject to falsification and there is no reason why this type of test is more likely to be falsified than others.

Some culture assessment tools are available that enable an organisation to determine its culture "type". For example, is the organisation more of a bureaucratic type or an entrepreneurial type? On the other hand, perhaps we could measure whether it is more a social or a relationship type, or if it is more a rules-following type? The Institute of Risk Management (2012), in its thorough and comprehensive review of risk culture, features a typology for risk culture in organisations. Type testing is common also in individual psychometric assessment and has a long history in psychology. However, our type is a strongly built in preference that will be hard to change, such as being right- or left-handed. Therefore, organisations may be interested to understand their culture type but will need to then consider carefully how they will assess routinely the effectiveness of their culture and progress towards culture goals.

One commentator (Tett, 2008) noted with sharp accuracy important cultural differences in some of the global banks of the day. Her prescience is quite shocking now that we know their fate during the latter part of 2008, when things came to a head. In January 2008, she wrote: "But what is crystal clear is that if you want to understand which banks will emerge as winners from the current mess, it is no longer enough to look at their computer systems and balance sheets. Now, more than ever, investors need to understand a bank's culture too – and the degree to which it is tribal."

Hence, in reviewing the culture of their organisation, the board should be considering many aspects of how people relate to each other, how much autonomy individuals believe they have, the extent to which people in one department need to take into account the needs of other departments, the degree of forgiveness if administrative requirements are not met, and so on.

Developing culture indicators for the board

Organisations may also choose to deploy a commercially available survey tool that could lead to a set of indicators being used to track developments in the company, or possibly to benchmark against other organisations. Power *et al.* (2013) list some of these culture surveys in an appendix to their review of risk culture in the financial sector. Changes in the organisation's own culture over time can be particularly useful as management and the board can identify different parts of the organisation that may have more risky cultures, or where new external pressures prompt changes in the culture. Benchmarking may be an attractive option, but managers should be careful to consider who they are benchmarking themselves against and whether that is a suitable goal for what they would like to achieve. Safety in numbers is rarely an answer to a weak culture, as has been demonstrated in industry-wide crises such as the financial sector Libor crisis or the cultural challenges throughout the UK National Health Service (NHS), as crystallised at Mid Staffordshire Hospital.

What indicators might be useful? Specific indicators, which have been used in my own work with organisations on risk culture, include:

❑ ease at which employees are able to speak out if they are concerned (no fear of reprisals);
❑ clarity of understanding of risk tolerances (no fuzziness on what can be done);
❑ consistency of practice between the top and the bottom of the organisation (no "them and us");
❑ collaboration between parts of the organisation (no success at the expense of others);
❑ proposals argued from an evidence base (no whims based on seniority);
❑ transparency if things going wrong (no fear of blame);
❑ taking accountability for mistakes (no hiding behind others);
❑ single rules for all (no allowances for favourites); and
❑ strength of managerial role models (no gaps in the hierarchy).

THE BOARD'S OWN CULTURE

It may seem strange to think of the board as having its own culture, potentially distinct from that of the organisation for which it has oversight. However, any group will develop its own norms, ways of working, habits and rituals. Indeed, many groups will deliberately develop particular ways of working so that the members of the group can feel a sense of belonging and loyalty, and so that outsiders can feel separate and not included.

Boards are effectively a senior team operating within an organisation and distinguished by their highly specific role and, sometimes, their specific legal duties. The dynamics and risks associated with senior organisational teams are therefore applicable to boards. On that basis, it is sensible for boards to consider, from time to time, whether or not their own dynamics and culture pose any particular risks to the organisation.

Board members are as likely as other individuals to be subject to common biases and social phenomena when it comes to decision-making, being not as rational as they might like to think. The development of behavioural economics and advances in the neurosciences have had a revolutionary impact in how we view individual decision-making, and indeed how social factors may come into play when decisions are made by groups.

PANEL 3.1: VIEW FROM WARREN BUFFETT, CHAIRMAN OF BERKSHIRE HATHAWAY

"Why have intelligent and decent directors failed so miserably? The answer lies not in inadequate laws – it's always been clear that directors are obligated to represent the interests of shareholders – but rather in what I'd call boardroom 'atmosphere' …

"Over a span of 40 years, I have been on 19 public company boards (excluding Berkshire's) and have interacted with perhaps 250 directors. Most of them were 'independent' as defined by today's rules … These people, decent and intelligent though they were, simply did not know enough about business and/or care enough about shareholders to question foolish acquisitions or egregious compensation. My own behavior, I must ruefully add, frequently fell short as well; too often I was silent when management made proposals that I judged to be counter to the interests of shareholders. In those cases, collegiality trumped independence."

Quoted from Berkshire Hathaway, "2002 Annual Report", chairman's letter to shareholders, pp 16–17.

The board as a role model for the organisation

The board environment and culture clearly needs to be as effective as possible in order for the board to add value to the organisation. However, the board culture provides a role model for the rest of the organisation. If in senior managers' experience the board is unwelcoming, aggressive or elitist, this will be communicated throughout the organisation. It is likely that ambitious managers will then emulate this behaviour as a perceived route to the top.

Without an effective culture, board members are also likely to want to leave the board early or fail to put in sufficient effort. The precise best culture may be hard to define as a chief executive is likely to want something different to the chairman or indeed to shareholders, and circumstance will dictate what is most effective. Executives often prefer supportive and trusting non-executives, although they may accept that non-executive board members will want to check assumptions and ask pertinent questions.

Board composition and its impact on board culture

As with any group, the membership of the board is clearly an important factor in shaping its culture. Intuitively, the backgrounds, specialisms and personal style of the board members must shape the way the board culture will develop. Hence, a board composed entirely of citizens of Germany, for example, would be expected to behave differently to one composed of US citizens, regardless of the country of registration of the company. Also, it is often assumed that board members from a commercial or private sector background will bring a different approach to a public sector organisation or to a charity than those who have only worked in the public or voluntary sector.

It is often assumed that a board needs a variety of types of people on it – ie, strong diversity. However, evidence concerning the impact of diversity on board effectiveness is patchy. This is to be expected to a certain degree, as measuring board effectiveness is anyway difficult and company performance is dependent on many other important factors, notably product and operational decisions.

The emphasis on appointing more women to board positions gained momentum in Europe following early moves in Norway to balance boards by gender more closely. Researchers at the Credit Suisse Institute (2012) studied over 2,000 global companies to determine whether companies with women on the board perform better than companies without. In their report on the period 2006–12, they stated: "In testing the performance of 2,360 companies globally over the last six years, our analysis shows that it would on average have been better to have invested in corporates with women on their management boards than in those without". Also it is not clear in which direction causation runs – better run companies appoint more women or more women lead to better run companies.

Boards will want to look at what diversity means in their own context. For some organisations, there may need to be greater diversity of previous experience that could take in experience in several different sectors, different functional expertise and different geographical expertise. If an organisation has complex risk management challenges such as in the financial sector, an independent director with risk management experience could be in a stronger position to challenge the internal head of risk than their other board colleagues. Similarly, organisations in the high-technology sector are likely to benefit from a number of independent directors with related although not necessarily identical technical expertise. Many boards have begun to seek expertise in social media marketing, as this has become a critical advertising and sales channel (see Spencer Stuart, 2014).

Although, generally, greater diversity is considered to lead to the potential of greater performance, there are many examples of where it has resulted in greater conflict and discord. Hence, diverse groups may require more expert leadership.

Common issues with board behaviour

Most board members aspire to entirely rational analysis and decision-making. If boards adopt a logical, detailed process to review assumptions and evidence and to select a preferred option, it is assumed that an entirely rational decision will be made. However, the quote from Warren Buffett in Panel 3.1 illustrates that cold-headed, rational decisions are not always the norm on boards. He was writing almost immediately after the collapse of US-listed company Enron, which was seen as a clear governance failure. Not surprisingly, shareholders at the time were concerned that such a pattern of behaviour might be found in other listed companies; in his chairman's report, Buffett sought to reassure through admitting past mistakes. Sutherland (2013) wrote the first synopsis of decades of psychological research that demonstrates the prevalence of irrational behaviour, which has become more widely accepted by the general public. He shows how readily we are influenced by irrelevant factors, common biases and false inferences. Ariely (2012) also examined the extent to which we deceive ourselves and others – our cheating is more common that we might admit; there are a large number of small acts of deception carried out every day in all organisations.

The key question for board members is how to steer their own behaviour towards a more positive or more sensible norm and to work together to avoid biases, false assumptions and blindness. If the board can operate as openly and effectively as a group of interdependent peers (after all, each is equally liable), board members can act as an effective role model for the whole organisation.

In the context of board behaviours, board members would be wise to familiarise themselves with some common challenges facing decision-making groups (see Table 3.2).

Table 3.2 Common challenges for board behaviours

Overconfidence It has been shown that professionals from many disciplines have a tendency to be overconfident in their own abilities, powers of judgement and control over external events. People pay too little attention to contrary evidence, often remember past events in a way that reinforces personal biases and can build up a causal story to show the strength of past judgements. A key role for board members is to challenge the plans of company executives, who are likely to predict an overly optimistic outcome. This is not wilful fraud or dishonesty on their part; it is a natural consequence of a successful professional career. Boards can be strong role models by being prepared to take feedback about their own behaviours.
Capture Capture refers to the phenomenon that people who work as regulators, auditors or inspectors can end up being overly sympathetic to those they regulate, audit or inspect; possibly, this occurred within financial regulators in the years before the 2007–08 banking crisis. It is not unlike Stockholm syndrome, where captives become sympathetic towards their captors. In the case of independent board members, it could involve a loss of independence and being overly influenced by strong-minded executives.
Free-riding This is a situation where several people are involved in making a decision but some of them choose not to participate actively. They justify this to themselves by arguing that others are more knowledgeable, concluding that they do not need to delve into analysis to form an independent view. They are taking a "free ride" on the back of the work of other people. The same phenomenon is also known as social loafing. Board members should avoid this laziness. They should also be wary of being "held hostage" by overly confident colleagues who may not be right all of the time.
Groupthink Groupthink is the tendency that, after a while, everyone in a group starts to think the same way on many issues. It can be the result of socialisation and the pressure to conform to the norms of the group. Diversity of members, regular renewal of independent directors and regular involvement of specialist advisers and employees can mitigate this tendency.
Wilful blindness This expression was first used in a legal context where an individual claimed in their defence that they were not aware that they were committing a crime. For example, someone found carrying illegal drugs in their luggage claiming that they did not put them there and were planted by someone else. This is rarely a successful defence in law. It has also been applied to boards that deliberately ignore key information – perhaps relevant inconvenient facts are known but no-one mentioned them at the crucial moment. Sometimes this phenomenon is referred to as selective attention.
Risky shift This is a phenomenon that can occur when people make a decision in a group; groups may take a more extreme or riskier position than if individuals were deciding separately. They may feel safety in numbers or greater confidence in our own beliefs if others appear to share them.

Geslevich-Packin (2013) makes an interesting case for applying what we know about behavioural risks in decision-making by boards and risk committees to financial regulatory practice, in the context of legal changes in the US such as the Dodd–Frank Act. She argues for more than the minimum requirements of the act, such as having one risk specialist and several independent directors on the risk committee, for example. This could enable greater awareness of decision biases such as the choice shift (similar to the risky shift phenomenon), and to much greater disclosure on risk matters with particular attention to written analyses and not just formulaic or mathematical approaches. She draws from Ariel Rubinstein's experiments on risk-taking behaviour in an interesting way in the context of corporate governance requirements for US significant financial institutions.

Applying what has been learnt about human perceptions of risk and propensity to irrational behaviour to board dynamics is an important next step. A useful introduction is provided in Annex 4 of the Walker Report (2009). Boards have been found to be at their most effective when making decisions if they apply considerable effort and adopt an open and investigative style (Forbes and Milliken, 1999). It is assumed that such behaviours help prevent some of the irrational analysis and decision-making traps that might occur otherwise. Along the same lines, McNulty et al. (2013) compared data on boardroom processes with financial risk outcomes in major non-financial company boards in the period 2008–09. Financial risk taking was found to be lower with boards where high effort is the norm and also where there is a higher level of cognitive conflict – ie, strong arguments over content. High levels of cognitive conflict do not mean that there is low mutual respect among directors; indeed,

PANEL 3.2: "VIEW FROM ALFRED P. SLOAN, CHAIRMAN OF GENERAL MOTORS"

"Gentlemen, I take it we are all in complete agreement on the decision here ... Then I propose we postpone further discussion of this matter until our next meeting to give ourselves time to develop disagreement and perhaps gain some understanding of what the decision is all about."

Alfred P. Sloan, Chairman of General Motors, as quoted in Drucker (2007), p 139.

the reverse is true and can lead to robust discussion and argument. Where boards have particularly high levels of cohesiveness (eg, non-executive and executive director co-working), there is less need for cognitive conflict. Therefore, it would seem that as well as working hard, boards must either adopt a high cognitive conflict mode or a high cohesive mode.

General changes in team working in organisations also apply to boards. Wageman (2012) argues that business collaboration has become more complex and will result in future teams being radically different, and not just an evolution, from how they have operated latterly. Complexity will lead to greater flexibility in ways of working, to team technology that will be constantly shifting. Team and board membership is likely to be more fluid, with more rotation and more frequent bringing in of others, such as experts and specialist employees, for specific decisions. Hence, boards may feel less like a fixed clique in the future.

Risk on the board agenda

Some may be concerned that boards devote too much time to compliance questions and insufficient time to business or growth matters. However, that is not the same as saying that boards devote too much time to matters of risk. The risk agenda is clearly a question of considering the business opportunities and ensuring that the organisation has the controls, checks and balances in place to ensure that opportunities are maximised. This means the iterative process of reviewing strategies and risks is at the heart of the board agenda.

Airmic, a specialist UK risk management association, has sponsored two important studies of how boards deal with risk. The first study (Airmic, 2011) was carried out by Cass Business School through a desktop-based review of 18 high-profile corporate crises, with a US and UK bias. The review came to the striking conclusion that boards (or at least the selected boards) have a blind spot with regard to risk management. The report highlighted that there were limitations to board members' skills and ability to monitor risk – indeed, that they were blind to risks in the business model, and that risk and internal audit managers failed to communicate risk effectively to the board. This is a stark review, although it is hard to calibrate how typical the findings might be of organisational boards. To some extent, every major organisational crisis must be related to failings at board level and in the organisation's culture. However, we must be careful how individual crises are judged, and not just jump to the top every time. The second report (Airmic, 2013), carried out by Cranfield University, highlighted some approaches to preventing crises through more effective risk management based on in-depth interviews at carefully selected organisations. From this research, a strong model for "high-resilience organisations" was developed. The authors claim that a focus on behaviours and culture is critical to building resilience., and highlighted the following features of high-resilience organisations:

❏ an effective risk radar – that is, an early warning system that anticipates risk;
❏ a well-diversified set of resources and assets to respond flexibly to crises;
❏ good risk communications so that information flow is effective throughout the organisation, and particularly to the board;
❏ rapid response capability in case of crisis; and
❏ an ability to learn from experience.

These very general conclusions may nevertheless be a useful starting point for boards to review what is in place in their organisation. They echo work carried out in the US by Weick and Sutcliffe (2007), who studied organisations and cases concerning major physical disasters. They applied the concept of mindfulness, which usually refers to individuals in a high state of awareness and attention, to organisations to describe one important characteristic of resiliency. Airmic (2013) developed the idea of organisational mindfulness and sense-making, showing that some successful project managers identify risks but do not mitigate them, which seems irrational. Instead, they are highly alert to early signs of risk crystallising, at which point they react extremely quickly in response – hence, the importance of a good risk radar and an effective rapid response capability.

TRENDS AT BOARD LEVEL

As industries and organisations change, so must the boards that run them. Therefore, as the task for boards becomes more complex and demanding, members are devoting more time to their roles. However, will more time and effort be enough? As the task also becomes more difficult – for example, in balancing strategic opportunities and business risk, and in developing risk culture – the board processes and dynamics will need to be sufficiently flexible and sophisticated to address multiple new tasks.

As our understanding of the behavioural aspects of decision-making from developments in neuroscience, psychology and behavioural economics increases, boards will need to consider their practices more carefully to improve their own performance. This will be helped by real-time and powerful corporate and external information, which will be easier to put together to aid fast decision-making. However, fast decision-making sessions will need to be balanced by other meetings primarily aimed at slow blue skies exploration, with more in-depth relationship building between members, internal managers and external advisers. More far-reaching analysis will be commissioned specifically for boards (as opposed to executive management) so that boards are able to consider longer-term challenges and the options to address them. Boards will be better versed in these longer-term issues than executive management, and hence will provide a more informed challenge as short-term decisions are made. This will be particularly useful to the board's deliberation of more complex matters, including values, behaviours and culture.

REFERENCES

Adams, J., 2013, "Risk: Perception, Measurement and Policy", presentation to What is Risk? conference, City University, December 13.

Airmic, 2011, "Roads to Ruin" (available at http://www.airmic.com/research/joint-research).

Airmic, 2013, "Roads to Resilience" (available at http://www.airmic.com/research/joint-research).

Alvesson, M., 2002, *Understanding Organizational Culture* (Sage).

Ariely, D., 2012, *The (Honest) Truth About Dishonesty: How We Lie To Everyone – Especially Ourselves* (HarperCollins).

Awrey, D., W. Blair and D. Kershaw, 2012, "Between Law and Markets: Is There a Role for Culture and Ethics in Financial Regulation?", LSE Law, Society and Economy Working Papers 14/2012.

Bloom, N., R. Sadun and J. Van Reenen, 2012, "Does Management Really Work?", *Harvard Business Review*, 90(11), pp 76–82.

Buffett, W., 2002, "Berkshire Hathaway Inc. 2002 Annual Report" (available at http://www.berkshirehathaway.com/annual.html).

Carroll, C., 2012, "The CEO of AngloAmerican on Getting Serious About Safety", *Harvard Business Review*, June.

Chen, Z., A. D. Morrison and W. J. Wilhelm Jr., 2013, "Investment Bank Reputation and 'Star' Cultures", *Review of Corporate Finance Studies*, online publication.

City Values Forum and City HR Association, 2013, "Performance with Integrity – Executive Overview".

Clarke, T., 2004, "Cycles of Crisis and Regulation: The Enduring Agency and Stewardship Problems of Corporate Governance", *Corporate Governance: An International Review*, 12(2), pp 153–61.

Combs, J., L. Yongmei, A. Hall and D. Ketchen, 2006, "How Much do High-performance Work Practices Matter? A Meta-analysis of their Effects on Organizational Performance", *Personnel Psychology*, 59(3), pp 501–28.

Credit Suisse Research Institute, 2012, "Gender Diversity and Corporate Performance", August.

Deal, T. and A. Kennedy, 1982, *Corporate Cultures: The Rites and Rituals of Corporate Life* (Reading, MA: Addison-Wesley).

Drucker, P., 2007,. *The Effective Executive (2e, revised)* (London: Routledge).

The Economist, 2013, "Robot Recruiters – How Software Helps Firms Hire Workers More Efficiently", April 6.

Financial Reporting Council, 2011, "Guide to Board Effectiveness".

Financial Reporting Council, 2012, "Comply or Explain 20th Anniversary of the UK Corporate Governance Code", November 5.

Financial Reporting Council, 2013, "UK Corporate Governance Code".

Forbes, D. P. and F. J. Milliken, 1999, "Cognition and Corporate Governance: Understanding Boards of Directors as Strategic Decision-making Groups", *Academy of Management Review*, 24(3), pp 489–505.

Geslevich-Packin, N., 2013, "It's (Not) All About The Money: Using Behavioral Economics to Improve Regulation of Risk Management in Financial Institutions", *University of Pennsylvania Journal of Business Law*, 2(15), Spring.

Group of Thirty Working Group on Corporate Governance, 2012, "Toward Effective Governance of Financial Institutions" (Chapter 7).

Guiso, L., P. Sapienza and L. Zingales, 2013, "The Value of Corporate Culture", NBER Working Paper No. 19557. October.

Hesselbein, F., 2011, *My Life in Leadership* (San Francisco, CA: Jossey-Bass).

Institute of Risk Management, 2012 "Risk Culture Under the Microscope: Guidance for Boards".

Lawler III, E. E., 2006, *Talent: Making People Your Competitive Advantage* (San Francisco, CA: Jossey-Bass), pp 106–20.

Lloyd's Emerging Risks Report, 2010, "Behaviour: Bear, Bull or Lemming?", March.

McNulty, T., C. Florackis and P. Ormrod, 2012, "Corporate Governance and Risk: A Study of Board Structure and Process", ACCA Research Report 129, issue 1–33.

McNulty, T., C. Florackis and P. Ormrod, 2013, "Boards of Directors and Financial Risk During the Credit Crisis", *Corporate Governance: An International Review,* 21(1), pp 58–78.

Power, M., S. Ashby and T. Palermo, 2013, "Risk Culture in Financial Organisations", Centre for Analysis of Risk and Regulation, London School of Economics.

Rubinstein, A., 2012, *Economic Fables* (Cambridge, UK: Open Book Publishers).

Rumelt, R. P., 2011, *Good Strategy/Bad Strategy: The Difference and Why it Matters* (London: Profile Books).

Salz, A., 2013, "Salz Review Report", Barclays.

Schein, E. H., 1984, "Coming to a New Awareness of Organizational Culture", *Sloan Management Review,* 25(2), Winter, pp 3–16.

Schein, E. H., 1996, "Culture: The Missing Concept In Organization Studies", *Administrative Science Quarterly,* 41(2), June, pp 229–40.

Shell Plc, "Code of Conduct" (available at www.shell.com).

Spencer Stuart, 2014, "What Directors Think".

Stanford, N., 2010, *Organisation Culture: Getting it Right* (London: Profile Books).

Sutherland, S., 2013, *Irrationality: The Enemy Within. (20th anniversary edition)* (London: Pinter and Martin).

Tett, G., 2008, "Insight: Anthropological Insights into Banking Behaviour", *Financial Times,* January 27.

Van Maanan, J., 2011, "Ethnography as Work: Some Rules of Engagement", *Journal of Management Studies,* 48(1), pp 218–34.

Wageman, R., H. Gardner and M. Mortensen, 2012, "Teams Have Changed: Catching Up to the Future", *Journal of Organizational Behavior,* 33(3), pp 301–15.

Walker, D., 2009, "A Review of Corporate Governance in UK Banks and other Financial Industry Entities".

Wee, H., 2013, "Korean Culture May Offer Clues in Asiana crash", www.CNBC.com, July 9 (available at http://www.cnbc.com/id/100869966).

Weick, K. E. and K. M. Sutcliffe, 2007, *Managing the Unexpected: Resilient Performance in an Age of Uncertainty (2e)* (San Francisco, CA: Jossey Bass).

4

The Views of the PRA on Risk Culture and Risk Governance in Banks and Insurers

Andrew Bailey and John Sutherland

Bank of England

This chapter introduces the role of the Prudential Regulation Authority (PRA) and its interest in risk culture. The importance the PRA attaches to those banks it supervises that have an effective risk appetite framework (RAF) is discussed, as is the role of the board in the overall context of risk management. The chapter also explores the kinds of questions that boards should ask, and looks at the issues raised by matrix management, covering business lines, entities and geographies. Finally, reference is made to insurance failures as seen through the problems those boards suffered, showing a close similarity with the failings seen on banks boards and the need for similar regulatory expectations regarding risk governance, risk appetite and risk culture for insurers as for banks.

THE ROLE OF THE PRA

Banks are essentially risk-taking businesses and this chapter concerns risk in banks, the presence of which defines the reason for having a prudential regulator such as the PRA. History abounds with examples of banks that have failed because they have taken on more risk than they had resources to manage. The shortfall in resources might have been in the balance sheet, not enough capital and liquidity, or it might have been in the boardroom, not enough people able to understand and direct appropriate mitigating action.

However, it is much more likely that it was an amalgam of both. This extract from the Federal Inquiry into the failure of Penn Square Bank in 1981 shows risk outstripping controls is not a new phenomenon:

> Well, sir, I guess the point that you are probably after, and maybe I can help you reach that point, is that the growth of the bank had been so dynamic that it had literally outstripped its management, its people, its personnel, its physical plant. That growth had been so rapid that the personnel had not been hired to cope with it.[1]

Following the catastrophic events of the 2007–08 crisis that led to the failure of RBS and HBOS, the two biggest UK bank failures but only two among many across the world, a complete review of prudential regulation and supervision led to the creation of the PRA. This work started in 2010 and led to the publication of the new approach the PRA would adopt in October 2012, shortly before it became an operating subsidiary of the Bank of England in April 2013. The PRA clarified the way it would work through its Approach Document:[2]

> The PRA will have a statutory objective to promote the safety and soundness of firms. It is required to pursue this primarily by seeking to avoid adverse effects on financial stability, and in particular seeking to minimise adverse effects resulting from disruption to the continuity of financial services that can be caused by the way firms run their business or upon their failure. A stable financial system, that is resilient in providing the critical financial services the economy needs, is a necessary condition for a healthy and successful economy.[3]

In setting out its stall, the PRA made sure that it was not viewed in any way as a no-fail regulator by rather clearly laying out its objective of containing failure and ensuring that critical economic functions would be protected:

> Firm failures happen, but the PRA seeks in particular to ensure that they do not result in significant disruption to the supply of critical economic functions, including depositors' ability to make payments. Assessing and planning to contain the impact of failure by developing feasible and credible resolution plans for its firms is a core part of the PRA's supervisory work. Its ability to do this depends on the efficacy of the statutory resolution regime, on which the PRA works with the rest of the Bank.[4]

The PRA was also clear about the standards it wished firms to hold themselves to: "The PRA will expect firms not merely to meet and continue to meet the letter of these requirements, but also to consider the overriding principle of safety and soundness."

The nature of banks is that from time to time markets offer returns that boards can find hard to turn away from. However, where there is return there is risk and the PRA approach places the responsibility for managing this risk with the firm, and responsibility for creating the culture that supports risk management with boards and senior management.

> It is the responsibility of each firm's board and management to manage the firm prudently, consistent with its safety and soundness, thereby contributing to the continued stability of the financial system. This goes beyond complying with the letter of the PRA's detailed requirements, for example, on adequate capital and liquidity and risk management and controls, and it often means firms acting more prudently than they would otherwise choose. It also goes beyond core responsibilities for all boards and management, such as ensuring that individuals appointed to senior management positions are competent to fill such roles, setting the firm's strategy and policies clearly, and ensuring that these are applied throughout the organisation, with responsibilities clearly apportioned.[5]

A final point to make is clarification of what the PRA means by "safety and soundness":

> "Safety and soundness" involves firms having resilience against failure now and in the future, and avoiding harm resulting from the disruption to the continuity of financial services, either in the course of business or in the event of failure.[6]

The Approach Document therefore sets the scene for how the PRA will operate and how it expects firms to operate, and to a very large extent there will be an overlap of interest as far as safety and soundness is concerned. There are nuances where, for instance, the board may view a loss of market share in a broad sense of how successful the bank is, whereas the PRA will ask in a more focused way what does this say about the business model of the bank, and does it indicate any threat to viability?

Another way of looking at nuanced differences between the bank and the PRA is to consider culture. The bank's board will properly consider the importance of culture in terms of customer fairness, staff morale and the acquisition and retention of business. The PRA will care about culture only to the extent it impacts upon safety and soundness.[7] In this context, it may well be the case that the PRA's

Figure 4.1 The PRA's risk framework

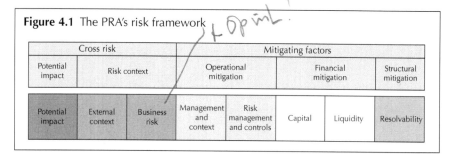

Cross risk			Mitigating factors				
Potential impact	Risk context		Operational mitigation		Financial mitigation		Structural mitigation
Potential impact	External context	Business risk	Management and context	Risk management and controls	Capital	Liquidity	Resolvability

interest is in the bank's risk culture rather than its overall culture. It is certainly not part of the PRA's brief to determine the rights and wrongs of culture, but it will be interested in how the bank's culture manifests itself in terms of risk management.

The PRA risk framework is shown in Figure 4.1. This framework enables the PRA to assess the gross risk the bank poses to its objectives of safety and soundness, and the mitigating factors that taken together allow the PRA to arrive at a net risk position for the bank.

Culture firmly sits within operational mitigation, but not just in "management and governance", as it also forms the part of "risk management and controls" that is the province of the board in setting the RAF. Setting this framework is a key activity for boards because in many ways it defines that part of the culture the PRA is most interested in: the risk culture.[8]

RISK CULTURE

The Financial Stability Board (FSB) has issued guidance to supervisors on this subject, which provides this definition: "While various definitions of culture exist, supervisors are focusing on the institution's norms, attitudes and behaviours related to risk awareness, risk taking and risk management, or the institution's risk culture."[9]

The PRA was already interested in the culture displayed by the banks it regulates, the state of health of a bank in the medium term being inextricably linked to the state of health of its culture today. The FSB guidance supports the PRA approach through its view on the consistency that a good risk culture provides: "A sound risk culture consistently supports appropriate risk awareness, behaviours and judgements about risk taking within a strong risk governance framework."[10]

PRA recognises that risk culture is not just about consistency, important though this is. There is a clear need to set standards in terms of the amount of risk a bank is willing to accept, as well as what happens if this risk is exceeded. The FSB lays out four themes in this respect:

❏ an appropriate risk–reward balance consistent with the institution's risk appetite is achieved when taking on risks;
❏ an effective system of controls commensurate with the scale and complexity of the financial institution is properly put in place;
❏ the quality of risk models, data accuracy, capability of available tools to accurately measure risks, and justifications for risk taking can be challenged; and
❏ all limit breaches, deviations from established policies and operational incidents are thoroughly followed up with proportionate disciplinary actions when necessary.

These are not just idle phrases. The PRA expects the boards of banks to have a firm grip on the risks being run and the forward-looking risks that may arise. This must include appropriate stress and reverse stress testing. It is inconceivable that the board of a bank can achieve this without the type of risk culture the FSB promotes being in place.

RISK GOVERNANCE

The PRA, as the prudential regulator of banks, is closely interested in how they manage their risk. In this context, the way the board engages with the RAF is critical. The FSB consulted with banks globally during 2013 to establish clarity around the RAF. This consultation dealt with taxonomy through to the very necessary delivery by the board of an effective risk culture.

The FSB define the RAF as follows:

> The overall approach, including policies, processes, controls and systems through which risk appetite is established, communicated and monitored. It includes a risk appetite statement, risk limits and an outline of the roles and responsibilities of those overseeing the implementation and monitoring of the RAF. The RAF should consider material risks to the firm, as well as to the firm's reputation *vis-à-vis* policyholders, depositors, investors and customers.[11]

Cutting to the chase, this means boards must be able to write down the risk it is happy for the bank to take and the controls that are

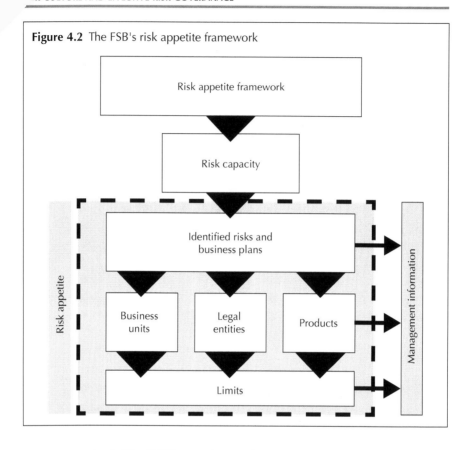

Figure 4.2 The FSB's risk appetite framework

required. The FSB's words are shown diagrammatically in Figure 4.2.

A brief description of each element is given below, again based on the FSB paper, with greater expansion on each later in this chapter. It is essential that the board grasp the mechanism of the RAF, as without this then any meaningful engagement and challenge with regards to risk is frankly impossible.

Defining risk capacity

A definition of risk capacity is: "The maximum level of risk the firm can assume before breaching constraints determined by regulatory capital and liquidity needs and its obligations, also from a conduct perspective, to depositors, policyholders, other customers and shareholders." In other words, does the bank have enough capital and liquidity now and in the future to meet its business plans?

How does this deal with
u-qualifub' inls? egt kep
opinh

As we know, having enough capital to absorb asset losses is essential for a bank. In abstract, it may seem somewhat surreal to suggest that a bank would take on more risk than it had capital to support. Except, unfortunately, as we have already seen in a number of well-recorded cases, that is exactly what did happen. This might come through decisions about the business model or acquisition of businesses. A bank may have the opportunity to buy a new earning asset (it may be a trading book or a mortgage portfolio), in which case the directors should know if this means dipping into existing capital to the extent the bank's safety is put at risk.

While this might all sound pretty obvious stuff, it is clear that in the run up to the crisis many firms had not carried out the basic analysis of their positions. In the case of a regional building society, a plan for them to buy a mortgage book in late 2007 ran into opposition from the regulator for this very reason. Converting low yielding liquid assets into higher paying but illiquid mortgage assets made sense from a profitability standpoint, but it made no sense in light of the extreme pressure on bank liquidity generally at that time.

Risk appetite is shown in Figure 4.2 to be an amalgam of several items. The FSB define risk appetite as: "The aggregate level and types of risk a firm is willing to assume within its risk capacity to achieve its strategic objectives and business plan." In other words, the board have to take the firm's business plan and risk-assess it, in the course of which they will assure themselves that the resources of the bank are sufficient not only to meet the plan, but also in the event that the plans go awry or some significant external event takes place that adversely impacts the bank.

Identified risks

The FSB noted the RAF should "determine for each material risk the maximum level of risk that the firm is willing to operate within, based on its risk appetite, risk capacity and risk profile".[12] The determination of material risks will include such areas as credit risk, basis risk, interest rate risk, market risk, operational risk, currency risk and foreign exchange risk.

It is not the purpose of this chapter to dive into each of these risks in any detail, but rather to highlight key points boards need generally to bear in mind. The first is to consider if commonly known risks that have not hitherto been relevant are now important because of a change in circumstances. For example, a small regional bank may not have intentionally taken foreign exchange risk in the past and therefore might have no risk treatment for it, but a change in business activity could have suddenly exposed the bank to this risk.

For instance, prior to the global financial crisis many UK building societies did not see basis risk as an exposure until very late. As is known, basis risk is simply that the interest received from assets is based on a different dynamic to the interest paid on liabilities. At the end of the 1990s, all of the societies' mortgage assets would have been on managed rates (determined by the society) and all of the savings' balances similarly. The basis on which interest was calculated was therefore the same for both assets and liabilities, and thus little or no basis risk existed. Progressively, the societies designed fixed rate mortgages that matured at the end of the deal onto the standard variable rate, which they managed. However, in 2003–05 this gradually changed such that the fixed rate mortgages matured onto a small margin above the Bank of England base rate, which the societies had no control over. Over time, more fixed rate mortgages matured in this way until in 2008 large swathes of their mortgage books had interest linked to the base rate.

When the base rate was quickly reduced to 0.5% in 2008, these societies found they had quantities of mortgages earning less than the society was paying to savers, giving a negative net interest margin. While the societies had their savings' balances on managed rates and could change them by taking action to bring these down below the mortgage rate, this would have left them hopelessly uncompetitive in the savings market and led to loss of funding. The basis risk had crystallised and was in the end pretty much the final nail in the coffin for a few societies.

The change in the pricing policy, maturing fixed rates onto a rate linked to the base rate instead of onto a rate they set themselves, went unnoticed in risk terms. This is a classic case of a risk that had in the past been regarded correctly as not applying to the societies, and therefore had not been managed, but when it subsequently appeared on the books it was not spotted until too late.

The next point about material risks is not to fall for equalisation. Let us say that a bank identifies seven material risks: the board should know which of these risks pose the biggest risk to the bank, and not accept any suggestion they all be treated equally. If it is determined that, of the seven, three pose 80% of the risk, then it is safe to assume this should be reflected in the resources the bank deploys in mitigation. A clue might be if there is one page per risk in the management information!

In supervising banks, the PRA requires its own supervisors to identify the top three risks every year that each supervised bank poses to the Bank of England's objectives for safety and soundness. This analysis is then backed up by the supervisors being required to reflect in their workplan for the next year mitigation of these three key risks. This may not be a bad yardstick for bank boards to consider within their own banks. What are the top few risks to the viability of the bank, and what are management doing to mitigate those risks?

Business plans

All firms, bank and non-bank, produce business plans but banks alone are prone to the twin attacks of asset losses leading to insolvency and/or runs leading to a liquidity crisis. This difference is what boards have to both understand and manage. The consequence is that bank boards must have forecasts of both capital and liquidity that are outputs of the bank's business plan.

Increased lending and/or the acquisition of other earning assets require financing. We know that increased leverage, borrowing to finance new assets, reduces the bank's capacity to absorb losses. This is shown through the example of a bank changing its business plan to increase its size. Figure 4.3 shows the evolution of such a plan, with the first focus on how to increase the assets, and then the decision on funding and the final shape of the balance sheet after expansion. This gives the movement in a bank's balance sheet over time.

In Figure 4.3, we can see at (1) the position of the bank at the start of the plan to increase in size while (2) shows the planned increased assets but without the planned change in liabilities. The bank has a clear plan for asset growth, but the funding gap has yet to be closed. At (3) the bank has set out the change needed to liabilities, and has chosen to close the gap with more wholesale funding. The net result is a bigger bank that, all other things being equal, will generate higher net interest income and thus profit. However, the leverage has increased (the same amount of capital is supporting a larger balance sheet) and it will take a smaller percentage loss in assets to render the bank insolvent.

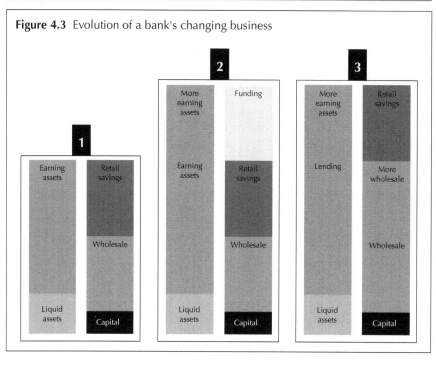

Figure 4.3 Evolution of a bank's changing business

The business plan question for the board is whether this dilution of capital to assets is within their risk appetite. If it is not, then the board must decide either to grow less quickly or finance part of the growth with additional capital. The board may also wish to debate whether they are happy to have less of the funding at (3) provided by retail savings – and, if not, then they may decide that in addition to raising more capital, more savings should be attracted to reduce the increase in wholesale funding.

This is not intended to be a treatise on bank funding, but the discussion should explain in a general way the vital link between the risk appetite of the bank and its business plans and the critical role of challenge played by the board, particularly the non-executives.

Business units, legal entities and products

The FSB sees the RAF being embedded into business units, legal entities and products. We should be clear on what these three are.

❏ Business units – this could be a geographical unit (eg, Europe, Middle East & Africa, EMEA) or a business line (eg, commercial lending, global custody management or personal banking).

❏ Legal entities – a legal unit that could be a bank holding company, a subsidiary or a branch of an overseas bank.
❏ Products – this might be specific, such as mortgages, or it could be a collection of individual products in a business line, such as fixed income, currencies and commodities (FICC).

The complexity in many banks, particularly large banks, is the three-dimensional overlap of business units, legal entities and products. It is quite typical for a bank to have a management line that heads up a product, selling into a management line that heads up a region, with that management line booking the product sales to one or more legal entities. The reasons are perhaps more obvious than the dangers.

A bank's clarity and focus around product profitability can be optimised using a management line that owns the product. Equally, the ownership in management terms of a country or geographic region optimises focus there, as does having a management line that focuses on, say, wealth management or commercial banking. The dangers were highlighted only too well in the failure of Barings in 1995 through the fraudulent activities of Nick Leeson:

> Barings employed a matrix approach to managing this global network. Traders reported to a local manager regarding operational and administrative matters and to product managers, who had responsibility for the profitability of their transactions. Proprietary trading reported to a different product manager than agency trading. Back-office managers reported to a local manager and their functional head in London. This matrix management structure fragmented the oversight of Leeson's activities. In principle, Leeson reported to product managers in London, a local manager at Baring Securities Singapore and a regional operations manager for Southeast Asia. In practice, Leeson evaded effective supervision altogether.[13]

The reasons for more than one legal entity are likely to stem from legal constraints and tax management. In the US under the Dodd–Frank Act (see endnote 12 for reference), a bank cannot generally deal in securities on their own account, but a bank holding company can own a bank and a non-bank securities company that does carry out proprietary trading. As a whole, the bank holding company is not different to the European universal bank but a legal constraint determines a specific legal entity structure. In addition to tax and legal constraints, a bank often has legal entities reflecting past mergers and acquisitions.[14]

It is not unusual for a global bank to have hundreds of legal entities in scores of jurisdictions. There are a number of implications, such as who is accountable for success or failure, the product line or the business line? In addition, legal entities have less importance when a bank is trading – however, if a bank fails everything focuses on the legal entities. "Global banks are global in life, but national in death" is a quote famously attributed to Sir Mervyn King.[15] More detail is found in the June 2009 Bank of England "Financial Stability Review", an extract from which is set out below:

> The legal structure of a banking group is important in a crisis because it is legal entities, not business functions, which go into insolvency. Because of that, the resolution authorities need to have access to information on a legal entity basis. But firms sometimes do not produce data in that form, given their day-to-day focus on business functions. That needs to be addressed.[16]

Part of setting out the bank's risk appetite involves the board deciding how much risk to allow individual business units and/or individual products. This will be highly complex in a global bank but much simpler in a regional building society. In either case, however, the board should be the arbiter of how the risk and thus capital is allocated to different parts of the bank.

The board also need to understand the importance of legal entities and the interest therein from regulators and governments. The likelihood is that, in the absence of a clear resolution plan, banks will be asked to hold more capital and liquidity in specific legal entities. This is to ensure that in the event of a resolution the authorities do not themselves face a disorderly failure of the bank in the absence of adequate capital and liquid assets. The danger of fragmentation of the bank's balance sheets is well understood, but in the absence of an effective resolution plan the authorities will have to take remedial action.

The final point of note is that there should be sufficient understanding, including by the banks' non-executive directors (NEDs), of how the legal structure works. BCCI was an extreme example of a legal structure designed to confuse and obscure from public view the workings of the bank. This description of BCCI, from a report produced after its failure, reveals the scale of the BCCI legal entity artifice:

> From the outset, BCCI adopted a dual banking structure. The non-bank holding company established in Luxembourg in 1972 (BCCI

Holdings SA), under the protection of very tight secrecy laws, owned two separate banks that were licensed and supervised in two separate jurisdictions, well insulated by bank secrecy laws: BCCI SA in Luxembourg and BCCI Overseas in the Cayman Islands. Although BCCI SA was registered as a bank in Luxembourg, its banking business was conducted not in Luxembourg, but through 47 branches in 13 countries. BCCI Overseas did conduct a banking business in the Cayman Islands as well as through 63 branches of BCCI Overseas in 28 countries. As the Shadow Financial Regulatory Committee (1991) noted, "BCCI's headquarters were established in countries with weak supervisory authorities, strong secrecy laws and neither lenders of last resort nor deposit insurers who would have financial reasons to be concerned about the solvency of banks that are chartered in their jurisdictions." Contrary to what the organisation chart seems to imply, neither Luxembourg nor the Cayman Islands was the operational headquarters of BCCI. Instead, most managerial decisions were made in London with oversight from the founder, Aga Hassan Abedi.[17]

This is not to imply that what turned out to be the fraudulent activities at BCCI are likely to be found in other institutions. However, as an example of how legal entities – particularly across borders – can be used to conceal trading activities, it is probably without parallel. Mapping the business onto the legal entities is a crucial part of business model analysis. If there is a lack of clarity in any part of the map, then boards do well to recall what was found on ancient maps when the cartographer was unclear: "here be dragons".

Risk limits

Figure 4.3 shows the risk appetite framework ending with limits. This is a translation of the words in various parts of the RAF into the limits that business units and product areas have to remain within. Simplistically, a statement in the RAF that the board wants to write low-risk mortgage business calls for loan-to-value and loan-to-income limits that reflect this. Allowing for unlimited amounts of 100% loan-to-value mortgages would mean the risk limit was at odds with such a RAF. The combination of the identified risks and business plans, the split of this by business, product and legal entity, and the attendant limits equals the risk appetite.

There is one final piece in the risk jigsaw and that is the risk profile. In summary, this is the risk the bank is actually running versus its risk capacity and risk appetite. It is expressed via the quantitative risk limits and, as needed, qualitative aspects of appetite, and by management information recording the risks taken.

This is the FSB version of risk profile:

> Point in time assessment of the firm's net risk exposures (after taking into account mitigants) aggregated within and across each relevant risk category based on forward-looking assumptions. The RAF sets the firm's risk profile in the course of implementation of the firm's strategy and the risks undertaken in relation to the firm's risk capacity.[18]

If that all sounds a mouthful, then what about: "how much risk is the bank taking against how much risk it planned to take and how much risk it can afford to take?" Or, "are we taking more or less risk than we planned and when do we run out of capital?" The real complication for many banks and thus their boards is the extreme difficulty of collecting all of the bank's risk positions and relating them to one another to get to this "magical" net risk position. This is Ben Bernanke on the subject:

> If you looked at the weaknesses in financial management, if you look at the private sector for a moment, there were a lot of problems. But I think a very important area was weakness of risk management. So these firms became very big and they became very complicated. They got involved in many activities. And they simply did not – and, of course, the supervisors bear some responsibility for not insisting appropriately that they do it – but they did not have, and some of them still don't have to our satisfaction, the management information systems, the techniques, and so on, in order to look at their risks across their entire business. Not just in each individual subsidiary, but across the entire firm.[19]

This discussion of the RAF is the essence of risk management in a bank from the board's standpoint. It does not mean there is not more to understand, but if directors do not understand the backbone of how risk is organised and monitored, then risk in the bank is simply out of control. Moreover, the PRA's interest in the risk culture of the bank is explained by the link between effective risk governance and risk culture. If the board is unable to comprehend the way the key components of the RAF interact, it is communicating loud and clear throughout the bank that risk culture does not matter.

The question to ask of any board is: "do you the board have a common risk language (including measurement) that you share with all others in the bank?" If not, then the bank either has a recipe for confusion or a number of people within it are pretending that all is well, or even fooling themselves.

This involvement of the board in the creation and agreement of the RAF is absolutely crucial. The FSB have this to say about it:

> The risk appetite framework explicitly defines the boundaries within which management is expected to operate when pursuing the firm's business strategy. Firms that implement a RAF most effectively are those that incorporate the framework into the decision-making process and into the firm-wide risk management framework, and communicate and champion the framework throughout the organisation, starting from the top.[20]

In other words, the RAF applies to the board downwards, not just below the board; the FSB emphasise this strongly:

> The board of directors must establish the firm-wide RAF and approve the risk appetite statement, which is developed in collaboration with the chief executive officer (CEO), chief risk officer (CRO) and chief financial officer (CFO). The CEO, CRO and CFO translate those expectations into targets and constraints for business lines and legal entities to follow. The independent assessment of the firm's RAF (ie, by internal audit, an external auditor and/or other independent third party) is critical to the ongoing maintenance of a firm's internal controls, risk management and risk governance. The strength of the relationships between the board, CEO, CRO, CFO, business lines and internal audit plays an instrumental role in the RAF's effectiveness. As such, distinct mandates and responsibilities for each of these levels of governance are essential.[21]

It is worth noting here that if only one NED on the board has this skill, then immense responsibility is placed on their shoulders, as all of the other NEDs will look to that person for reassurance. This whole debate about the importance of the board as a group being able to grasp the essentials of risk management is of great importance, as returning to the Barings failure highlights only too well:

> The Board of Banking Supervision concluded there was a near total failure of risk management systems and controls as well as confusion within the management group. The Singapore inquest on Barings securities Ltd was less charitable (Lim and Tan, paragraph 36 (vii)) concluding that managers of Barings "could have remained ignorant of the account up to the time of collapse only if they had persistently shut themselves from the truth … [The] explanation that Mr. Leeson's trading activities posed little (or no) risk to the Barings Group, but yielded very good returns, is implausible and in our view, demonstrates a degree of ignorance of market reality that totally lacks credibility."[22]

If the board do not confidently grasp the knowledge of risk such that they can challenge the executive effectively, then risk – which is at the core of any bank – is out of control and trouble over a period can be expected. The PRA recognise this very clearly, and supervisors have frequent opportunities to assess the risk culture in a bank. In fact, every interaction with the people in a bank from top to bottom is an opportunity for supervisors to ask themselves: "how is this informing my opinion of the culture in the bank?"

THE SENIOR MANAGEMENT REGIME: ROLE OF THE BOARD AND SENIOR EXECUTIVES

The responsibility of bank boards has been put firmly in the spotlight. The Parliamentary Commission on Banking Standards, which produced its fifth and final report in June 2013, noted what it called the dismal feature of lack of personal responsibility:

> One of the most dismal features of the banking industry to emerge from our evidence was the striking limitation on the sense of personal responsibility and accountability of the leaders within the industry for the widespread failings and abuses over which they presided. Ignorance was offered as the main excuse. It was not always accidental. Those who should have been exercising supervisory or leadership roles benefited from an accountability firewall between themselves and individual misconduct, and demonstrated poor, perhaps deliberately poor, understanding of the front line. Senior executives were aware that they would not be punished for what they could not see and promptly donned the blindfolds. Where they could not claim ignorance, they fell back on the claim that everyone was party to a decision, so that no individual could be held squarely to blame – the Murder on the Orient Express defence. It is imperative that in future senior executives in banks have an incentive to know what is happening on their watch – not an incentive to remain ignorant in case the regulator comes calling.[23]

This view manifested itself in a key recommendation of the Commission: the creation of the Senior Management Regime (SMR). The idea is estimably simple, the clarification and acceptance of the responsibilities of board directors, executive and non-executive, together with key below-board executives such as the head of internal audit and the chief risk officer.

The PRA's challenge is to create the rules that define how the SMR will operate. It also has to take into account in its rule-making the additional Commission recommendation that in a failed bank it will be the senior person's responsibility to explain why they were not culpable for the failure, thus reversing the burden of proof from the existing position where the regulator has to prove culpability.

The SMR is elegantly simple in concept. However, the PRA has to tread a fine line between clarifying where individual responsibility sits, on the one hand, and leaving directors to question why they would want to take on this additional regulatory burden, on the other. In managing this overarching risk to the SMR, namely that bank directors become an endangered species, the PRA needs to make clear its expectations with respect of governance. What is it reasonable to expect directors to be responsible for? This work will unfold throughout 2014, with the final policy statement and rules expected towards the end of the year. Big questions abound, such as the technical knowledge the PRA will expect of bank directors.

The previous discussion about the FSB RAF gives some clue in that direction. It is not a technical challenge to understand how such a framework should help a board to mitigate risk. It may well be a technical challenge to understand complex derivatives and models. It will certainly be a challenge if the information provided to the board is so poor as to render any analysis a dead letter.

The PRA, FSB and Parliamentary Commission on Banking Standards are at one on the responsibilities of the board, with the final clear word provided here by the FSB:

> A key value that should be espoused is the expectation that staff act with integrity (doing the right thing) and promptly escalate observed non-compliance within or outside the organisation (no surprises approach).[24]

Underlying any debate about risk is analysis of incentives. To what extent and how are the executives of the bank incentivised to take risk to maximise their income? The 2007–08 crisis showed clearly enough the impact short-term incentives could have on the risk profile of banks. Too often the short-term profitability of the bank was built upon medium-term risk. It was therefore quite possible for executives to be rewarded for income generation that would ultimately be lost several times over as these medium-term risks crystallised:

> … the nature of compensation systems at banks, particularly those that were based on short-term performance targets, provided incentives for bankers to assume additional risk via leveraging the capital base.[25]

These two examples in isolation – the technical demand of understanding risk models and the demand to understand the holistic impact of incentive schemes – highlight the broad skillset banks need with which the SMR should be consistent.

CULTURE OR RISK CULTURE FOR BANKS AND INSURERS?

Another area of concern in terms of responsibilities is in culture related to conduct, which many banks are grappling with. The Libor traders, rate setters and Nick Leeson were all relatively junior managers. How, therefore, can a director accept responsibility for the culture throughout the business? Here we need to differentiate clearly between what is reasonable and what is unreasonable. It is not reasonable for directors to be responsible for the behaviour of everyone in the business, whether small and regional or massive and global. However, it is reasonable for them to be accountable for the control framework in the business, the communication of the culture and to have several independent forms of feedback on how the culture is manifest in the business.

Was it reasonable for bank directors caught out by the Libor rate setting scandal to avoid responsibility? After all, it was the front line that did it, but it was the first-line management who did not spot it or did not act, then middle management who did not spot it or did not act, followed by the senior management who did not spot it or did not act and, finally, risk, compliance and internal audit who did not spot it or did not act; and all of that failure is nothing to do with the board?

The PRA is very clear that it cannot set unreasonable goals for directors, but in turn banks cannot be run on the basis that any infraction is OK at a junior level, no matter how big the cost, because it is effectively in the "too difficult to do" pile.

So far, apart from the quotation regarding culture from the inquiry into the failure of HIH Insurance, we have talked exclusively about banks. However, the PRA is also accountable for the regulation and supervision of insurers operating in the UK. Is it worthwhile, therefore, reading across from the narrative above to see how this might apply to insurers?

The question of whether we want insurers to have a sound risk culture, a knowledgeable board, NEDs who are able to challenge effectively and an embedded RAF should all easily be answered "yes". It would be wrong for the PRA to hold the boards of insurers to different standards than those to which boards of banks are held.

However, the Parliamentary Commission into Banking Standards has put forward its views on responsibility within the proposed SMR. This by definition will not apply to insurers.

It does not require much research to find examples of risk failure among insurers, and descriptions of failure that are redolent of those we have seen in banks. Here is a quote from Judge Owen in Australia:

> The problematic aspects of the corporate culture of HIH – which led directly to the poor decision-making – can be summarised succinctly. There was blind faith in a leadership that was ill equipped for the task. There was insufficient ability and independence of mind in and associated with the organisation to see what had to be done and what had to be stopped or avoided. Risks were not properly identified and managed. Unpleasant information was hidden, filtered or sanitised. And there was a lack of sceptical questioning and analysis when and where it mattered.[26]

Further evidence comes from the US concerning the failure of AIG:

> Our examination revealed stunning instances of governance break-downs and irresponsibility. You will read, among other things, about AIG senior management's ignorance of the terms and risks of the company's US$79 billion derivatives exposure to mortgage-related securities.[27]

In the UK, the failure of Equitable Life led Lord Penrose to make this comment about the skills of NEDs:

> None of the non-executive members of the board had relevant skills or experience of actuarial principles or methodologies over most of the reference period. They were generally experienced in the financial services industry, but specialists, where they had specialist knowledge, in general finance, in investment and banking rather than life assurance.[28]

It is abundantly clear from just these three extracts that failure to mitigate risks by the boards of insurers has the same root causes found in bank failures. Mark Carney, governor of the Bank of England, set out this position in *The Times*:

> What the Bank of England won't do is protect insurance companies from the consequences of their own decisions. It is for boards to run their companies, and for those who manage insurers to be account-able for their actions if things go wrong. So alongside reforms that Parliament has asked us to make to hold senior bankers to account, we will create a similar regime for senior managers in the insurance industry. Integrity, honesty and skill are not optional, whether you

run an insurance company, global investment bank or building society.[29]

With this in mind, the PRA will as far as possible seek to emulate where it can the key parts of the SMR in the governance, culture and, especially, risk culture of insurers.

CONCLUSION

The PRA expects all the firms it supervises to have sound risk practices. These risk practices must emanate from a board that is equipped with the ability to lead a clear and coherent risk culture that contains a robust, continuously improving and workable risk appetite framework.

These expectations are not only because the PRA has to meet its statutory objectives, but also because the culture of the PRA itself must first and foremost believe in the spirit of regulations that are there to protect the stability of the UK economy. The PRA expects no less of the boards of the firms it supervises; it is looking to the spirit of the rules not just obeying the rules, that is the difference between success and failure.

1 Testimony of Eldon Beller, President, Penn Square Bank, before the Committee On Banking, Finance And Urban Affairs House of Representatives 97th Congress Second Session – Part 1, August 1982.
2 The PRA's Approach to Banking Supervision 19 June 2014.
3 ibid.
4 ibid.
5 ibid.
6 ibid.
7 Guidance on Supervisory Interaction with Financial Institutions on Risk Culture June 2014.
8 ibid.
9 Financial Stability Board, 2014, "Guidance on Supervisory Interaction with Financial Institutions on Risk Culture – A Framework for Assessing Risk Culture", April.
10 ibid.
11 Financial Stability Board, 2013, "Principles for an Effective Risk Appetite Framework", October.
12 Financial Stability Board, 2013, "Principles for An Effective Risk Appetite Framework – Consultative Document", July 17.
13 D. D. Evanoff and G. G. Kaufman (Eds), 2005, Systemic Financial Crises: Resolving Large Bank Insolvencies (Hackensack, NJ: World Scientific), pp 321–45.
14 SEC, 2014, "Prohibitions and Restrictions on Proprietary Trading and Certain Interests In, and Relationships With, Hedge Funds and Private Equity Funds", April.
15 Quoted by Adair Turner, press conference, March 18, 2009.
16 Bank of England Financial Stability Report, June 2009.
17 Evanoff and Kaufman (2005), pp 321–45.
18 Financial Stability Board, 2013, "Principles for An Effective Risk Appetite Framework – Consultative Document", July 17.

19 Financial Crisis Inquiry Commission, closed session: Ben Bernanke, Chairman of the Federal Reserve, November 17, 2009.

20 Financial Stability Board, 2013, "Principles for An Effective Risk Appetite Framework – Consultative Document", July 17.

21 ibid.

22 Evanoff and Kaufman (2005), pp 321–45.

23 House of Lords, House of Commons, Parliamentary Commission on Banking Standards, Report 5, "Changing Banking for Good", session 2013–14.

24 Financial Stability Board, 2014, "Guidance on Supervisory Interaction with Financial Institutions on Risk Culture – A Framework for Assessing Risk Culture", April.

25 Emilios Avgouleas and Jay Cullen, 2013, "Excessive Leverage And Bankers' Pay: Governance And Financial Stability Costs of a Symbiotic Relationship".

26 HIH Royal Commission, 2003, "The Failure of HIH Insurance", April.

27 Financial Crisis Inquiry Commission, 2011, "Final Report of the National Commission on the Causes of the Financial and Economic Crisis in the United States", pursuant to public law 111–21, January.

28 The Right Honourable Lord Penrose, 2004, "Report of the Equitable Life Inquiry", March.

29 Mark Carney, 2014, "Regulating the Insurance Industry to Support the Real Economy", *The Times*, May 22.

5

Risk Appetite and Risk Culture: A Regulatory View

Michael Alix

Federal Reserve Bank of New York

Financial organisations seeking to instill a strong risk culture – behaviours among business leaders, risk managers and risk takers that align with the expectations of directors and senior management – need to provide clear and consistent leadership, guidance and incentives to shape attitudes and achieve acceptable long-term results. Supervisors increasingly expect boards of directors and senior management to communicate guidance on strategy and risk taking clearly and effectively, and to test whether the actions taken and risks assumed are within levels desired. Since the early 2000s, for many firms this process has been either ineffective or non-existent.

The experience of the financial crisis of 2007–08 and beyond has demonstrated the need for stronger articulation by directors and senior management of desirable and undesirable risks, explained in the context of the firm's business model, strategy and external conditions. Careful articulation of so-called "risk appetite", and effective processes to ensure that any risks taken are within the set of acceptable risk parameters, are necessary for regulators and supervisors to gain comfort that the organisation is reasonably governed and risk managed. Risk appetite statements and frameworks have emerged as an intuitive and potentially effective way to express, record and manage types and levels of risk. Properly implemented and cascaded throughout the organisation, these statements and frameworks benefit all stakeholders.

The term "risk appetite" conveys different meaning to different audiences. While regulators have been using the terminology for many years, at times loosely or inconsistently, global supervisors have latterly clarified their objectives and definitions, provided high-level principles, and pushed directors and senior managers of firms to better articulate the relationship between strategy and risk taking. The regulatory efforts coincided with private sector initiatives intended to improve governance and risk management practices. This chapter will review ongoing development of risk appetite as a key governance process – defining terms and describing the roles of directors, management and risk takers – and highlight how the process can both promote and benefit from a supportive culture. The development of clear, straightforward institution-wide risk appetite statements and comprehensive implementing frameworks, with data and communication and modelling behaviours that embed the risk appetite throughout the organisation, should be an urgent priority for firms to satisfy stakeholder desires for strong and effective governance – and not just to "tick the box" to placate regulators.

This chapter sets out the history of the developing thinking on risk appetite, and then proceeds to define commonly used terms and describe the critical and distinct roles of various actors inside organisations. The chapter will further elaborate on elements of strong risk appetite statements and frameworks, and highlight the essential complementary link with culture.

HISTORY OF REGULATORY AND PRIVATE SECTOR INITIATIVES ON RISK APPETITE

In assessing safety and soundness, financial regulators and banking supervisors must understand a banking firm's governance and risk management processes. Historically, the discussion among regulators, directors and managers of significant banking risks was dominated by the identification, measurement and management of credit risks. Traditional lending risks posed the greatest threats to a bank's viability, and those credit risks – when well understood and reasonably well measured – were often controlled via simple concentration and sector limits and ratings requirements set and enforced by a chief credit officer. The advent of more complex risks in banking organisations – for instance, trading and counterparty risks associated with derivatives – led to attempts to quantify potential or loan equivalent exposures, first in industry (through what was called daily-earnings-at-risk) and then through regulation (with proba-bilistic model-based measures incorporated in the Basel Capital Accord market risk rule). However, firms' ability to measure and roll-up risks at the enterprise level, and to contain risk taking relative to the capacity and willingness of directors to accept that risk, was shown for many to be weak and ineffective by the financial crisis. This could be attributed to, in part, increasing complexity in banking business models and strategies that drove changes in the types of risks that were undertaken, and to market forces that enabled substantial growth in leverage.

Supervisors and banking managers have used varying and impre-cise language to refer to banks' ability and willingness to accept credit and other significant risks. The term "risk appetite" was used by supervisors as early as the 1990s. It was then that the Joint Forum on Financial Conglomerates, a working group of global banking, securities and insurance supervisors, asked large complex institu-tions about risk appetite in a survey on risk management. The surveyors sought to understand, in part, the firms' current and future risk appetite, parenthetically defined as "management's views as the conglomerate's willingness to accept risk".[1] However, the term "risk appetite" did not become part of the day-to-day vocabulary among bankers and supervisors until much later, and emerged far more prominently in the immediate aftermath of the financial crisis. In its third paper on improving industry risk prac-tices,[2] published in mid-2008, the private sector Counterparty Risk Management Policy Group argued that weaknesses in governance exacerbated problems among financial firms, and in response urged firms to better articulate and measure risk appetite.

In January 2009, the Basel Committee on Banking Supervision proposed enhancements to its Pillar 2 supervisory review process to examine governance and risk management to ensure that boards of directors and senior management, among other responsibilities, "define the risk appetite in a manner that considers the long-term performance over the cycle; and to set clear incentives across the firm to control risk exposures and concentrations in accordance with the stated risk appetite."[3]

The Senior Supervisors Group (SSG), comprised of supervisors of many of the largest banking organisations in the world, followed up an early 2008 report, in which the group differentiated among risk governance, risk management and measurement practices at large firms ahead of the most difficult period in the crisis, with a October 2009 report that considered the factors that contributed to most significant stress in 2008 and early 2009 for firms and markets. This report called out "the failure of some boards of directors and senior managers to establish, measure and adhere to a level of risk acceptable to the firm …",[4] and also cited material deficiencies in the ability of firms to gather relevant data and aggregate risks across the enterprise as an impediment to effective risk governance. The SSG added:

> A key weakness in governance stemmed from what several senior managers admitted was a disparity between the risks that their firms took and those that their boards of directors perceived the firms to be taking. In addition, supervisors saw insufficient evidence of active board involvement in setting the risk appetite for firms in a way that recognises the implications of that risk taking. Specifically, only rarely did supervisors see firms share with their boards and senior management a) robust measures of risk exposures (and related limits), b) the level of capital that the firm would need to maintain after sustaining a loss of the magnitude of the risk measure, and c) the actions that management could take to restore capital after sustaining such a loss. Supervisors believe that active board involvement in determining the risk tolerance of the firm is critical to ensuring that discipline is sustained in the face of future market pressures for excessive risk taking.[5]

A year later, members of an SSG working group met with 14 global firms in 10 different jurisdictions to determine progress made in developing effective risk aggregation and risk appetite frameworks (RAFs). While acknowledging that many firms had made progress in developing RAFs and improving IT infrastructure, the SSG noted that "considerably more work is needed to remediate risk management practices that were revealed as particularly weak during the height of the crisis".[6]

Nearly all firms produced a risk appetite statement, using a wide variety of approaches, but the statements were quite new and untested – having been in effect for a year or less at more than half of those firms. While the SSG working group found strengths and weaknesses in the implementation of RAFs among firms, no single firm demonstrated all best practices identified.

In 2011, the Institute for International Finance (IIF), a private sector organisation representing many large global banks, itself cited weak governance as a factor leading to the crisis and promoted the development of robust risk management frameworks. "One of the key lessons of the financial crisis was that some firms took more risk in aggregate than they were able to bear given their capital, liquidity and risk management capabilities, and some took risks that their management and boards did not properly understand or control."[7]

Despite both official and private sector pushing for better RAFs, progress remained slow, with apparent confusion among institutions and supervisors about what risk appetite statements should say and how effective RAFs should be designed and constructed. Referring to an October 2011 Financial Stability Board (FSB) progress report on enhanced supervision, the FSB's Supervisory Intensity and Effectiveness group noted that "effective risk appetite frameworks that are actionable and measurable by both financial institutions and supervisors had not yet been widely adopted. It concluded that the development of an effective risk appetite framework is important for financial institutions and supervisors, and needs attention by both." The 2011 report recommended that supervisors discuss expectations for what a "good" RAF entails and how to supervise these expectations.[8]

Banking supervisors in the US have similarly stressed the crucial need for directors to set strategy and clearly link to risk appetite. As part of its heightened expectations for large complex firms, the US Federal Reserve requires that boards of directors, with support of senior management, "establish and maintain the firm's culture, incentives, structure and processes that promote its compliance with laws, regulations and supervisory guidance". The supervisory guidance advances an expectation that boards "maintain a clearly articulated corporate strategy and institutional risk appetite", and goes on to make clear that "the board should set direction and oversight for revenue and profit generation, risk management and control functions, and other areas essential to sustaining the consolidated organisation".[9]

Similarly, the Office of the Comptroller of the Currency (OCC), which oversees national banks in the US, set heightened expectations "that pertains to risk appetite (or tolerance) and involves institutions defining and communicating an acceptable risk appetite across the organisation, including measures that address the amount of capital, earnings or liquidity that may be at risk on a firm-wide basis, the amount of risk that may be taken in each line of business, and the amount of risk that may be taken in each key risk category monitored by the institution".[10]

Even with the various attempts by supervisors to clarify expectations, Tapestry Networks, a governance consultancy that runs the Bank Governance Leadership Network, cited discussions among directors of large banks, risk managers and regulators that revealed "an enduring lack of clarity" regarding the objectives and core elements of a RAF.[11]

Therefore, in an attempt to clarify the language of risk appetite, and the expectations of various actors within financial organisations, in late 2013 the FSB's Supervisory Intensity and Effectiveness (SIE) group published principles designed to guide supervisors in assessing governance and risk appetite across jurisdictions.[12] The next sections will draw heavily on the FSB SIE's work in defining terms and setting out the responsibilities of board members and key executives.

KEY DEFINITIONS

Some uncertainty about the meaning of important terms used in describing RAFs, with perhaps slightly different definitions across jurisdictions and financial institutions, contributed to the confusion in conversations about risk governance among industry and regulators. For example, some firms used risk appetite and risk tolerance interchangeably, while others attributed different meanings to the two terms. After reviewing the literature and conferring with industry and supervisors, the FSB provided its own consensus definitions, detailed in Panel 5.1, with an aim to "establish a common nomenclature for supervisors and financial institutions to facilitate discussions on risk appetite".[13]

Among the noteworthy elements of the FSB SIE group's definitions, the group highlighted the importance of considering difficult-to-measure risks in all of the measures. It also chose not to separately define risk tolerance and instead clarify its meaning of risk appetite. The FSB included the important concept that risk appetite statements should express not only those risks that an institution is willing to accept, but also those risks an institution intends to avoid.

The FSB SIE group's definitions suggest a relative ordering of the measures of risk profile, risk appetite and risk capacity in a properly

PANEL 5.1: FSB DEFINITIONS

Risk appetite = positive articulation of desired
risk profile on a forward-looking basis

Risk profile < Risk appetite < Risk capacity

Risk appetite ≠ a simple definition of a buffer
between risk profile and risk capacity

In its principles,[14] the FSB SIE group provided the following definitions:

Risk capacity
The maximum level of risk the financial institution can assume given its current level of resources before breaching constraints determined by regulatory capital and liquidity needs, the operational environment (eg, technical infrastructure, risk management capabilities, expertise) and obligations, also from a conduct perspective, to depositors, policyholders, shareholders, fixed income investors, as well as other customers and stakeholders.

Risk appetite
The aggregate level and types of risk a financial institution is willing to assume within its risk capacity to achieve its strategic objectives and business plan.

Risk appetite statement
This is the articulation in written form of the aggregate level and types of risk that a financial institution is willing to accept or to avoid in order to achieve its business objectives. It includes qualitative statements, as well as quantitative measures expressed relative to earnings, capital, risk measures, liquidity and other relevant measures, as appropriate. It should also address more difficult-to-quantify risks such as reputation and conduct risks, as well as money laundering and unethical practices.

Risk appetite framework
This is the overall approach, including policies, processes, controls and systems, through which risk appetite is established, communicated and monitored. It includes a risk appetite statement, risk limits and an outline of the roles and responsibilities of those overseeing the implementation and monitoring of the RAF. The RAF should consider material risks to the financial institution, as well as to the institution's reputation *vis-à-vis* policyholders, depositors, investors and customers. The RAF aligns with the institution's strategy.

Risk profile
This is the point-in-time assessment of the financial institution's gross and, as appropriate, net risk exposures (after taking into account mitigants) aggregated within and across each relevant risk category based on forward-looking assumptions.

functioning RAF. The definitions suggest that, in practice, firms should ensure that risk appetite does not exceed risk capacity, and that risk profile remains within risk appetite.

ROLES OF THE BOARD AND SENIOR MANAGEMENT

Supervisors in the US and elsewhere are stepping up their engagement with both boards of directors and so-called "C-suite" management – primarily the chief executive officer (CEO), chief risk officer (CRO) and chief finance officer (CFO) – looking for more robust and more consistent discussions of the links among business strategy, competitive choices and the vulnerabilities that result. While it is also critical to continue to improve the stature and influence of the risk management organisation led by the CRO, responsibility for enhancements to risk governance should not be fully delegated to them. The board must articulate both the business strategy and the risk appetite against which strategy will be assessed, and senior management – including the CRO – must implement processes and systems that ensure that the board's wishes are followed in every aspect of business activity.

A financial organisation's highest-level governance body, typically the board of directors, should own both the business strategy and risk appetite. The manner in which directors achieve ownership varies. In some cases, the board merely accepts the risk appetite statement as crafted by senior management, while in other cases directors actively engage with management and drive the statement. The FSB's principles suggest that the board approve the risk appetite statement rather than simply acknowledge management's views, and establish an institution-wide RAF. Both the risk appetite statement and its supporting framework should be developed in collaboration with C-suite management. These managers translate the board's expectations into targets and constraints for risk takers in the business lines and legal entities to follow.

Strong internal controls, risk management and risk governance are essential for the implementation and operation of an effective RAF. As a check on these key requirements, independent assessors – including internal and external auditors or other third parties – perform a crucial role. Their initial and ongoing independent review of the design and execution of the RAF is closely linked to their customary responsibilities for ongoing monitoring and evaluation of the design and overall effectiveness of internal controls, risk management and risk governance. Each member of the board, C-suite, business line management and internal audit plays important, and distinctive, parts in the execution of the RAF, and collaboration among those parties will further enhance the framework's effectiveness.

Examples of responsibilities under FSB SIE group's principles[15]
Board of directors
❏ Approving the financial institution's RAF, developed in collaboration with the CEO, CRO and CFO, and ensuring it remains consistent with the institution's short- and long-term strategy, business and capital plans, risk capacity as well as compensation programmes.
❏ Holding the CEO and other senior management accountable for the integrity of the RAF, including the timely identification, management and escalation of breaches in risk limits and of material risk exposures.
❏ Ensuring that annual business plans are in line with the approved risk appetite and incentives/disincentives are included in the compensation programmes to facilitate adherence to risk appetite.
❏ Including an assessment of risk appetite in their strategic discussions, including decisions regarding mergers, acquisitions and growth in business lines or products.
❏ Discussing and monitoring to ensure appropriate action is taken regarding "breaches" in risk limits.
❏ Obtaining an independent assessment (through internal assessors, third parties or both) of the design and effectiveness of the RAF and its alignment with supervisory expectations.
❏ Discussing with supervisors decisions regarding the establishment and ongoing monitoring of risk appetite, as well as material changes in the current risk appetite levels, or regulatory expectations regarding risk appetite.

Chief executive officer
❏ Establishing an appropriate risk appetite for the financial institution (in collaboration with the CRO and CFO) that is consistent with the institution's short- and long-term strategy, business and

capital plans, risk capacity, as well as compensation programmes, and aligns with supervisory expectations.

❏ Ensuring, in conjunction with the CRO and CFO, that the risk appetite is appropriately translated into risk limits for business lines and legal entities, and that business lines and legal entities incorporate risk appetite into their strategic and financial planning, decision-making processes and compensation decisions.

❏ Ensuring that the institution-wide risk appetite statement is implemented by senior management through consistent risk appetite statements or specific risk limits for business lines and legal entities.

❏ Providing leadership in communicating risk appetite to internal and external stakeholders so as to help embed appropriate risk taking into the financial institution's risk culture.

❏ Setting the proper tone and example by empowering and supporting the CRO and CFO in their responsibilities, and effectively incorporating risk appetite into their decision-making processes.

❏ Dedicating sufficient resources and expertise to risk management, internal audit and IT infrastructure to help provide effective oversight of adherence to the RAF.

Chief risk officer

❏ Developing an appropriate risk appetite for the financial institution (in collaboration with the CEO and CFO) that meets the needs of the institution and aligns with supervisory expectations.

❏ Obtaining the board's approval of the developed risk appetite and regularly report to the board on the financial institution's risk profile relative to risk appetite.

❏ Actively monitoring the financial institution's risk profile relative to its risk appetite, strategy, business and capital plans, risk capacity, as well as compensation programmes.

❏ Establishing a process for reporting on risk and on the alignment (or otherwise) of risk appetite and risk profile with the institution's risk culture.

❏ Ensuring the integrity of risk measurement techniques and management information systems (MIS) that are used to monitor the financial institution's risk profile relative to its risk appetite.

❏ Establishing and approving, in collaboration with the CEO and CFO, appropriate risk limits for business lines and legal entities that are prudent and consistent with the financial institution's risk appetite statement.

❏ Independently monitoring business line and legal entity risk limits and the financial institution's aggregate risk profile to ensure they remain consistent with the institution's risk appetite.

❏ Acting in a timely manner to ensure effective management and, where necessary, mitigation of material risk exposures, in particular those that are close to or exceed the approved risk appetite and/or risk limits.

❏ Escalating promptly to the board and CEO any material risk limit breach that places the financial institution at risk of exceeding its risk appetite and, in particular, of putting in danger the financial condition of the financial institution.

Chief financial officer

❏ Incorporating risk appetite into the financial institution's compensation and decision-making processes (in collaboration with the CEO and CRO), including business planning, new products, mergers and acquisitions, and risk assessment and capital management processes.

Business line leaders and legal entity-level management

❏ Being accountable for effective management of the risk within their business unit and legal entity.

❏ Ensuring alignment between the approved risk appetite and planning, compensation and decision-making processes of the business unit and legal entity.

❏ Embedding the risk appetite statement and risk limits into their activities so as to embed prudent risk taking into the institution's risk culture and day-to-day management of risk.

Internal audit (or other independent assessor)

❏ Routinely including assessments of the RAF, identifying whether breaches in risk limits are being appropriately identified, escalated and reported, and assessing the design and effectiveness of risk measurement techniques and MIS used to monitor the institution's risk profile in relation to its risk appetite.

RISK APPETITE STATEMENTS: QUALITATIVE AND QUANTITATIVE

The FSB and other bodies have stressed that risk appetite statements should address both the type and level of desirable risks. The FSB's elements of an effective risk appetite statement are detailed in Panel 5.2.

The risk appetite statement can highlight the types of risk firms will actively manage to fulfill their strategic objectives, and could specifically identify undesirable risks, particularly if those risks might be encountered normally in the execution of the business strategy. Critically, risk appetite statements should consider the ability of senior management and the board to fully understand the nature and dynamics of the risks, and of the firm's information technology infrastructure to provide timely and accurate information about those risks. Statements should describe acceptable risk types at a level of granularity sufficient to communicate the board's wishes. If, for instance, institutions are willing to accept one type of credit risk but wish to avoid another, the risk appetite statement should make that clear. If there is a risk that is an inevitable by-product of an important business activity, but which the board believes is undesirable, the expectation of mitigating that risk should be apparent. The statement should explicitly link to the firm's strategy, describing the types of risks the board wants to take, contrasted with the types of risks it wants to avoid. Properly crafted, this part of the statement will inform decision-making throughout the organisation, helping to determine whether it makes sense for the organisation to pursue new opportunities ranging from an individual transaction to a potential acquisition.

Once the board, working with management, has articulated the type of risk that the organisation may take, it must attempt to describe the appropriate level of such risks. In general, boards will need to weigh the returns expected from an activity against the potential downside, typically measured as the loss under stress, driven by the risk factors associated with that activity. However, they should also consider that there is an upper capacity for risks associated with even the most attractive business. In describing the level of risk that they will tolerate, boards should be mindful of the challenges in measurement. Boards should be careful to articulate their key assumptions in describing the level of acceptable risk.

If risk appetite statements are to resonate with individuals throughout an organisation, they must contain both qualitative and quantitative features, and promote holistic rather than silo-based evaluation of risks. A risk appetite statement that features a clear and positive statement about acceptable risks can guide actions throughout an organisation. It should be sufficiently well understood from the top to the bottom of an organisation, so that directors, C-suite management, risk managers and line risk takers are on the same page. According to the FSB, "The risk appetite statement should be easy to communicate and therefore easy for all stakeholders to understand."[16] A compelling risk appetite statement should be easily summarised.

PANEL 5.2: RISK APPETITE STATEMENT

According to the FSB's principles,[17] an effective risk appetite statement should:

❏ include key background information and assumptions that informed the financial institution's strategic and business plans at the time they were approved;

❏ be linked to the institution's short- and long-term strategic, capital and financial plans, as well as compensation programmes;

❏ establish the amount of risk the financial institution is prepared to accept in pursuit of its strategic objectives and business plan, taking into account the interests of its customers (eg, depositors, policy-holders) and the fiduciary duty to shareholders, as well as capital and other regulatory requirements;

❏ determine for each material risk and overall the maximum level of risk that the financial institution is willing to operate within, based on its overall risk appetite, risk capacity and risk profile;

❏ include quantitative measures that can be translated into risk limits applicable to business lines and legal entities as relevant, and at group level, which in turn can be aggregated and disaggregated to enable measurement of the risk profile against risk appetite and risk capacity;

❏ include qualitative statements that articulate clearly the motivations for taking on or avoiding certain types of risk, including for reputational and other conduct risks across retail and wholesale markets, and establish some form of boundaries or indicators (eg, non-quantitative measures) to enable monitoring of these risks;

❏ ensure that the strategy and risk limits of each business line and legal entity, as relevant, align with the institution-wide risk appetite statement as appropriate; and

> ❑ be forward looking and, where applicable, subject to scenario and stress testing to ensure that the financial institution understands what events might push it outside its risk appetite and/or risk capacity.

The FSB also notes:

Some better examples of risk appetite statements include a summary statement that is easy for all stakeholders to understand and addresses the levels and types of risk the financial institution is willing to accept to achieve its business objectives. Risk appetite may not necessarily be expressed in a single document; however, the way it is expressed and the manner in which multiple documents form a "coherent whole" need to be carefully reviewed to ensure that the board obtains a holistic, but compact and easy to absorb, view of the financial institution's risk appetite.[18]

RISK APPETITE FRAMEWORKS

The RAF should be directly linked to the financial institution's strategy, address the institution's material risks under both normal and stressed market and macroeconomic conditions, and set clear boundaries and expectations by establishing quantitative limits and qualitative statements. It should establish quantitative measures of loss or negative outcomes that can be aggregated and disaggregated. These measures may be expressed in terms of earnings, capital, liquidity-at-risk or other appropriate metrics (eg, growth, volatility).

What does an effective risk appetite framework look like?

❑ Establishes risk appetite consistent with business strategy.
❑ Provides a strategic decision-making tool for considering new businesses, appropriate to the overall business mix to achieve risk and revenue goals.
❑ Achieves:
  ○ a balance between flexibility and responsiveness to environmental changes; and
  ○ consistency to ensure movement away from strategy is deliberate, guarding against strategic drift.
❑ Establishes clear areas of responsibility and governance structure.
❑ Communicates leadership's risk expectations throughout a firm:
  ○ provides a clear "mission statement for risk" that clarifies

firmwide goals and boundaries relative to strategic risk-taking; and
- ○ establishes incentives for staff to incorporate risk appetite into daily work.
- ❏ Incorporates formal monitoring of actual risk profile versus risk appetite, as well as expectations for the risk profile under multiple scenarios.

From a financial planning perspective, it is useful to set targets, but the risk appetite statement has to be more than an expression of numerical targets.

THE LIMITS OF LIMITS

Risk limits are a critical component of an effective RAF. The FSB defined risk limits as "quantitative measures based on forward-looking assumptions that allocate the financial institution's aggregate risk appetite statement (eg, measure of loss or negative events) to business lines, legal entities as relevant, specific risk categories, concentrations and, as appropriate, other levels".[19]

Since at least the 1980s, limits have been used as the primary means of control for risk taking at larger financial firms, whether for credit or trading or other risks. In building out RAFs, some firms have focused on incorporating within the frameworks ever more elaborate limit structures. Typically, the limit system is designed and implemented by the CRO's organisation, and reflects interpretation by the risk professionals of the risk appetite statement. In theory, the combination of limits will, if respected, ensure that risk taking, in the aggregate, will not exceed risk appetite.

In practice, measures and limits may proliferate to the point that directors and senior managers find it difficult to relate the specific limits, and that activity measured against those limits, to the desired risk management outcome. Moreover, some risk types are not particularly well measured and therefore are not easily limited, quantitatively. Effective risk appetite statements must address the appropriate level of risks, and limits on the right risk measures will serve to help implement the statements.

Practically, risk limits cannot possibly be fully comprehensive. There are risks that are difficult to measure, that are not easy to describe crisply in a limits framework, but which are nonetheless important. One obvious example is reputational risk. How do you set a limit on reputational risk? While boards and managers are quick to state that damage to franchise from reputational risk is unacceptable – many risk appetite statements set a zero tolerance for reputational damage – it is impossible for financial firms to operate without absorbing some reputational risk. Therefore, firms should find other ways of describing and communicating limits on reputational risk, and a supportive risk culture is critical to this.

Limits mean different things at different organisations. Quantitative constraints may be expressed at the firm level, at the business unit level and at the risk factor level. They may set at the higher absolute risk tolerance level, where they pose few practical constraints, or at a low level, well below actual risk tolerance, and calibrated to expected activity. They may be a speed bump – a breach prompts a discussion, and perhaps a change in the limit – or a stop sign, which cannot be run. Whether and how limits can be tied to risk appetite depends importantly on how risk limits are used and viewed within the organisation. Given the diversity of risks faced by complex institutions, and the difficulty in measuring some important risk factors, a proliferation of limits raises the prospect that RAFs will be overly focused on some types of readily measurable risks at the expense of others. Conversations between risk managers and risk takers can focus so much on the micro limits that the macro risks are missed.

Ideally, the RAF will be sufficiently well understood that risk takers and managers can understand whether a particular risk is acceptable, even where no explicit limit applies.

CASCADING RISK APPETITE

Once firms have settled on effective quantitative and qualitative measures, and descriptions of risk appetite at the enterprise level, they need to determine the best ways to cascade and embed that risk appetite at the local level – for example, at a business line, geographic region or legal entity. Rather than simply repeating the risk appetite statement and subdividing detailed enterprise risk type limits into very granular limits – for instance, loan or interest rate limits – institutions can provide higher-level constraints, often framed as stress loss tolerances that each local level must operate within. For example, headquarters executives can provide to local businesses and control management an outline of acceptable and unacceptable activities, and a financial loss tolerance, and task them with translating those constraints into a tailored local risk appetite statement, and more detailed RAF and limits structure that resonates with the local staff. The local business unit head must work with local control managers to ensure that appropriate incentives and limits are in place to keep risk of future loss in an extreme environment within the portion of the appetite allocated by headquarters. The local managers remain accountable for reporting adherence with risk appetite to headquarters. Firm management and the board remain accountable for ensuring that the aggregation of local-level appetite frameworks will keep total risk within acceptable levels.

LINK WITH CULTURE/EMBEDDING

Regulators and industry leaders alike see a critical link between implementation of an effective RAF and supportive attitudes and behaviours among all actors in an organisation. The IIF noted that:

> A strong risk culture is a prerequisite to eventually putting in place an effective risk appetite framework, and is also itself reinforced by the introduction of such a framework. Firms with demonstrably robust risk cultures that support "tone from the top" are best equipped to build engagement and put in place effective structures. One important implication of this is that a risk appetite framework should not be seen as a discrete set of mechanisms or processes, but rather as something inextricably linked to a wider set of issues that govern a firm's risk culture.[20]

Therefore, the best RAFs will be ineffective if not supported by the right risk culture. Culture means the shared attitudes and behaviours of risk takers and risk managers (and, for that matter, really all employees) responsible for the analysis, decision-making and reporting necessary to adhere effectively to risk appetite and support the organisation's strategic mission. Staff in a good culture will smoothly and effectively fill in the inevitable gaps in risk policies and procedures, promoting actions that are fully consistent with the spirit, and not just the letter, of the risk appetite statement. Those in a weaker culture may seek to exploit opportunities to take risks that are not expressly prohibited, or to work around the constraints that are designed to reinforce risk appetite. Staff in a good culture will identify new and unexpected risks, and will escalate problems quickly and clearly. Those in a weaker culture will stifle bearers of bad news. Risk managers will know, without a lot of new research, where on the continuum of risk culture their organisation falls; it is equally important for boards to understand the strength of the risk culture, and the support and reinforcement it provides their vision of risk appetite.

To improve risk culture – that is, to better align the actions of individuals with the wishes of the board – boards and managements must take stock of the incentives and penalties in place. Does the performance management and compensation system reward good risk behaviour, and punish bad or unethical risk behaviour? Are whistleblowers encouraged and protected? How are disputes escalated internally? How are audit or supervisory concerns handled? Are new products or businesses openly vetted, directly considering risk appetite, and considering the views of all internal parties? How are customer suitability issues handled?

A strong risk culture will judge the wisdom of opportunities by looking well beyond the nominal profits those opportunities may bring. Firms should decide what is right or wrong without deferring to lawyers or regulators. A weak risk culture, by contrast, may allow the risk appetite process to devolve into a "tick-the-box" compliance exercise, where lower-level control personnel test whether the policy is being followed.

CONCLUSION

Better articulation of risk appetite, facilitated by appropriate infrastructure and supported by a strong culture, should improve firm governance and performance. With the proper emphasis and focus from the top, the risk appetite framework should lead to clearer and better decisions and stronger, sustainable results. While global regulators, led by the FSB, have pushed for progress, this cannot be viewed as simply a regulatory compliance exercise – or it will be doomed to fail.

The opinions expressed in this chapter are the views of the author and do not necessarily represent the views of the Federal Reserve Bank of New York, the Federal Reserve Board or the Federal Reserve System. The author would also like to acknowledge Emily Yang for her contribution to this chapter.

1 "Supervision of Financial Conglomerates", papers prepared by the Joint Forum on Financial Conglomerates, February 1999 (available at http://www.bis.org/publ/bcbs47.pdf).

2 Counterparty Risk Management Policy Group, 2008, "Containing System Risk: The Road to Reform", The Report of the CRMPG III, August 6.

3 BIS, Basel Committee on Banking Supervision, 2009, "Proposed Enhancements to the Basel II framework", January (available at http://www.bis.org/publ/bcbs150.htm).

4 Senior Supervisors Group, 2009, "Risk Management Lessons from the Global Banking Crisis of 2008," October 21 (available at http://www.sec.gov/news/press/2009/report 102109.pdf).

5 ibid.

6 Senior Supervisors Group, 2010, "Observations on Developments in Risk Appetite Frameworks and IT Infrastructure", December 23 (available at http://www.newyorkfed.org/newsevents/news/banking/2010/an101223.html).

7 Senior Supervisors Group, 2009, "Risk Management Lessons from the Global Banking Crisis of 2008", October 21 (available at http://www.sec.gov/news/press/2009/report 102109.pdf).

8 FSB, 2011, "Intensity and Effectiveness of SIFI Supervision Progress Report on Implementing the Recommendations on Enhanced Supervision", October (available at http://www.financialstabilityboard.org/publications/r_111104ee.pdf).

9 Board of Governors of Federal Reserve System, 2012, "Supervisory Letter SR 12–17, Consolidated Supervision Framework for Large Financial Institutions", December 17.

10 Department of the Treasury, 2014, "OCC Guidelines Establishing Standards for Certain Large Insured National Banks, Insured Federal Savings Associations, and Insured Federal Branches", January (available at http://www.occ.gov/news-issuances/news-releases/2014/nr-occ-2014–4a.pdf).

11 Tapestry Networks, Bank Governance Leadership Network, ViewPoints, 2013, "Enabling More Effective Risk Appetite Frameworks", September 30 (available at http://www.ey.com/Publication/vwLUAssets/EY_Building_more_effective_risk_appetite_frameworks/$FILE/EY-BGLN-ViewPoints-Enabling-more-effective-RAFs-30-September2013.pdf).

12 FSB, 2013, "Principles for an Effective Risk Appetite Framework", November 18 (available at https://www.financialstabilityboard.org/publications/r_131118.pdf).

13 ibid.

14 ibid.

15 ibid.

16 ibid.

17 ibid.

18 ibid.

19 FSB, 2013, "Principles for an Effective Risk Appetite Framework", November 18 (available at https://www.financialstabilityboard.org/publications/r_131118.pdf).

20 IIF, 2011, "Implementing Robust Risk Appetite Frameworks to Strengthen Financial Institutions", June (available at http://www.iif.com/regulatory/article+968.php).

6

The Investor Perspective on Risk Culture

Peter Montagnon

Institute of Business Ethics

This chapter looks at the role of shareholders in contributing to risk management and oversight. It begins by considering the overall attitude of investors in terms of time horizons and investment approach, noting that shareholders are not a homogeneous group. While there are many, often egged on by sell-side analysis, who seek short-term returns and encourage leverage, there is also a substantial body that takes a long-term view and would prefer to engage. This community has developed a clear understanding of what to expect from companies in terms of risk management and oversight, as exemplified in the work of the International Corporate Governance Network (ICGN) and the Financial Reporting Council (FRC). The chapter examines these conclusions, before moving on to consider shareholder expectations of company reporting and the impact of the UK Stewardship Code. It concludes that, while shareholders will not be a first line of defence in risk management and oversight, they can make an important contribution and should be encouraged to do so.

SHAREHOLDER TIME HORIZONS AND INVESTMENT APPROACH

Rightly or wrongly, a substantial portion of blame for the 2007–08 financial crisis was directed towards shareholders. In the preamble to its April 2014 announcement proposing changes to the Shareholder Rights Directive, the European Commission did not mince its words. The financial crisis has revealed, it says, that shareholders in many cases supported excessive risk taking by management. Moreover, it adds, there is clear evidence that existing levels of monitoring by institutional investors and asset managers of the companies they own is "sub-optimal." It does not say what this evidence is, but goes on to assert that investor focus on share price movements leads to short-term pressure on companies and lack of focus on the long-term prospects for companies resulting from their appetite for the management of risk.

The UK Parliamentary Commission on Banking Standards argued that the expectation that banks would be bailed out if they got into difficulty encourages shareholders to support increased leverage in boom conditions. Royal Bank of Scotland told the Commission that "in some instances investors pressed for what were arguably unsustainable levels of return, creating pressure to increase leverage and take on additional risk". Douglas Flint, chairman of HSBC, told the Treasury Committee that "there was a great deal of pressure coming from shareholders who were looking for enhanced returns and were pointing to business models that have, with hindsight, been shown to be flawed and in particular very leveraged models".[1]

This view of shareholder behaviour is commonplace among policymakers and some companies, and it certainly embodies at least a partial truth despite it being easy for regulators and company executives to blame others for their own mistakes. Many shareholders do seek short-term returns and, in the run-up to the financial crisis, many encouraged companies in which they held stakes to gear up in order to improve their return on equity. If that led the share price to outperform the market in the short run, then so much the better, especially for institutions that measure their performance against the short-term movements of a market index. The basic proposition for the purposes of this book might therefore be that we cannot rely on shareholders to do much about risk oversight. That has to be left to corporate boards and management and, where necessary – as in the case of the banks – to regulators.

This is, however, perhaps too gloomy a view. Shareholders are not a homogeneous group, and some of what appears among their most egregious failures in terms of short-term focus in fact reflects the attitude of sell-side analysts purporting to know what shareholders want. The sell-side has a natural interest in promoting fee income from the financial engineering and trading that would result. Investment banks that thrive on dealing commissions want shareholders to take a short-term view and churn their positions. Pressure from them on both shareholders and companies is constant. To that has to be added pressure for return from asset owners such as pension fund trustees. It is not surprising that many shareholders respond accordingly, especially now that the market structure has changed.

The latest figures from the Office of National Statistics confirm that long-term institutions, notably pension funds and insurance companies, held only a small portion of the market, 4.7% and 6.2% respectively, in 2012, while over half the shares listed in London, or 53.2%, are now held by foreigners.[2] While the market used to be dominated by long-term institutional investors, the gap now appears to have been filled by investors with a much shorter-term trading interest.

Even so, not all these foreign holders are fly-by-night, short-term speculators or even passive investors who do not care to act as owners. A fair proportion of them are long-term investors, including overseas pension funds such as Calpers of the US and Ontario Teachers of Canada, who tend to take an active view of investing. Some are also sovereign wealth funds. The precise total is uncertain, but the Norges Bank Investment Management that administers that country's sovereign wealth fund has claimed that it alone owns roughly 2% of the London market. These are long-term investors who have a natural interest in how companies handle risk.

Some of these overseas investors have given their funds to UK-based asset managers to invest on their behalf. Where these asset managers are also investing their own insurance funds, they have a built-in interest in taking a longer-term view. Also, contrary to the generally received wisdom among academics, tracker funds do not always ignore the importance of engagement out of an obsession to keep costs down. Since they cannot sell their shares, they are the ultimate long-term investors. The only way they can preserve value for their clients is to engage, and their ability to do so effectively is enhanced when they are large holders. This is why Legal & General, one of the largest UK tracker funds, is also actively engaged in corporate monitoring, and why BlackRock is increasingly making its presence felt on the international stage.

Therefore, it is reasonable to suppose that, notwithstanding the absolute decline in UK long-term institutional holdings, there is still a critical mass of shareholders with a long-term investment interest that can be mobilised to deliver in ways that the European Commission sought but did not find. The UK Stewardship Code, which is discussed further below, is an attempt to identify and galvanise this group. Indeed, from the point of view of policymakers concerned with companies and risk management, there is every incentive to draw in the long-term holders and encourage them to take a more active role. This is one of the main purposes of the EU package.

While the institutions largely failed to deflect the banks from their worst excesses in the run-up to the crisis, they clearly were not blind to what was going on. Examination of the relative share price performance of Northern Rock against its peers would reveal a significant period of decline before disaster struck. Moreover, there clearly was a significant change in the shape of its shareholder register. By the end, the traditional institutions had largely all sold out, apart from the tracker funds required to hold onto their position for index-matching purposes. This suggests that a significant portion of the shareholder community was worried by the extent of the leverage in the system rather than inclined to encourage it. There should have been a lesson in that for supervisors, but they ignored it and thus were taken unnecessarily by surprise.

Those investors who did sell out have some right to be offended by the Commission's strictures. Having tried but failed to register their concerns with a determined management, they did at least succeed in preserving value for their beneficiaries only to find themselves being blamed for the crisis because of their supposed apathy. It follows from this that investors are aware of risks, even when they do not engage with companies, or, as was the case with Northern Rock and Royal Bank of Scotland, cannot do so effectively because the company will not engage with them. Peter Chambers, then chief executive of Legal & General Investment Management, told the Treasury Select Committee in 2009 that his company had tried repeatedly to engage with Royal Bank of Scotland but been rebuffed.

Companies that want a stable shareholder base would do well to recall that shareholders can choose to exit rather than engage. When they do so on a large scale, it is usually because they have weighed up the risks and found them excessive. It follows also that companies that want to manage risk effectively can be helped through dialogue with shareholders, provided they can find the right ones to talk to and are prepared to listen.

SHAREHOLDER EXPECTATIONS IN CORPORATE RISK MANAGEMENT

Shareholder groups, such as the Association of British Insurers (ABI, whose investment division is to merge with the Investment Management Association), the Investment Management Association (IMA), itself and the National Association of Pension Funds, have been actively involved in the debate on risk for a long time. All three have supported the so-called Turnbull Guidance requiring boards to state that they have monitored the effectiveness of their internal controls, although there is a general disappointment with the boiler-plate nature of the resulting disclosers. Shareholder bodies have also generally been supportive of efforts to persuade companies to set out more detail about material non-financial risks in their annual reports. Indeed, the ABI began asking companies to do so in the early 2000s – well before the introduction of the business review under European directives made this a formal requirement. It is worth noting, when it introduced this requirement, the ABI made it clear that when companies were discussing material risks (ie, those that could have a significant impact on the business) the right place to discuss them was in the annual report. There was little enthusiasm among shareholders for the separate glossy corporate responsibility reports that were fashionable at the time.

In the wake of the financial crisis, long-term investors became more interested in risk. There is some evidence from company chairmen that shareholders are more interested in discussing risk and how the company manages it. There is also a greater focus on understanding the business model and the risks inherent in it, as well as an awareness of the importance of the link between risk and remuneration that has been reflected in ABI statements on remuneration. Shareholders have also been supportive of regulatory efforts to raise the standard of narrative reporting, as well as more discursive reporting by audit committees on the issues they have encountered when drawing up the accounts.

A clear view of what long-term shareholders want in terms of corporate risk management is set out by the ICGN. This investor-led organisation, with around 500 members from over 50 countries, is the closest one can get to a global consensus buy-side view. In the wake of the crisis, it published a paper based on extensive consultation with its members on dialogue between shareholders and

companies over risk, and a set of guidelines on risk oversight from an investor perspective.[3]

Strategy, risk and risk tolerance are inseparable, the ICGN maintains. Capital allocation and capital structure should be visibly aligned with strategy and risk tolerance. The ICGN is clear that boards as a whole are responsible for risk oversight. Even where some of the work is delegated to committees, this does not absolve the other directors from their responsibility. The board's culture should encourage "openness, dynamic dialogue on risk and strategy, and constructive challenge of judgement and assumptions". Non-executive directors should be actively involved and the board should seek to ensure that it has sufficient information to address risk properly. Once it has that information, it should not be afraid to act: "The board should recognise that failure to act on information it has can be just as damaging as not having the information at all."

Further, boards should set an example to management through decisions that show they weigh up risk–return considerations; they should proactively shape management's process of managing risk so that it is integrated into their daily activities and decision-making; and compensation should be aligned to risk and return at every level. Managers should not be incentivised to take risks that are excessive from the investor or company perspective.

One of the hallmarks of the ICGN is that it is comprised of shareholders who recognise the importance of dialogue with companies that go beyond efforts to prise out more and more financial detail. Another organisation that champions this approach, although from a regulatory and standard setting perspective, is the UK FRC. In the wake of the financial crisis, it convened a series of discussion groups involving both companies and senior investors to discuss how companies should approach risk. The result was a paper summarising the issues from a joint perspective.[4]

The paper drew three main conclusions. First, there had been a sharp change in the board focus on risk over the preceding three years. Second, there might be a need to modify existing guidance[5] to take account of the changing environment. Third, there was a need for greater sharing of information about differing approaches. One size does not fit all, the report said, but there are common themes and techniques that merit consideration.

RISK APPETITE

Both investors and companies agreed in the ICGN dialogue that better risk taking should not necessarily mean less risk taking, as this was necessary to entrepreneurial activity. Boards need, however, to agree their appetite or tolerance for key individual risks. They need to understand the company's exposure to risk and how this might change as a result of changes to strategy and the operating environment. Reputational risk had grown in importance and required greater attention, especially since the development of social media meant that problems could become public very quickly, even when they had occurred in a remote location. Companies therefore need robust crisis management plans, including clear prior agreement on the respective roles of the chairman and chief executive. As a general point, boards should focus especially on those risks capable of undermining the strategy or long-term viability of the company, or damage its reputation. Good corporate culture was widely seen as essential to good risk management, and boards need to set the tone from the top.

A key point, which is also echoed in the ICGN document, is that boards needed to take an overall view of risk and how one set of risks might combine with another in order to design effective mitigation policies. Boards should not assume that they only had to deal with net risk – ie individual risk seen in isolation after the adoption of mitigation policies. They should look at gross risk as well so that they have an idea of the company's overall maximum exposure to risk.

RISK GOVERNANCE

At the governance level, the FRC paper[6] concluded that transparency and clear lines of accountability throughout the organisation were essential for effective risk management. Within the company, risk management and internal audit functions continued to play a vital role, so their reporting lines to board committees must be clear. Different board committee structures might be appropriate to different industries and companies. The decision should be up to individual boards, rather than impose a risk committee on all companies.

While views differed on the exact dividing line between audit committee and the board, and between audit and risk committees, the essential requirement was clarity. There should also be a clear link between the remuneration committee's work and risk management. Responsibility for reviewing internal controls and the process of risk management might be delegated to board committees, but this did not detract from the board's strategic responsibility for risk decision-taking.

RISK REPORTING

Boards were becoming more proactive in seeking to assure themselves about the risk and control culture in the company, but in a conclusion that also found its echo in the ICGN paper, the FRC found lack of meaningful reporting about these issues – for example, through an integrated discussion of the company's business model, strategy, key risks and mitigation. Some investors said they placed more importance on the assurance they received from discussions with management and boards than on words in the annual report. This was particularly the case when it came to considering the quality of risk management and internal control, for which their main source of assurance was the quality of the board.

One of the big complaints of the ICGN paper was the lack of information flow to shareholders. The ICGN says an understanding of the way companies manage risk is key to their valuations. Companies that both manage risk well and communicate this will benefit from higher valuations. Ensuring transparency to investors requires the board itself to have knowledge of all material risks facing the company. These need to be seen not in silos, but in the round so that boards are aware of the interplay between different, seemingly unconnected, risks. Boards should be aware of how the risk environment is changing, and take account of non-financial, as well as financial, risks.

The FRC cites a number of obstacles to risk disclosure and dialogue with shareholders. One reason for boilerplate disclosures, it says, is a compliance mindset on the part of company secretaries who often have a legal background and find it difficult to see the investor perspective. Another big factor is fear of legal liability on the part of the company and its directors. This needs to be addressed, and shareholders who recognise the value of good disclosure and dialogue should be prepared to work with companies to find solutions. A starting point for this is a better system for allowing companies to find out who their shareholders really are.

None of the investors consulted for the FRC paper valued the tendency for companies to produce long lists of risks with little or no qualitative discussion. Investors felt that boards should focus especially on strategically important risks, and that this might be achieved by linking the discussion of risk more specifically to the business model. Discussing changes to the strategy and how the company might develop in the future, and explaining the implications for the company's exposure to risk, might enable companies to air some key risks in a way that did not raise commercial sensitivities.

Suggestions for improving reporting included: integrating commentary on risk rather than treating it as a standalone section; specifically linking reporting of risk to discussion of the strategy and business model; explaining changes in the company's risk exposure over the previous 12 months as a result of changes to the strategy or business environment, and indicating if it might change in the future; and, finally, companies should disclose how key risks were being mitigated.

Subsequently, the FRC sought to pull these issues together in a consultation paper[7] that proposed linking the Turnbull Guidance to the existing requirement on companies to state as part of their accounts that they were a going concern. This paper, which emerged in November 2013, was the product of a long and intensive debate within the FRC on both the future development of the Turnbull Guidance and of Lord Sharman's proposals on going concern.[8]

Lord Sharman's report concluded that the assessment of threats to a company's solvency and liquidity should be broadly based. Similarly, the FRC's report on companies' and investors' approach to risk highlighted that the board's responsibilities for risk management are not limited to oversight of the internal control system. Taken together, it said the two reports had concluded that the board must determine its willingness to take on risk and the desired risk culture within the company. Risk management and internal control should be incorporated within the company's normal management and governance processes, not treated as a separate compliance exercise. The board must make a robust assessment of the principal risks to the company's business model and ability to deliver its strategy, including solvency and liquidity risks. In making that assessment, the board should consider the likelihood and impact of these risks materialising in the short and longer term.

Once these risks have been identified, the board should agree how they will be managed and mitigated, and keep the company's risk profile under review. It should be satisfied that management's systems include appropriate controls, and that it has adequate sources of assurance. The assessment and management of the principal risks, and monitoring of associated controls, should be carried out as an ongoing process, not seen as an annual one-off exercise.

The FRC said it had therefore decided to bring together guidance on these matters in one place. This would replace the previous guidance both on internal control and going concern. However, investors were cautious about the detail. In its response, the IMA stated that "in the current economic climate it is particularly important that investors, as the providers of risk capital, understand the risks to a company being able to continue as a viable business and meet its liabilities as they fall due". Investors have been concerned about the lack of transparency as to the uncertainties that underlie a company's viability, it continued, but they had reservations about certain of the FRC proposals. It should be clearer how these fit in with the new narrative reporting requirements under the Strategic Report, that the guidance as drafted drew too heavily on the experience of financial services companies and companies should disclose material uncertainties that could threaten its ability to meet its liabilities and continue in operation.[9]

At the time of writing, the FRC had not yet decided how to proceed. While the active participation of shareholders in the debate shows their concern about risks, the question remains as to how far policymakers can rely on shareholders to pick up risks and take decisive action to ensure that companies in which they hold stakes can deal with them.

THE UK STEWARDSHIP CODE

Thus, while shareholders form one potentially powerful line of defence, the banking crisis has shown that it is not impregnable. On the other hand, the generally positive reception given to the Stewardship Code is a good sign. This has around 290 adherents and is a model that has been replicated in countries ranging from Japan, to South Africa to the Netherlands, with a code also under active preparation in Italy.

The Stewardship Code was launched in 2010 and revised in 2012.

It lays out a series of principles about the responsibilities of institutional investors. They should:

❏ publicly disclose their policy on how they will discharge their stewardship responsibilities;
❏ have a robust policy on managing conflicts of interest in relation to stewardship that should be publicly disclosed;
❏ monitor their investee companies;
❏ establish clear guidelines on when and how they will escalate their stewardship activities;
❏ be willing to act collectively with other investors where appropriate;
❏ have a clear policy on voting and disclosure of voting activity; and
❏ report periodically on their stewardship and voting activities.

Guidance in the section on escalation lists the company's approach to risks, including those that may arise from social and environmental matters, as one of the triggers for escalation. The others listed are strategy, performance, governance and remuneration.

In the report on "Developments in Corporate Governance", published in December 2013, the FRC said that the quality of engagement between companies and shareholders was improving, with shareholders moving beyond remuneration to address a broader range of issues, including strategy, board and committee composition, and succession. Interestingly, however, risk was not specifically mentioned by those surveyed as an investment engagement priority. Also, the FRC said that the higher standards reflected greater effort by those that had always engaged rather than those engaging for the first time. Moreover, most of the dialogue was around larger companies. There was an "engagement deficit" with medium-sized companies, including those at the bottom of the FTSE 100, and below. Many companies in this group "reported frustration that their requests for engagement with investors were sometimes rebuffed."

EU governance initiatives on shareholder rights and proxy advisers
The stewardship concept has been taken up by the European Commission, which proposed a series of revisions to the Shareholder Rights Directive in April 2014.[10] As mentioned at the beginning of

the chapter, the Commission's underlying thinking is that the financial crisis did reflect a failure of governance. The right response is both to ensure that shareholders have sufficient powers and that they are encouraged to use them. Thus, the package would give shareholders new rights to vote on remuneration and related party transactions, and new obligations to disclose their investment and engagement policies and their voting record.

It remains to be seen what the outcome of this package will be. The timing of the launch, shortly before the dissolution of the European Parliament for fresh elections and the renewal of the Commission, has created uncertainty. It is not clear whether the new Commission and Parliament will put corporate governance very high on the agenda, or how the package will be amended in the course of dialogue between member states. Nonetheless, the Commission proposal goes quite a long way towards bringing the stewardship concept into the legal framework, and introduces a degree of prescription – for example, around disclosure of mandates – not hitherto seen in initiatives such as the Stewardship Code.

One other important concern raised by the Commission is the role of proxy voting advisers. These organisations – the dominant ones being ISS of the US and Glass Lewis, which is headquartered in the US but owned by a Canadian pension fund – provide institutional investors with voting advice on company resolutions at general meetings. They have been criticised for the superficiality of their judgements, their perceived lack of flexibility and unwillingness to drill down into the real issues facing companies whose annual meetings they advise on. Shareholders have been criticised for following their advice uncritically. Critics say that the proxy advisers thus steer shareholders towards particular answers, and provide an excuse for them not to engage directly with companies at whose meetings they are voting. The Commission proposals therefore oblige proxy advisers to adopt and implement measures to guarantee that their voting recommendations are accurate and reliable, and to provide information on conflicts of interest that they may face and how these are managed. Separately, under the guidance of the European Securities and Markets Authority (ESMA), proxy advisers have established three voluntary principles to guide their work.[11] These are, however, rather weak, and do not go much further than describing their existing procedures.

CONCLUSION

The debate about proxy advice is quite instructive as to the role and attitude of institutional shareholders. On the one hand, many shareholders would like to take risk more directly into account and recognise its relevance to value. They recognise also that failure to do so may cause loss of value to them and their clients. On the other hand, they are overwhelmed by the size of their portfolios, which is why they tend to rely on the recommendations of proxy advisers. This tendency has increased with the fragmentation of the equity markets. In the old days when UK pension funds and insurance companies collectively owned the majority of UK industrial companies, it was much easier for them to impose their will through engagement. With the portfolio becoming large and international, it is much harder. Norges Bank Investment Management, which manages Norway's sovereign wealth fund, has stakes in over 8,000 companies in markets around the world. It simply cannot engage with every single one of them.

The lesson is that we cannot rely on shareholders to do all the work of monitoring the quality of risk management and risk oversight in companies in which they invest. Were we to expect this, we would also have to expect a radical shift in the business model of most asset managers who believe they add value by economies of scale in investment when they are offering passive products or their ability as active managers to pick stocks and trade in and out of the market, depending on their perception of value. Large-scale investment in corporate governance resources make little sense when there is no direct return to asset management firms apart from a marginal increase to the value of assets under management on which their fees are based.

However, the authorities are almost certainly right to push shareholders to do more. Active shareholder engagement is not the whole solution, but it is certainly part of it. One of the most encouraging, and perhaps surprising, consequences of the results of the Stewardship Code has been a growing awareness on the part of asset owners – pension funds and others, such as charitable endowments – of the value of engagement. The Code has given them an ability to insist that their asset managers take engagement more seriously, and this is beginning to have some effect on the market. Investors who have done serious work on risk may still be in a minority, but the work of the ICGN and others is still significant. They should be encouraged to do more, not dismissed as irrelevant.

1 http://www.publications.parliament.uk/pa/cm201011/cmselect/cmtreasy/uc612-ix/uc61201.htm
2 Office of National Statistics, "Ownership of UK Quoted Shares 2012".
3 ICGN, 2010, "Dialogue in Corporate Governance Risk Oversight: Corporate Risk Oversight Guidelines".
4 Baroness Hogg, 2011, "Boards and Risk: A Summary of Discussions with Companies, Investors and Advisers", September.
5 "Internal Control Revised Guidance for Directors", known as the Turnbull Guidance.
6 The Sharman Inquiry, 2011, "Going Concern and Liquidity Risks: Lessons for Companies and Auditors", FRC preliminary report, November.
7 "Risk Management, Internal Control and the Going Concern Basis of Accounting", November 2013.
8 The Sharman Inquiry, 2011, "Going Concern and Liquidity Risks: Lessons for Companies and Auditors", FRC preliminary report, November.
9 For a full list of responses, see consultations section of the FRC website.
10 Proposal for a Directive of the European Parliament and of the Council amending Directive 2007/36/EC as regards the encouragement of long-term shareholder engagement and Directive 2013/34/EU as regards certain elements of the corporate governance statement, April 9, 2014.
11 "Best Practice Principles for Voting Research and Analysis", published March 5, 2014.

7

Values-driven Performance Management

Robert Potter and Miriam Earley

Hays Plc and JLT Group

This chapter discusses the issues concerning the development and the maintenance of a values-driven performance management environment within organisations. Values-driven performance management infers a people management philosophy that seeks to ensure that employee actions and behaviours are driven by the values and culture of the organisation, as well as by the desire for organisational success. As such, it is also a key tool in the management of risk, in particular the risks that emanate from employee behaviour that we term simply as "people risk".

It is a process that is driven from, and owned by, the most senior individuals within the organisation. Driving and embedding values-driven performance management starts with the board and senior executives, which may subsequently be facilitated by functions such as human resources (HR) through the governance of programmes ranging from recruitment processes to performance appraisals, to leadership development and succession planning.

This chapter therefore examines people risk as a concept, and how the potential risks associated with employees can be measured and managed. The importance of understanding organisational values is discussed, as well as how they link to values-driven performance management. The responsibilities with regards to values-driven performance management are also examined, starting with boards and cascading to functional specialisms.

A performance roadmap is presented, detailing how a values-driven performance management process might be operationalised, and finally, the chapter explores some of the challenges that can be encountered when seeking to develop and maintain a values-driven performance process.

CORPORATE CULTURE AND VALUES

Values-driven performance management and its place in the management of risk is a concern for all organisations. Examples within the financial services sector have illustrated this keenly. Surveys such as the Edelman 2013 Global Trust Barometer[1] have shown that trust in the banks and other financial services providers eroded following the crisis in 2007–08, although matters associated with risk and trust are pertinent to all sectors.

Corporate culture is defined by a shared set of beliefs, myths and practices. As in any other social system, this shared culture binds people together. In some industries, a strong corporate culture can positively affect a firm's economic performance, but there is no guarantee that a strong culture automatically assures high performance in all industries.[2] Any corporate culture is likely to have within it characteristics from which behavioural risk can manifest. Such risk may arise as a consequence of factors that are intrinsic or extrinsic to the company, and may even arise from the disengagement of a single employee. Traditional hard audit and risk management controls are not sufficient to manage these risks adequately; however, the risks embedded within cultures can be assessed and monitored.

Cultures will evolve "Darwinistically", responding to a variety of impulses. Organisations can monitor such impulses and assess whether likely outcomes (be they short or long term) will be positive or otherwise. A lack of alignment to the values of society poses a long-term risk for companies. Companies that allow behaviours that are not in line with accepted beliefs or conduct within the societies within which they operate are likely to be sanctioned in some way or other by that society. For all these reasons, a values-based performance and risk management regime provides companies and boards with an additional tool and safety net. Although developing a values-based performance and risk regime takes time and effort, such effort will always be less costly than the efforts required to respond to a crises generated from people risk.

Following the global crisis of 2007–08, the financial services sector provided a good example of the dangers associated with people risk. The sector came under intense scrutiny from governments, policy-makers, regulators and investors, as evidenced by a number of reports and investigations, as well as by the media and general public. Reports in the UK included the Parliamentary Commission on Banking Standards, the Salz Review and the Walker Report, alongside major governance guidelines emanating from the Financial Reporting Council's guide on board effectiveness and the Association of British Insurers. While each report makes its own recommendations, all place high value on ensuring that the right culture prevails within organisations. Such reports have encouraged organisations to examine their processes and tools with a view to ensuring that they are suitable, and work to support the desired organisational culture and behavioural outcomes. Although the focus of these reports has been on banks, the risk of behaviour out of line with the values of society applies to all organisations and sectors.

While it is a cliché to say that, in many organisations, people are the greatest asset, history tells us that asset comes with considerable risk. Inappropriate employee behaviour can cause long-term damage to organisations (Enron, Arthur Andersen, BP, RBS, Barings Bank, to name but a few), even more so in terms of reputational damage when it becomes public. This is particularly the case in an era where trust in organisations has been eroded. Organisations have to find a way to manage more effectively the risks posed by the behaviour of their employees. Values-driven performance management is a fundamental tool that can be used by organisations in the management of people risk.

Defining people risk and the link to values-driven performance management

In order to provide the context for values-driven performance management in relation to employee generated risk, it is important to first establish a shared understanding of what constitutes people risk. People risk represents the "soft factors" of operational risk management (the "hard factors" being the mechanisms frequently embodied in systems, processes and information flows).[3] People risk can be defined as "the risk to the firm caused by its people and the risk to the firm caused by what the firm does to its people".[4]

While this provides a definition of people risk, the range of circumstances where risk can crystallise because of the behaviour of individuals can be seen from a variety of examples – which extend from the Libor-rigging scandals, to the Deepwater Horizon disaster, to payment protection insurance (PPI). It also includes failure within organisations where the lack of development of talent can result in an inability to drive change in technological times (eg, Polaroid), and the stark illustrations of the grave impact of the rogue trader (eg, UBS and Société Générale). These examples show employees have the capacity to engage in activities with consequences that can be potentially fatal for a company. This capacity is quantifiable and, if measured, can be managed. It is for this reason that values-driven performance management is an important risk management tool for organisations. It ensures that the quantifiable and measurable data needed to anticipate and mitigate areas of risk can be collated, and appropriate processes to manage behaviours deployed.

Defining values and expected behaviours

In the main, employees will engage in behaviours and practices that they perceive the organisation expects of them. While Gordon Gecko's "greed is good" mantra may be fictional, it is an extreme example of a culture that encourages behaviours which can lead employees to excel financially and provide strong returns to shareholders and bonus pools, at the risk that those same behaviours could expose the employee and the organisation to great damage.

Notorious cases, such as that of Nick Leeson at Barings or Jérôme Kerviel at Société Générale, provide real-life examples of individual behaviour that damaged organisations; and Enron is also arguably an example of an organisation brought down by its culture. Latterly, the global financial crisis and its devastating effects on organisations such as Lehman Brothers and many other banks has raised broader questions regarding risk-taking behaviour. This, taken together with problems in pharmaceutical and petrochemical businesses, may lead to the conclusion that risky, and arguably occasionally inappropriate, behaviour within organisations may lean towards the rule rather than be the exception. While research and political commentary largely concerns the financial services sector, it is noted that behaviours not aligned to the long-term interests of companies are not limited to that sector.

The BP Deepwater Horizon disaster was a clear example of poor governance of people and people processes. The 2013 National Energy Board of Canada (NEB) report suggested that part of the cause lay in production pressures where organisational goals and performance metrics were weighted towards commercial output, encouraging leaders to make short-term decisions against long-term safety considerations. Lower down the organisation it had become acceptable to deviate from policies and procedures. There was high regard for safety procedures on the rig, but at a strategic level the focus of the operator was on undertaking a series of time- and money-saving decisions with limited regard to risk. However, the reaction of the then CEO Tony Hayward, as he publicly stated "There's no one who wants this thing over more than I do, I'd like my life back", demonstrated a top-down culture that was out of touch with the expectations of society, given the damage to the physical environment and people's livelihoods. While this may not have had a terminal impact on BP, it undoubtedly damaged the organisation's reputation for a generation.

In April 2014, Toyota announced the recall of 6.4 million vehicles across more than 20 models due to potential problems with airbags, steering columns and brakes. In 2012, they recalled over seven million vehicles, and in March 2014 paid US$1.2 billion to US authorities in connection with charges that the firm had lied about problems with faulty accelerators associated with a series of traffic accidents, some of which included fatalities.[5] While analysts noted that the April 2014 recall had been prompt, and therefore may not have proved too damaging to the company, the question must be asked: what led to incorrect information being given to regulators? In order to mitigate people risk, there are two things that employees need to understand: what are the overriding values of the organisation for which they work, and what behaviours that demonstrate those values are expected of them as they go about their work?

One of the five values articulated by BP is:

Respect [BP]: We respect the world in which we operate. It begins with compliance with laws and regulations. We hold ourselves to the highest ethical standards and behave in ways that earn the trust of others. We depend on the relationships we have and respect each other and those we work with. We value diversity of people and thought. We care about the consequences of our decisions, large and small, on those around us.[6]

The words of Tony Hayward following the Deepwater Horizon disaster arguably failed to demonstrate support for what BP now terms the value of "respect". The values of BP as an organisation are now very clearly and publicly set out – it takes just a few seconds to locate them by conducting a basic Internet search. It is obvious that following the events in the Gulf of Mexico in 2010, senior leaders within the organisation recognised a need for clarity on how the company expressed its values and leadership framework. As a result, as part of its "Sustainability Report 2010",[7] BP announced that the organisation was going to conduct a review of how the company's values and leadership framework were expressed. Unless leadership and management live the values and reinforce them and their purpose, other truer values supplant the rhetoric that is often to be found on websites or framed on walls within building receptions. A set of articulated behaviours must be underpinned by a true overriding set of values that are embedded within all people management processes, and constantly reinforced by leadership, if the organisation aims to reduce people risk.

Values-driven performance management

A values-driven performance management process can assist in managing risks driven by behaviour because it constantly reinforces and emphasises the worth to the organisation of individuals behaving in a manner consistent with the firm's values by making clear what behaviour is expected. What behaviour is expected will depend on the values of the organisation, as well as what is seen as appropriate and acceptable within the organisation's culture. By setting out the expected behaviours of those in the organisation and constantly reinforcing them, the required values and culture will emerge if they have not already been set out. This alignment of culture, values and behaviour will lead to long-term sustainable benefits, whether financial (from reduced risk of reputation damage or financial damage from incidents) or from softer benefits, such as a more positive view of the brand from customers or a less adversarial relationship with regulators.

This emphasises an important point. Which comes first: an articulation of values or an articulation of required behaviours? There are many tools and methodologies that can assist organisations in identifying, developing and communicating values and, as is the case in many areas of organisational development, necessity becomes the mother of invention. It is suggested that if organisations set out which behaviours are required, then employee values will become aligned over time. Where alignment is not achieved – in other words, employees have not adopted the values – providing the correct controls are in place, the desired behaviours are still more likely to be delivered because those exercising the controls will have a clear view of what is expected. However, where employees have not adopted the values, there is a risk that when controls fail, or if exceptional events occur, there may be "exceptions" in conduct that could be counter to the long-term interests of the organisation.

Required behaviours are not necessarily fixed over time. A crisis, a change of senior leadership, development of a new strategy, a regulatory concern or some other factor may spur an organisation into examining the required set of behaviours or the underpinning corporate values. Whether a top-down or all employee bottom-up approach is taken, it is critical that a consistent rigorous methodology is used. It is also important that the process incorporates both challenge and review to ensure that every effort is undertaken to pursue the truth of the organisation and avoid the process being superficial.

Values should not be engineered in order to fit a partial or false view of reality – for example, a business that is not customer focused putting that as its top value. They must reflect the way in which the organisation does business, and how it wishes to continue to do business. Values can be aspirational and should be expressed as such, reflecting a view of where the organisation wants to be, as opposed to where it is. Leaders need to convey that there is a journey that has to be followed to reach the desired behaviours that are associated with those values. However, if the fact that values are aspirational is not clearly articulated, cynicism and confusion is likely to arise. The following comments, gathered during an organisation-wide project to define a set of organisational values, demonstrate the importance of a process of challenge throughout projects in order to avoid the values being artificial.

❏ "It's true, but we can't say that."
❏ "Now we have been trained, who will train the leadership?"
❏ "Let's put this in as a value and perhaps one day we will become like this."

- ❏ "Well, this works for all departments except …"
- ❏ "The truth is this all of this goes out of the window if we are not making budget."
- ❏ "In normal circumstances these values are the good ones, but we still need to be able to trade with [name of country]."
- ❏ "Commercially, there are circumstances where we need to make third-party payments."

The examples of BP, Enron and others demonstrate that the culture of an organisation is influenced by what leaders and managers say and allow to be said and reward, not just what the firm chooses to measure or set out as its values on the website.

The performance management regime within an organisation can provide powerful reinforcement of expected behaviour, playing a fundamental role in the formation of the psychological contract between the organisation and the employee. It provides an ideal platform for a commentary on conduct between managers and employees, and can establish metrics that lead to the definition of desired behaviours and required conduct of employees. By providing such a structured commentary and predetermined metrics on behaviours, the performance management process can become a driver of required values, as well as itself being values-driven.

RESPONSIBILITIES FOR VALUES-DRIVEN PERFORMANCE MANAGEMENT

Organisations do not exist within a vacuum, and behaviour in partic-ular can be driven by reaction to outside influences. Without clearly articulating the behaviours and conduct required of employees, companies are exposed to risks emanating from external factors. These can be difficult to foresee, assess the consequences of, or control. History tells us that external socio-political factors have serious consequences for organisations if they fail to align to society's expectations and the current political climate.

In 2013, as part of a study into values-driven performance manage-ment, the City HR Association[8] reviewed a number of industry reports and also conducted structured interviews with more than 20 financial institutions across all disciplines, as well as five leading blue chip organisations from outside the sector. The study was supplemented by the results from an HR policies benchmarking survey that was completed by 52 participants comprising investment banks, corporate and retail banks, together with asset management companies. The survey explored organisational practice with regard to values, performance and reward, and provided important information regarding the roles of various sections within organisations with regard to the management of performance. This data, combined with secondary research from other sources, allowed the following roles and responsibilities in the orchestration and maintenance of values-driven performance management to be identified.

Boards

The data gathered suggested that boards and executive teams across the financial services sector were actively reviewing their practices and relationships to determine their organisation's purpose, values and strategy with regard to people and risk in order to deliver sustainable performance and rebuild trust with stakeholders. Strong leadership was identified as critical in creating the organisation's culture, setting the right values and ensuring that performance and behaviour are measured in this context.

Research from CapGemini has also shown that boards are actively considering strategic risks such as lack of clarity on responsibilities, or where leadership attitudes may be out of alignment with organisational long-term interests.[9]

The study by the City HR Association reinforced the recommendation by from the Financial Reporting Council's "Guide on Board Effectiveness" (2011), that the board was entirely responsible for the culture, values and behaviours associated with the conduct of its business. The study found that the tone needs to be set from the top, but also that most boards were ill-equipped to do so, lacking information, metrics and failing to set aside time within board meetings to complete this task.[10]

Such research indicates, therefore, that whether boards decide to focus on desired behaviours and then shape values from those behaviours, or conduct discussions related to strategy that uncover values and then define behaviours, is somewhat irrelevant. It is the result that matters, and whether boards gather and monitor information that equips them to do so and spend the time to complete this important task.

Research suggests that the board also has a role in "future proofing" the organisation with regard to people-related risk through the identification and management of macro strategic risks that may affect the organisation in the longer term.[11]

Senior executive teams

While the board is responsible for the identification of risk at the strategic and pan-organisational level, the chief executive officer (CEO) and executive team plan the management of targeted risks, including focusing on those key groups or individuals who have the potential to create high value as well as deep impact risks. Data from processes such as succession planning, organisational health checks and, vitally, performance management, will inform senior teams of any potential risks, allowing them to take action to prevent the consequences of risky behaviours.

Functional specialisms

While the internal audit and risk functions play a vital role in ensuring that fit-for-purpose processes and systems exist, and are adhered to throughout the organisation, it can be accepted that the breadth of issues concerning people risk are not fully understood by these specialisms. Therefore, it is necessary for one function to act as the guardian of data and processes associated with people risk, and to work with the HR, audit and risk functions to ensure data and processes are used appropriately and effectively.

Traditionally, for instance, audit have worked to ensure compliance with processes such as performance management, and to address questions regarding whether appraisals are being completed and if objectives are in place. In more advanced organisations, audits of objectives to ensure that they are specific, measurable, actionable, relevant and timely (SMART) take place. However, the objective for such reviews is rarely associated with people risk, but more often associated with a need to comply with a process or to ensure that evidence can be produced to justify the payment of a bonus or a salary increase. By adding behavioural objectives, or the assessment of behaviours against a set of standard criteria, specialist functions can help to provide data that will support risk management processes.

NORMALISING VALUES-DRIVEN PERFORMANCE MANAGEMENT

A values-driven performance management regime is about much more than a performance management appraisal. Appraisal processes are commonplace, but alone are not effective in the management of people risk. A values-driven performance management regime should be governed from the very top of the organisation, and that is where performance across the organisation should be continually monitored against well-articulated sets of behaviours. Annual objectives are not just SMART, but include evidence of behaviours and practices that reflect the manner in which the company wants its employees to operate. Data from other processes and systems such as customer management tools, business management tools and HR information systems should be drawn upon at the level of individual employees to assess compliance with behaviours and to mitigate people risk. Such a holistic approach is what ensures that performance management becomes values-driven. HR information systems can allow organisations to gather this data in a systematic fashion, which should reduce the burden on those conducting the analysis and make it an efficient process. In some companies, managers will claim frequently that they do not have the time to spend conducting appraisal processes. However, when the time taken to manage crises is considered, it is arguable that a well-run process is less time-consuming overall.

The research undertaken by the City HR Association in 2013 indicated that organisations that are serious about being values-driven regard the performance management process as an essential leadership tool – that, in essence, performance management becomes part of the way in which the company "does business".

There is an important caveat, however: creating a performance management appraisal framework with clearly stated behavioural metrics will not give rise to a values-driven performance management process alone. Too often, organisations devise highly mechanistic tools that may give comfort to boards and senior executive teams seeking to manage people risk, but which are in reality ineffective. This is because, while the perception is that they focus on risk, they are designed to focus on short-term performance goals rather than specific targeted risks. It is also likely that the set of risks is not comprehensive and can quickly become outdated because the approach did not take a holistic strategic and environmental risk management approach. It is through a holistic approach, regularly reviewed through organisational health checks, that the long-term suitability of the performance management process becomes cemented.

Linking performance to values: The performance roadmap

Practically speaking, how can organisations set out to manage performance in a values-driven context, thus mitigating people risk? Approaches will vary according to the stage of the organisational life cycle at which the company finds itself, but the principles outlined below can assist when planning a wholesale change to a system or an update of existing practices.

The performance roadmap was developed by the City HR Association to help organisations to navigate the process of linking individual performance to corporate values, and using the process to effectively manage behaviour. It captures the full process of developing, communicating and embedding values within key people management activities. This roadmap illustrates the point that values-driven performance management does not refer to the performance appraisal process alone, but is an integral part of people management throughout the employee life cycle.

Additionally, such a roadmap provides ample opportunity for risk management, in both a proactive and reactive manner. It ensures that expectations of employee behaviour are set out and can be clearly measured. It also allows the organisation to compile quantitative and qualitative data on employee behaviour, as well as monitoring objectives and goal setting.

Roadmap step 1: Identification of values

"If you want to change attitudes, start with a change in behaviour."
William Glasser

It has been demonstrated that all organisations have a set of values from which employee behaviours arise, some of which will carry a degree of potential risk. Through analysis of behaviours, organisations can identify their values, seek to influence them and mitigate risk in a manner that is conducive to protecting the company and the attainment of strategic goals. There are many tools and organisational health processes that can be used to identify values.

When values have been identified, many organisations choose to

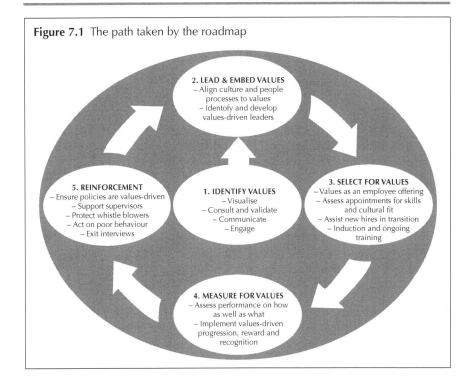

Figure 7.1 The path taken by the roadmap

2. LEAD & EMBED VALUES
– Align culture and people processes to values
– Identofy and develop values-driven leaders

3. SELECT FOR VALUES
– Values as an employee offering
– Assess appointments for skills and cultural fit
– Assist new hires in transition
– Induction and ongoing training

1. IDENTIFY VALUES
– Visualise
– Consult and validate
– Communicate
– Engage

5. REINFORCEMENT
– Ensure policies are values-driven
– Support supervisors
– Protect whistle blowers
– Act on poor behaviour
– Exit interviews

4. MEASURE FOR VALUES
– Assess performance on how as well as what
– Implement values-driven progression, reward and recognition

run roadshows, conduct publicity campaigns and embed messages concerning values into communications with employees. While helpful to focus the minds of employees for a short period, such campaigns rarely assist with real behaviour change. By embedding values-driven behaviour into performance management processes, the expected conduct of employees is reinforced on a consistent basis and becomes normalised.

Organisational health tools that aggregate data for use by boards can assist in ensuring that the values of the organisation are still fit for purpose, and indicate any modifications in behaviour that are necessary.

Roadmap step 2: Lead and embed values

It is also commonly held that strong leadership enhances organisational performance. Masaru Ibuka, the founder of Sony, outlined the values he wanted for the organisation (teamwork, technological innovation, ethical and fair practices, and emphasis on ability and performance) and these have remained in place for over three decades.[12] It makes sense that the behaviours required of leaders, to reflect the organisation's values, are an integral part of any framework that supports leadership development. Such leadership behaviours can be reinforced through stated requirements for promotion, through leadership development centres and through senior management's evidenced behaviours in employee interactions. This, in turn, makes leadership values an aspirational concept, gives employees something to strive for and enhances the worth of such behaviours in the eyes of all employees.

Roadmap step 3: Select for values

Clearly laid out behavioural expectations, detailed in everything from job descriptions, to interview questions, to induction materials, mean that the right people are hired into the organisation and are clear from the outset on what is expected of them. It is essential that management and process owners, whether HR or recruitment teams, remain the guardians of this process. Care needs to be applied to ensure that selection processes do not become weakened. Untrained or unschooled selectors will allow processes to become diluted; in essence, the organisation leaves it up to individuals to communicate their interpretation of values and required behaviours to prospective employees. In order to maintain strength and consistency in the process, rigour is necessary.

Roadmap step 4: Measure for values

This step is based around the performance appraisal process. As with all people management processes, the performance cycle and risk management process will be determined by the business, and the size and complexity of the organisation. That said, there are key characteristics that, if embedded, will assist in the management of behaviours. Table 7.1 shows the characteristics of such a system.[13]

As organisations are living entities and subject to constant change, the performance management process is also a living process. While the framework may stay the same (timings of the process, style of documentation or system used, ratings scales, etc), the content of the system must be reviewed frequently. As part of the organisational health check conducted annually by the board, required behaviours may be amended and updated. It is then the responsibility of the HR function to, in turn, update the performance management system,

Table 7.1 Characteristics of values-driven performance management system

Respectful of the individual	At the outset, the employee and supervisor agree: ❑ what performance will be delivered; and ❑ what support the organisation will provide to help the employee achieve the performance. The agreement is documented. The employee receives regular feedback throughout the year about how they are performing. The employee has the opportunity to sign off on the supervisor's assessment of performance, and to register their views in the event of a difference of perception.
Holistic	The assessment of performance notes all of the value which that the employee creates, not just obvious criteria like such as financial performance. Required performance is documented as a balanced scorecard of value creation. The assessment gives equal value to what was achieved and how it was achieved, enabling an assessment of how well the employee's behaviour upholds the organisations core values.
Transparent	The employee understands what is expected of them in practical terms against which delivery can be objectively measured. Performance can be defined as: ❑ a set of targets to be achieved; ❑ a set of skills to be mastered; and ❑ a set of behaviours or competences that can be observed.
Evidence-based	The assessment of performance should be supported by reference to examples of actual work done. The supervisor should take formal or informal note of the evidence gathered from others – peers, internal clients, subordinates – to develop a balanced perspective of the employee's performance.
Consistently applied	So that the employee can have trust in the process, assessments should be reviewed to identify and address errors, e.g,. poor ratings discipline, unsubstantiated ratings.
Serve a purpose	It must be seen as a valuable tool by supervisors and employees alike. It should provide a body of evidence on which decisions on the employee's reward and future progression are made.
A primary tool for managing the business	The process should be initiated and led by the CEO, and implemented by successive layers of management with HR in a supporting and advisory role, not owners of the process.
Be easy to use	The process should be readily accessible and not be overly complex or time-consuming to complete.

and ensure that managers and employees are equipped to manage such changes. Boards and senior management are not fulfilling their role as organisations guardians if HR teams are allowed to design, alter and change appraisal processes without their involvement.

Roadmap step 5: Reinforcement of values

Reinforcement of values and required behaviours occurs in a myriad of ways. Above, we have referred to recruitment processes, briefly discussed roadshows and internal marketing campaigns, high-lighted leadership development tools, as well as examining the characteristics of values-driven performance appraisals. Three further methods of values reinforcement merit attention: whistle-blowing procedures; reward mechanisms; and how organisations manage and monitor employee engagement.

Whistleblowing procedures — *Lot reimrtj agthk emr Lot hem*

In an imperfect world, even with careful management of behaviour, it is inevitable that there will be examples where employees, and indeed senior leaders, will engage in behaviour that is potentially damaging to the organisation. In such cases, whistleblowing proce-dures will enable others who are aware of such occurrences to inform the organisation of concerns. The existence of such a process, clearly understood, will act as a deterrent, as it provides a safety net for employees with fears or concerns. Unfortunately, statistics show that too often whistleblowing procedures lead to sanctions against whistleblowers, and lack management and leadership support. Where this occurs, organisations can be sure that in all likelihood they have failed to embed values.

Reward mechanisms

Reward mechanisms are traditionally used to drive performance in the form of results: in essence, ensuring that individuals achieve the "what". However, the behavioural aspect of the achievement of goals (the "how") is not usually sufficiently addressed within incen-tive plans. Variable compensation schemes that have a behavioural component act as a quantifiable incentive for employees to conduct themselves appropriately within the workplace, and encourage them to pay attention to "how" they are achieving the "what". It does of course require that behaviour is measured quantifiably. The

degree to which behaviour is rewarded monetarily as a proportion of overall variable compensation can be varied according to the risks associated with inappropriate behaviour in a particular role.

Within the UK, the Financial Conduct Authority (FCA) and Prudential Regulation Authority (PRA), as with their predecessor, the Financial Services Authority, provide guidance and regulation on this very point in order to assist organisations in the management of risk. The FCA/PRA Remuneration Code, which covers the financial services sector, requires that employees in high-risk positions have their bonuses capped at 100% of salary in most circumstances, that a proportion is deferred and is not paid in cash, but awarded in shares or other instruments that would lose value if the organisation suffered a reversal in fortune. It also requires, importantly, that malus (the ability to not pay a deferred portion of bonus) and clawback (the ability to recoup already paid compensation) are put into place for such payments and awards.

While this is a regulatory concern for the firms encompassed by the code, and indeed is only required for the staff deemed to fall within the terms of the code within those firms, other organisations are implementing such policies as part of good practice and, in some cases, extending the provisions of the Remuneration Code beyond the staff to whom the FCA and PRA deem that it applies. In order to invoke malus or clawback, behaviour by employees needs to be particularly egregious and have a material impact on the organisation. Evidence suggests that malus and clawback are two instruments taken seriously by employees. While such policies and procedures are a requirement for many organisations, interestingly other organisations are also using this mechanism as a method of reinforcing the consequences of a misalignment between employee behaviour, the company's values and the ensuing risk.

Employee engagement: The individual career equation
Theories relating to employee engagement have become popular, and frequently propose that employee engagement is correlated with productivity. There is value in monitoring and managing employee engagement in the light of the potential propensity for disengaged employees to commit multiple types of unethical behaviour, self-serving decision-making in the workplace or, at an extreme, fraud. A study on "why employees do bad things",[14] explains how a host of

ethical debacles across a wide range of industries has inspired growing interest in studying and understanding why individuals engage in the kind of behaviour that leads to enormous risks and cost. Interestingly, it can be argued that this latent risk to companies among morally disengaged employees cannot be measured satisfactorily using traditional employee engagement survey methods. Traditional engagement survey methods frequently aggregate anonymous responses to questionnaires, which may result in identifying broad trends but fail to provide information that has the capacity of predicting potential risk by specific individuals.

This study claimed the moral disengagement of employees, which can drive unethical risk-related behaviour, was linked to how individuals process, frame or understand information relevant to ethically meaningful decisions. This plays an important role in their ethical and unethical choices, and suggests that companies should attend more carefully to the way that individuals take decisions and what they see as relevant information. As moral disengagement can result in an individual taking unethical decisions without the usual self-censoring mechanisms kicking in, it is therefore important that employers can identify this behaviour pattern, assess whether training can change the pattern and also introduce controls so that this kind of reasoning cannot go unchecked. One suggested way in which this can be achieved is through increasing individual accountability. This study on "why employees do bad things" argues that increasing individual accountability would make it harder for an individual to justify behaviour to themselves by blaming others or regarding others as responsible. It also suggests that managers should encourage the use of ethical language and discourage the use of euphemisms that cloud judgements, and that managers should make harm to other stakeholders more real to employees to make it less likely, for example, that customers or other stakeholders are simply blamed for bringing harm onto themselves.

This points to the need for a range of actions to reduce the likelihood of this behaviour. Another aspect that should be considered is some form of assessment relating to this type of risk, being undertaken with individual employees directly or through discussion with their managers. Almost all companies have in-depth interviews and assessments of employees at the point of entry. It is possible to include a component of the assessment considering how an individual would react given certain information. This could be repeated regularly post-hiring. Companies such as JLT Group have introduced a "career review process", which they operate with employees post-recruitment and throughout their employment. The career review process serves a number of purposes, including an assessment of the degree to which an individual is engaged. The process contains a predictive element that enables a forecast to be maintained, suggesting when a re-measurement of the engagement and potential risk of an employee should be conducted. The JLT career review process is supported by a number of proprietary psychometric tools that assist in understanding preferred styles of working which, in tandem with the study on individual engagement, can help the organisation to predict how individuals are likely to behave and how likely they are to pose a risk.

QUESTIONS TO CONSIDER FOR VALUES-DRIVEN PERFORMANCE MANAGEMENT

Developing a performance management regime that is values-driven is a more complex process than may at first be assumed, and cannot be delegated to functions such as HR alone. The following set of questions is designed to assist organisations in developing and maintaining a values-based performance management regime. These questions can be used at the start of the process of developing values-driven performance management, and also during organisational health checks to assess whether or not the values-driven performance regime and processes are working correctly.

Identify values

❏ Are the values current and real, and have they been comprehensively reviewed by the board in the last 24 months?

❏ Do they meet the expectations of all stakeholders, including shareholders and regulatory bodies?

❏ Are the values in line with the strategy of the organisation?

❏ What behaviours are required of individuals in order to achieve the organisation's aims in a manner that does not expose the organisation to unnecessary risk?

❏ Is it clear what behaviours are expected of leaders?

Understanding the culture

❏ What information has been collated and analysed to understand current behaviour in the organisation and its alignment with the values?

❏ Are behaviours regularly checked to ensure that they are in line with the organisation's expectations?

❏ Are leaders selected, promoted and recognised for their values-driven behaviours?

❏ Do leaders behave in a manner that is in line with the values?

❏ Is there evidence that sanctions are consistently applied where any employee behaves in a way that is not values-driven?

❏ Is performance defined as "what has been achieved and how" in terms of work output and behaviour?

❏ Are suppliers and contractors expected to behave in accordance with the values?

Recruit, select and induct for values

❏ Are external and internal appointments assessed against the organisation's values and behaviours? Are external headhunters and agencies briefed on the values and behaviours required of all staff? Do internal recruiters assess people in accordance with these values and behaviours?

❏ Are integrity testing techniques used in the selection process for internal and external appointments, and as part of succession planning?

❏ Are all new hires (and contractors) inducted on the corporate values and expected to behave accordingly?

Measure for values

❏ Are the values and resulting culture regularly reviewed and measured?

❏ Are misalignments to the corporate strategy actively managed?

❏ Is individual behaviour reviewed, assessed and rated in the performance management process?

❏ Do the audit/compliance/people sub-committees of the board actively manage culture and risk, and monitor these through employee surveys, succession plans and other relevant sources?

❏ Are metrics undertaken on the effectiveness of linking people and performance management to values, and are these reported to the board or contained within the annual report?

Reinforcement

❏ Are all people processes regularly assessed for their alignment with the values by the board using a consistent framework?

❏ Does the talent management programme attract, retain, develop and promote employees who exhibit values-driven behaviour?

❏ Is reward allocated with reference to desired behaviours as well as financial contribution delivered?

❏ Is there a "speak up" mechanism in place that allows those with concerns about inappropriate or unethical behaviours to voice their concerns, and is it effective?

❏ Are exit interviews used to elicit insights into how the values and desired behaviours are perceived and practiced?

❏ Are individuals engaged, and is the "deal" between employee and employer in line and consistent with organisational need?

CHALLENGES IN ACHIEVING VALUES-DRIVEN PERFORMANCE MANAGEMENT

Achieving values-driven performance management is not easy. Too often, performance management is seen as a mechanistic process, owned by HR and not an essential organisational tool. The link between the management of people risk, and the organisation's ultimate aim (to make a profit in most cases) is not clearly understood. This is despite the fact that the public cases of failure (as discussed above) are epic in proportion for individual organisations and the individuals who perpetrate the failures. Although organisations are clearly aware of the consequences that have befallen others where a failure in employee behaviour has occurred, it could be argued that these occurrences are considered unusual and unfortunate, and not of concern for the majority of companies.

However, such failures, when they occur, are transformational for organisations, and the risk does need to be managed and mitigated by all organisations. So, what are the challenges faced by companies?

Lack of an organisational development or HR lexicon within leaders and managers

CEOs not versed in the language of finance are rare; other disciplines, such as operations and technology, are more frequently found within the lexicon of leaders. A clear challenge in achieving a values-driven performance regime is that many CEOs have still not grasped the techniques, methods and theories that underpin organisational development and strategic human resourcing activities.

Lack of organisational alignment between behaviours and organisational strategy

Lack of alignment leads to lack of clarity regarding required behaviours in the organisation. Without such clarity, it is impossible to design and implement an effective values-driven performance management system. The solution is potentially time-consuming but essential, and involves boards investing time in conducting an organisational health check.

Lack of consistent behaviour within the organisation

If leaders and line managers are not "on-boarded" effectively with the values and behaviours required of the organisation, and their own orientation is not in line with the organisation's needs, the result may be that they will engage in behaviours that carry potential risk.

Lack of the monitoring of external factors

External socio-political factors, particularly in our rapidly paced information age, have the potential to cause upset to an organisation's equilibrium and therefore the behaviour of employees. Ensuring constant risk monitoring at the strategic, targeted and environmental level can help to mitigate these external factors, and ensure that internal systems are updated and modified to manage them.

CONCLUSION

Over time, corporate cultures can be influenced by establishing standards of acceptable behaviour for employees. Underpinning values are likely to change over time in line with those standards, but a lag in the change in values means that in the interim companies carry a residual risk.

Human resource functions may not be the right starting point in the development of a values-based performance risk management regime. The standards of conduct, behaviour and underpinning values need to originate from the board and leadership of an organisation. Behaviour and values need to be aligned to the strategy and competency of the company, and it is only with the commitment and knowledge of the leadership that a true and meaningful values-based performance and risk management regime can be developed within an organisation.

The roadmap steps contained within this chapter provide a useful starting point for companies that recognise the importance of positively managing the culture existing within their organisation. The process of developing a values-based performance and risk management regime will only be successful if undertaken with rigour and a willingness to encourage challenge throughout the process to avoid sycophantic or shallow outcomes.

Inappropriate behaviour by employees is often cloaked and disguised, and certainly not easily recognisable from the boardroom. There are, however, obvious cues that are easy to find within the rhetoric and language in all companies, and if one decides to tune into them, such cues can inform senior management about whether the values written on the website, or on the wall in the reception, are the true values that underpin the behaviour of the employees as they go about their work. It is for the board and top management to decide if employees are creating a risk or not. This chapter suggests that employee-related risk can be accessed, monitored and influenced.

One starting point in establishing a people risk management regime is to establish standards of behaviours, and to understand how organisational values link to these behaviours. The performance roadmap shows that values-driven performance management covers much more than a performance appraisal process, and should be considered a part of the whole employee life cycle. Organisational values should be reinforced through all people management processes, which importantly includes reward mechanisms, whistle-blowing procedures and employee engagement activities.

Data from people management processes can be effectively aggregated to provide effective monitoring and controls. Where possible, data analysis should have the ability to drill down to individual employees.

There are undoubtedly challenges to the successful achievement of values-driven performance management, including – in some circumstances – a lack of understanding of people management techniques and organisational development among senior leadership, and the lack of alignment and consistency between organisational behaviours, processes and organisational strategy.

1 Edelman Insights, 2013, "Global Deck: Edelman Trust Barometer 2013", 21.
2 Ronald S. Burt, 2000, *Capital Ideas Journal*, 2(3), Chicago Business School.
3 Deloitte, 2007, "Defining and Understanding People Risk".
4 Helen Sharp, 2013, "People Risk and the Transformational Agenda", Capgemini.
5 Rebecca Clancy, 2014, "Toyota Recalls 6.4 Million Cars Globally", *Daily Telegraph*.
6 BP, 2014, "Our Values".
7 BP, 2010, "BP Sustainability Report 2010", 18.
8 City HR Association, 2013, "Performance with Integrity: Linking Performance to Values: A Toolkit".
9 Capgemini Consulting and Quinnity Limited, 2013, "Your People are Your Biggest Asset and Your Biggest Risk", 4.
10 Financial Reporting Council, 2011, "Guidance on Board Effectiveness".
11 Capgemini Consulting and Quinnity Limited, 2013, "Your People are Your Biggest Asset and Your Biggest Risk".
12 See Alagse, 2014, "Promoting Thought Leadership: Leadership and Organizational Values".
13 City HR Association, 2013, "Performance with Integrity: Linking Performance to Values: A Toolkit".
14 Celia Moore, James R. Detert, Linda Klebe Treviño, Vicki L. Baker and David M. Mayer, 2012, "Why Employees Do Bad Things: Moral Disengagement and Unethical Organisational Behaviour", *Personnel Psychology*, 65, pp 1–48.

8

Creating a Culture of Success: Reducing the Likelihood of Conduct Failures

Brendon Young
ORRF Risk Research Foundation

The banking and financial services industry suffered substantial reputation damage in the years since the 2007–08 global financial crisis due to concerns about conduct. Initially, the reputation damage stemmed from the size of losses in the crisis and concerns about the magnitude of risk being taken by the industry pre-2008. However, this has been exacerbated by a range of conduct issues that have come to light that have severely affected the way the industry is viewed. These cases have arisen in both wholesale and retail product markets, and have affected banks across the global financial centres. Blame has been placed on the culture of the banks, with the reform of culture being widely acknowledged as essential to restore trust and confidence in the industry. In October 2012, the chief executive officer of RBS, Stephen Hester, stated: "Banks must undergo a wholesale change in their culture and refocus their behaviour on meeting the needs of customers to restore trust in the industry" (Reuters, 2012). Similarly, António Horta-Osório, the group chief executive of Lloyds Banking Group, told the UK Parliamentary Commission on Banking Standards in July 2012 that the banking industry was facing a "deep crisis of confidence and trust" and "needed cultural change".[1]

Trust lies at the heart of financial services, determining its success and sustainability, and this has been undermined by conduct failures. Deregulated capitalism, promoted for example by the Washington Consensus (Bremmer, 2009), was expected to deliver better outcomes for society but has started to be challenged in the light of the financial crisis. Stiglitz (2010) visualises an industry beset by conflicts of interest and argues for this reason that activities of commercial and investment banks should not be comingled.

It is clear that when problems in the banking industry reach the point of widespread failure, even the social fabric can start to be undermined. An example is Iceland, which although a peaceful country with a democratic tradition dating back over a thousand years, experienced rioting following the collapse of Icelandic banks during the crisis. Iceland's President Grímsson stated in a speech covering the Icelandic banking crisis: "These dramatic events demonstrated that the failure of the financial sector can indeed threaten the very foundations of our societies, of our democratic values."[2]

Regulators are taking an increasingly active role in terms of the culture of the financial services industry and, in particular, the conduct of firms and employees. In the UK, the Financial Conduct Authority (FCA) has adopted a "Conduct Agenda" and globally different authorities are moving to take action on conduct issues. This chapter will therefore look at the shape of the regulatory conduct agenda globally, before examining the range of conduct issues and ways in which conduct risk can be influenced. Subsequently, the chapter considers why a change in tools and indicators is needed, and the likely characteristics of successful organisations in this area in the future.

Many of the findings are applicable to a wide range of customer-focused industries; the chapter draws parallels between financial services and the UK National Health Service (NHS), and explores examples of techniques used in the nuclear power industry.

REGULATORY FOCUS ON CONDUCT

The issue of conduct risk is high up the agenda of many regulators globally. The authorities have been wrestling with the aftermath of the global London Interbank Offer rate (Libor) manipulation scandal, as well as money laundering and financial crime incidents. The UK has gone further than most countries with the FCA setting the conduct agenda, placing particular focus on behaviour towards customers. The FCA has stated that the conduct agenda is central to its overarching strategic objective of ensuring markets function well.

This objective is supported by three operational objectives: to secure an appropriate degree of protection for consumers; to protect and enhance the integrity of the UK financial system; and to promote effective competition in the interests of consumers.

Put simply, the conduct agenda is about:

❏ how firms treat customers;
❏ how firms behave towards one another; and
❏ how firms behave in the wider market.

The FCA's view is that in order to regain trust and restore confidence in the sector, the customer must be put at the heart of a firm's strategy, taking an end-to-end approach. A holistic view is required that goes beyond systems, but concerns culture, staff behaviour and rewards. The FCA has also shifted focus to outcomes. To achieve this change, firms need to consider, for example, if particular products will be advantageous to investors. Firms must structure their business to focus on the customer. Martin Wheatley, chief executive of the FCA, stated in October 2012: "From the boardroom to the point-of-sale and beyond, firms' behaviour, attitudes and motivations must be about good conduct."[3]

This will require a change throughout the organisation. The FCA has indicated that it expects to discuss with the senior management and boards of firms how business models and strategies meet the conduct agenda. Boards can no longer rely upon formal annual reviews in order to identify inappropriate behaviours or practices. Instead, they need to apply the same level of rigour to reviewing likely customer outcomes as they do to monitoring the financial performance of the business.

The UK regulations protecting customers of financial services firms is more extensive than for almost any other country, and a number of mis-selling cases have been brought against firms over retail products. However, other countries have also been tightening up conduct expectations and imposing large penalties for misbehaviour. All major banks will need to address, going forward, how to avoid customer-focused conduct issues in order to reduce the risk of reputation damage. Approaches adopted in one country are likely to influence the global agenda, so there are therefore wider lessons to be drawn from the FCA's approach.

The FCA is intending to take a holistic approach to assessing conduct issues in firms, and will be reviewing the way that a product is managed through its lifecycle – from design through to sale and post-sale servicing, then handling of any complaints. Instead of simply setting standards, then looking back at what has been achieved, the FCA's assessment will delve into the attitudes and behaviours that shape how the firm treats customers and makes money. A firm's business model and strategy will be assessed on an ongoing basis. The assessment will begin with the tone and objectives set by the board, before filtering down to frontline teams directly engaged with customers. Unidentified and future risks will require risk-based assessment of the portfolio, applying approaches such as scenario analysis to ensure preparedness. This may result in the firm having to change future product design, together with approaches to customer engagement and remediation. Fundamentally, the conduct agenda requires a firm to raise potential issues with the regulator *ex-ante* rather than the regulator having to find and deal with problems *ex-post*.

Globally, action is being taken by many different regulatory bodies where they see conduct that is affecting investors or markets. In the US, this involves bodies such as Financial Industry Regulatory Authority (FINRA), a self-regulatory organisation that regulates member brokerage firms and exchange markets, and has a mission to protect investors by making sure that the US securities industry operates fairly and honestly, providing oversight over all securities firms that do business with the public.

In addition, the US Securities and Exchange Commission (SEC) sees its mission as protecting investors as well as maintaining orderly and efficient markets. It too is taking action in various cases where they believe that investors have been misled. However, many other authorities are also involved, including state securities regulators and the Justice Department. In announcing findings against UBS during the Libor scandal, Attorney General Eric Holder said: "The Department of Justice will continue to stand vigilant against corporations or individuals who threaten the integrity of our financial markets."[4] The Federal Reserve Board is also concerned. In 2008, they defined their compliance risk agenda as covering areas such as anti-money laundering, privacy, affiliate transactions, conflicts of interest and fair lending (SR 08–08).

Going beyond assessing conduct in firms, regulators globally are also intending to be more intrusive in terms of reviewing indicators of culture in different firms. In November 2013, the Financial Stability Board released a consultation paper setting out "Guidance on Supervisory Interaction with Financial Institutions in Risk Culture" (FSB, 2013). This paper proposes a "more intense and effective approach to oversight ... proactively assessing the decisions of the financial institution."

In the UK, Hector Sants, chief executive of the Financial Services Authority (FSA), gave a speech in October 2010 that sought to ask the question: "Can culture be regulated?"[5] In this speech, he stated that we must ensure that "firms have the right culture for their business model – the right ethical framework – to facilitate the right decisions and judgements, and we (the regulators) should intervene when we find those frameworks are lacking". However, there are different views on whether culture can be changed by the authorities. With regard to the NHS, Darzi (2008) stated that the government's role in this is limited.[6]

The FCA will also be focused on the wider indications of a firm's culture in terms of conduct. The FCA's director of supervision, Clive Adamson, said in a speech at the CFA Society in April 2013: "The key drivers of culture at a firm include: setting the tone from the top; translating this into easily understood business practices; and supporting the right behaviours through performance management, employee development and reinforcing through reward programmes."[7] He stressed that the FCA would draw conclusions about culture from what was observed about a firm covering the following areas:

❏ how it responds to regulatory issues;
❏ what customers experience when they buy a service;
❏ how the product approval process is run;
❏ the behaviour of the firm in particular markets;
❏ remuneration structures – alignment between incentive structures and corporate values;
❏ how the board engages with issues – for example, if it probes high-return products or business lines;
❏ if the board understands strategies for cross-selling;
❏ how fast growth is obtained; and

❏ whether products are being sold to markets they are designed for.

The FCA has also made the point that there will be an emphasis on individual as well as corporate accountability.

The range of conduct issues and the implications

Conduct issues

It is notable that the financial services industry has faced a wide range of different types of conduct issue, with many types of firm having been drawn into the fray. In the UK, where regulations to protect retail investors are wide reaching, there have been a number of major mis-selling cases where firms have been held to account (both in terms of fines and compensation) for selling products that were deemed unsuitable for some of the buyers. These cases have cost the industry some tens of billions of pounds since the turn of the century. For example, in the case of payment protection insurance (PPI), borrowers purchased credit insurance for loans but in some cases could not themselves benefit or were unlikely to need to benefit. There were a number of other factors too, including borrowers being led to believe that taking out payment insurance was mandatory.[8] Mis-sold PPI could cost the industry approximately £20 billion in total in fines and remediation, making it the UK's worst-ever consumer scandal.[9] Overall, it is not clear what the net cost to the banks will be because of the high profits made from PPI. It could be argued that the real impact relates to reputation.

A number of post-crisis investigations of US firms into sales of structured products have also focused on unsuitability. These investigations have also gone wider to include broader forms of investment. For example, the Massachusetts Securities Regulator is investigating a range of major firms over the sale of alternative investment products to elderly investors. The products being reviewed include oil and gas partnerships, private placements, structured products and hedge funds (Maddox Hargett & Caruso, 2013). Some investigations are focused on the misleading of investors. The SEC charged Merrill Lynch in December 2013[10] with misleading investors over two collateralised debt obligations.

The issue of the disclosure of risks to investors has been at the heart of other investigations. FINRA carried out a review of the sales of structured products by Morgan Stanley,[11] and fined the firm US$600,000 for failing to have a firmwide structured product-specific suitability guidelines policy. Concerns about some international banks supporting tax evasion by US citizens have also led to a probe by the US Senate.[12] Wholesale markets have also been affected by conduct issues, with investigations regarding the manipulation of the Libor rate by a range of international firms, as well other benchmark rates and possibly FX rates.

Reputation damage

Firms have the potential for reputation damage from conduct cases. One of the most extreme examples of reputation damage following a conduct event was the experience of Salomon Brothers in 1991. A flagrant breach of the rules for US Treasury bond auctions, which led to Salomon's controlling US$10.6 billion of the US$11.3 billion issue in the May auction, led to an investigation by the authorities. Reputation damage led to a sharp loss of liquidity. The investment bank had to be saved by Warren Buffett (Instefjord *et al.*, 1998).

The cases of conduct problems in Libor and now possibly FX have damaged the reputation of individual firms and the market as a whole. Banks have acknowledged that the reputation damage has been costly. The language used to describe various events by the authorities increases the risk of reputation damage. In December 2012, HSBC was fined US$1.9 billion in a money laundering case and was criticised in the US Senate for a "polluted culture". Douglas Flint, the chairman, has acknowledged that the "last two years have been extremely damaging to HSBC's reputation and to our own perception of ourselves". HSBC is just one bank among many that have faced public criticism for their actions.

Firms are also vulnerable to the risk of misbehaviour by employees. In banking, rogue trader risk is an ever-present threat. Annex 4.1 to this chapter sets out some rogue trader cases, and these too can create significant reputation damage and even failure, as in the case of Barings.

Higher capital requirements

One result of the number and size of conduct events is that banks have to allocate significant amounts of capital to cover the risk of potential claims. Indeed, some UK firms are starting to set aside capital to cover the risks associated with new products sold. The primary difficulty in this area is how to properly assess these risks and therefore the amount of capital to be held. Whereas taking market and credit risks are an intrinsic part of banking, the appetite for conduct risk is zero. This has led to a difference in the way this risk is treated. Whereas credit risk and market risk were recognised risks and are quantified, operational risk was tackled much later as a risk type and tends to be treated as a "catch-all category". Indeed, the application of operational risk management has often led to elaborate frameworks and overly detailed non-directional analysis, requiring the collection of large quantities of data. Conduct risk has been one of the weakest areas in operational risk. Banks are starting to break down the components of operational risk to try to assess the drivers of risk factors more effectively – for example, rogue trader risk, systems risks and the risk of mis-selling. Conduct risk needs to be treated more clearly as a risk type, with different drivers from other aspects of operational risk and with different drivers for different aspects of conduct risk.

WAYS TO INFLUENCE CONDUCT RISK
Customer-centric approaches

One factor that seems to have exacerbated retail product conduct issues in the UK is a change in UK retail banking. In the period between the early 1990s and 2000s, there was a shift from a customer-centric branch banking approach to a more transactional focus, where emphasis is placed upon how quickly new products can be sold. Over this period, there was an increasing shift towards centralised marketing. The role of the central marketing teams was to maximise sales and the compliance department was charged with assuring regulatory acceptability. This has meant that compliance departments have become less part of the independent second line of defence but perhaps facilitators of the first line, working with the front office to try to ensure regulatory acceptability. Incentives structures in many banks are more focused on supporting growth in sales of products.

The conduct agenda requires a different approach. Going forward, the firm needs to ascertain first what is required by the customer and the related customer sector. This should then be carefully considered by the firm's governance committee, which needs to be assured that the customer requirements will be properly met and serviced, both now and into the future. Emphasis needs to be placed on whether financial outcomes will be appropriate for the customer. Clearly, this is not just a regulatory tick-box exercise that can be bolted onto an existing risk management framework, as it will require a substantial change in approach within the industry.

A similar shift towards a customer focus is also seen as imperative in other industries. For example, in the UK, the NHS has also suffered conduct failings, and Professor Lord Darzi has recommended "putting patients first", effectively inverting the organisational pyramid. This thinking will have a profound effect upon the NHS, which is undergoing a change-management process based upon continuous improvement in order to meet extremely challenging current and future demands. Darzi has also called for much greater openness in terms of what works and what does not.

One issue is uncertainty over how long it will take to create a more customer-centric approach and to achieve wider conduct changes. However, it is clear that firms will be required to commit very considerable effort and resources over what will inevitably be an extensive period.

Evaluating value to customers

The FCA outcome-based approach shines a spotlight on a particularly difficult area in the conduct arena: what constitutes value to the customer and, in particular, what features of products customers would regard as worth paying for. With regard to the FCAs approach and also various types of legal challenge, there are significant concerns that value will be judged in hindsight, raising the possibility of reaching a different answer to the one that would have been concluded at inception. Outcome-based regulation does require a different approach, with firms carrying out stress tests on products to consider different outcomes in different environments. Nonetheless, judgement in the light of hindsight does create a major risk for firms and lack of clarity *ex-ante* over what is appropriate and what is not.

While this is clearly a challenge, it could provide a valuable opportunity for those firms that use their understanding of customers to better tailor products and target services more effectively. Customer engagement therefore represents a competitive opportunity and not merely an exercise in compliance.

Simpler products or smarter ways of doing business?

One risk is that the conduct agenda will lead firms to retreat towards a much smaller range of simple products. This is one way of containing conduct risk, but it would impede innovation, product differentiation and speed-to-market, thus potentially failing to meet the increasing expectations of customers.

A better, and "smarter", approach would be to seek to understand customer needs and risks and let these drive product design. This does mean identifying conduct risks entailed in more complex products and underpinning decisions with an appropriate conduct risk appetite, management framework, key indicators and controls. This would require a more collaborative approach with customers to ensure products did meet their needs. The customer would be central to the product design process. Such an approach would not discourage product innovation; indeed, it could encourage greater product differentiation and should make it easier for firms to secure an appropriate risk-adjusted return. However, this approach will require new tools to be developed and new approaches to be adopted.

Incentives

Incentives in the form of various types of reward have a critical role to play in terms of conduct risk. The FCA has found examples of remuneration structures that have increased the risk of product mis-selling. In one example, in the case of Lloyds bank[13] the FCA noted that for sales of protection premiums (630,000 products sold to 399,000 customers) many of the products were found to be unsuitable or potentially unsuitable. The FCA highlighted a range of elements in the incentive arrangements that were at fault, in particular how the incentives were managed. Managers responsible for ensuring the good practice of advisers had their performance measured against sales targets, creating a clear conflict of interest. Although, on the face of it, advisers were required to meet competency standards to receive promotions or bonuses, a high proportion who had been rewarded were found to have sold unsuitable products. The FCA has made clear that while incentive arrangements are acceptable, there must be systems and controls to mitigate risks.

In September 2012, the FCA released details of poor sales staff remuneration practices. Some of the worst examples included:

❏ one-off payments and prizes – operating a "first past the post" system (where the first 21 sales staff to reach a target could earn a "super bonus" of £10,000);

❏ variable base salaries – basic salaries of sales staff moving up or down by a significant amount depending upon the level of sales achieved;

❏ product bias – excessively incentivising one product over another, therefore, despite claiming to offer impartial advice, there was a clear risk that advisers would sell the product that earned them more money; and

❏ bonus thresholds – allowing sales staff to earn a bonus of 100% of their basic salary for the sale of loans and PPI (the bonus only being payable to those who had sold PPI to at least half their customers).

Whistleblowing

One area where there needs to be a shift is the attitude within firms to the willingness to report misbehaviour. The Parliamentary Commission on Banking Standards found that many people "turned a blind eye to misbehaviour and failed to report it". They said that "institutions must ensure their staff have a clear understanding of their duty to report an instance of wrongdoing or 'whistleblow'".[14] Some consider that the unions have a potentially important role to play in supporting staff who need help and guidance with misconduct issues. One of the more controversial proposals for encouraging greater transparency is the use of financial incentives for those who report issues of concern, an approach used in the US.

In the NHS, it has been recognised that encouraging staff to report failures and risks leads to continuous improvement of the system as well as improving staff capability – ie, a supportive learning organisation is created. The NHS maintains a league table,[15] with low reporting hospital trusts being required to take appropriate action in order to positively encourage staff at all levels to report and learn from risks and failures. The NHS also operates mentoring and buddying schemes. Even so, there have been complaints that whistleblowers have been penalised.

Drivers of culture

Reducing the risk of conduct failings will take broader cultural change. Although the FCA conduct agenda supersedes the earlier FSA "treating customers fairly" programme, McConnell (2013) for example has suggested that the earlier programme still warrants further consideration by firms. It identified six main drivers of culture, together with a number of possible key indicators, the drivers being:

❑ leadership;
❑ strategy;
❑ decision-making;
❑ controls (including management information);
❑ recruitment, training, and competence; and
❑ reward.

Leadership and tone from the top require clear principles covering conduct. Globally, a number of leading firms have already produced sound conduct statements (eg, Goldman Sachs, 2013) designed to reduce the likelihood of conduct failings. However, as the Parliamentary Commission on Banking Standards (2013–14) pointed out, it has yet to be seen whether such actions represent a genuine commitment to improvement of conduct or is merely window dressing for regulatory purposes.

Achieving cultural change

An important part of the cultural change will be balancing the search for profit by the conduct risks entailed and a willingness to turn away business that could be to the customers' detriment. This gets to the heart of the business models that firms adopt. The UK PRA stresses that profits should be sustainable. In other words, business models should not be designed to produce high profits in some periods at the risk of substantial losses in others. The UK FCA goes further and stresses the need for "good profits" that will deliver sustainable returns. By "good" they mean profits that come from making sure that products and services are suitable for the people they are being sold to, that those people understand what they are buying, that they are getting appropriate value for money and that the product or service remains suitable as the client's needs and expectations change.

Beyond this focus on suitability, across all markets wholesale and retail it will be important for firms to assess the conduct risk entailed in different areas. This goes beyond checking compliance with the rules to a focus on the intrinsic risk in certain types of activity. The industry is already taking action to reduce reliance on methods of boosting income that could prove damaging in the long run. In February 2013, Antony Jenkins, chief executive of Barclays Bank, announced closure of its controversial tax planning unit in its structured capital markets division. While the tax unit was generating significant profits for the bank, it was accused of orchestrating tax avoidance on an industrial scale (The Guardian, 2013). The tax planning operation was one of several areas reviewed, with a view to assessing the potential impact upon the bank's reputation.

The difficulty in changing culture should not be underestimated, particularly in countries such as the UK and the US where free market forces have tended towards the creation of plutonomies. Indeed, "the failure rate of most planned organizational change initiatives is dramatic" (Quinn and Cameron, 2011). Organisational culture is a complex phenomenon and is in a constant state of flux. The effective management of this change involves not only overt rules and regulations, but also shared tacit assumptions that may well be in conflict. A change in culture often involves altering individuals' deeply entrenched underlying assumptions, with complexity invariably leading to unintended consequences. Among the many issues that need to be addressed when implementing cultural change, two factors stand out as being of particular importance: (i) education and learning; and (ii) remuneration and reward (IIF, 2009; Quinn and Cameron, 2011; CIPD, 2012).

Anthony Jenkins has also indicated that a period of five to 10 years may be necessary to bring about cultural change, whereas Archbishop Welby (non-affiliated member of the UK Parliamentary Commission on Banking Standards) believes a generational time-frame of 30 years may be needed. One concern is that there is a lack of clarity over what is required by the regulator; indeed, we ask again – what does "good" look like?

A CHANGE IN TOOLS AND INDICATORS
Forward-looking metrics for conduct risk

To deal with the new agenda, financial services firms will almost certainly need to put in place new tools and techniques to consider the broad suitability of products and the supporting governance structures. However, better analysis of data by firms will be advantageous. Within a national market, a firm can aggregate its indicators of conduct issues such as customer complaints and termination of products. The advantages of such measures are that they are very simple to collect and are "outcome-based".

The disadvantage is that they are backward looking. Many problems only come to light when there is a market break and the product returns are lower than expected. For example, endowment mortgages proved advantageous for many customers and only later, with weaker profits for insurers, did they prove a poor investment for others. This makes the development of more forward-looking metrics important. Firms need to develop indicators that the risks of a future conduct issue are rising – for example, if more complex products are being sold or more opaque products. This will be quite a new departure for the industry given that conduct is not treated as a risk type. Mystery shopper evidence, net promoter scores and the results of industry surveys, which give a more forward-looking perspective can also provide some information.

Indicators of behaviour

However, at its heart, "conduct" is concerned with culture and ethics – ie, people's behaviour, beliefs and motivations. Culture cannot be captured fully by metrics; these elements are almost impossible to measure directly, although proxies such as staff growth and turnover, attendance (ie, sickness and absenteeism) and education and training levels can be used, as can achievement against set objectives and self-assessment (including competence levels and future personal development). Firms need to be aware of those human factors that may lead to deviation from expected norms.

Behavioural economics is broader than the approach of more traditional economics, which is rationally based and considers factors of cost and reward. People may be swayed by a much wider variety of factors than are captured in economics. Traditional key indicators of risk and performance are therefore unlikely to prove sufficient. This is not entirely to dismiss existing risk methodologies, but to recognise the need to adapt them appropriately. The need is to develop forward-looking (leading rather than lagging) indicators, with advanced predictive tools being used to give early warnings. When identifying and evaluating possible future outcomes, it is necessary to consider broad holistic indicators and their inter-relationships (Young, 2013). Then, where appropriate, apply scenario and Bayesian approaches, with emphasis being on preventing problems rather than fixing them *ex post facto*.

In other sectors, such as the aerospace, nuclear and petrochemical industries, emphasis is placed on the use of a wider set of tools to consider behaviour and influences on behaviour. One aspect of this work is how organisations should respond to the unexpected and improve their resilience. This is a core part of the work on high-reliability organisations. Weick and Sutcliffe (2001) look at how unexpected events can test a firm's resilience, and focus on the importance of creating a "mindful infrastructure" that, among other things, tracks small failures. The emphasis is on different types of behaviour. They stress that high-resilience organisations reflect "lessons the organisation has learnt the hard way". The best high-resilience organisations know that they have not experienced all the ways that their system can fail, and appreciate the dangers of over-confidence. They look at the experience of forest fire fighting. Rather than being purely reactive, firefighters are becoming more proactive. Crews ignite pre-emptive fires to clear tinderbox debris, and then contain them within a particular area. However, this requires careful contingency planning.

The above study sees some of the key attributes of high-resilience organisations as a capacity to anticipate problems through: (i) preoccupation with failure – any lapse is treated as a symptom that something may be wrong; (ii) reluctance to simplify – ie, taking deliberate steps to create more complete and nuanced pictures of what they face;[16] and (iii) sensitivity to operations – ie, they are attentive to the front line, where the real work gets done. Anomalies are noticed while they are still tractable.

Another core principle is commitment to resilience. High-resilience organisations "develop capabilities to detect, contain and bounce back from inevitable errors". There are lessons here for the conduct agenda. One of the striking features of some of the retail mis-selling events is that it was only after regulatory focus had been turned to a particular product that poor sales practices by some staff were identified. In business as usual, there had been insufficient sampling and perhaps inadequate follow up of individual complaints. Weick and Sutcliffe (2013) suggest that one important aspect of high-resilience organisations is that they notice accumulating events at odds with what they expected faster than other organisations. One example of an area where the financial services industry has been weak has been in exploring the risks in high-profit areas, whether from a retail product such as PPI or from a trading operation. Alertness to information coming in, and a reluctance to see it as just confirming priors, is important. Understanding expectations is important – "expectations act like an invisible hand that guides you towards soothing perceptions". In other words, you explain away the data – the high level of complaints, the unexpectedly high profits.

Responsiveness and resilience of organisations requires well-trained and educated employees who are well motivated, dedicated and honest, and are capable of dealing rapidly and effectively with unexpected situations. In financial services, existing approaches (such as enterprise risk management) that have relied on hierarchical principles and frameworks of control have not provided adequate protection against conduct issues. Indeed, the traditional "three lines of defence" approach – comprising: (i) business operations (ie, line management); (ii) oversight staff functions, including the risk function; and (iii) independent assurance, ie, including internal and external auditing – has proved inadequate and been criticised by the UK Parliamentary Commission on Banking Standards (2013–14).

To achieve a highly resilient organisation, the various silos responsible for risks in a bank need to be broken down. This is starting to happen. Pre-crisis, chief risk officers were responsible for credit and market risk, and had no say on new products or strategy. Latterly, in general, they have a seat at the table on both new products and strategy, and are involved in operational risk and liquidity risk. Conduct risk, however, often still sits in a silo.

In industries such as nuclear power where errors can be catastrophic, there has been a considerable focus on the drivers of individual behaviour. Human behaviour is regarded as a key risk factor and is analysed in detail. The likelihood of failure is assessed using probabilistic risk analysis, underpinned by human reliability analysis. Human reliability analysis techniques, such as SPAR-H (Boring and Blackman, 2007), can be used to estimate the probability of human error. The method used in the nuclear industry was related to aspects of human error rate prediction and human reliability analysis. The SPAR-H framework decomposed probability of an error into contributions from diagnosis failures and actions failures. The context for events is included by using performance-shaping factors – ie, factors that influence the probability of an error (Idaho National Laboratory, 2004), For example, the Idaho report quotes that in the 1999 version of SPAR-H, eight performance-shaping factors had been identified: available time; stress and stressors; experience and training; complexity; ergonomics; procedures; fitness for duty; and work processes.

Hollnagel (1998) suggested an alternative approach, beginning with consideration of the context and the common performance conditions. Each target event is then analysed taking account of the context. Therefore, the list of possible causes of failure will contain those that are likely, given the conditions prevailing. In general, without determination of a substantive qualitative base that identifies possible dependencies between actions, quantification is considered inappropriate. While quantitative performance prediction is the *sine qua non* for human reliability analysis in probabilistic risk analysis, behavioural scientists consider quantification to be impossible and question its validity, particularly when critical tasks can be identified and failure modes determined. Human reliability analysis is a development from efficient scientific process analysis, enhanced to facilitate human capability and behaviour limitations. In the nuclear industry, maximum risk is found typically to occur when the system undergoes change, particularly that requiring human intervention. Other industries, including financial services, have not gone anywhere near as far in using human behaviour techniques to identify the risk of mistakes or poor behaviour.

Other techniques can also help to identify behaviour risks. In the NHS, staff surveys are carried out that identify behavioural factors such as high stress levels, excess drinking of alcohol and unexpected levels of depression or suicidal feelings. It has been found that these factors are predictive of higher risk with a less safe environment and poorer patient experience.

SUCCESSFUL ORGANISATIONS OF THE FUTURE

Cultural change, as suggested by the conduct agenda, requires full commitment. However, "best practice" has yet to be determined and, indeed, there is unlikely to be one single solution, although there are some interesting developments beginning to emerge. In the future, good companies that have successfully implemented the conduct agenda are likely to have the following:

❑ A strong and balanced board of directors, with a well-regarded and visionary chairman, a highly effective chief executive and a well-informed, challenging but supportive influential group of non-executives. In addition, it is likely that there will be a senior executive responsible for conduct.

❑ A customer-orientated culture, embedded throughout the organisation. Establishing the appropriate tone will require creation of a culture where everyone has ownership and responsibility for doing the right thing. This requires the CEO, with support from all members of the senior management team, to set the key company values and translate them into behaviours. This can only be achieved effectively by personally demonstrating the values through their actions. This is particularly the case when profit maximising would point to a different course to that indicated by following the firm's values.

Role of the board

As stated, conduct is concerned with setting the right tone at the top and then embedding it into behaviour through the organisation. In 1990, E. J. Schein stated, "the only thing of importance that leaders do is create and manage culture". The board needs to take an active role in setting and ensuring the right culture. The FCA has indicated that the board cannot rely simply upon formal annual reviews to identify inappropriate behaviours or practices. To ensure success, culture must properly underpin all levels of the organisation, given that strategy determines structure and structure determines systems. A customer-orientated culture applies to the actions of all and must be embedded throughout the firm.

In this, the board has a key responsibility. The Federal Reserve Board (FRB) made clear in their letter (SR08–8) to supervision staff in reserve banks[17] that their boards are responsible for setting an appropriate culture of compliance in their organisations, "for establishing clear policies regarding management of key risks, and for ensuring that these policies are adhered to in practice". They see it as essential for the board to promote a culture that encourages ethical conduct and compliance. This requires an understanding of the risks faced, together with ensuring that senior management is capable and motivated to fulfil its responsibilities.

One complexity is that the culture of an organisation does not remain fixed, but continuously changes over time in response to numerous internal and external factors (IIF, 2009) – ie, market forces, technological advances, regulation and legislation, as well as external pressures from investors and other stakeholders. In other industries, tools have been developed to assess the external factors that affect an organisation. For example, in marketing PESTEL analysis is used to consider the impact of political, economic, social, technological, environmental and legal impacts on organisations.

Another issue is that, in large dispersed organisations, culture may not be homogeneous throughout. This is particularly evident in global financial services groups having both investment banking and retail banking operations. The management of conduct risk therefore requires careful consideration of all interacting factors in order to establish continuity and consistency.

Structure and approach of the board

The conduct agenda will have a direct influence on the structure of the board, its responsibilities and its priorities. It is therefore necessary to consider what changes may be required at board level.

Understanding the conduct agenda

It is essential that the board fully understands the need for cultural change, and is totally committed to successfully implementing and embedding the conduct agenda. The firm's vision for the future, and its mission, should express continuously the intended desire to provide customers with excellent service. The organisation must have a clear statement of purpose and identify its core values, which must be properly reinforced, with good behaviour being appropriately rewarded. The fundamental aim is to put the customer at the centre of the business and create competitive advantage. Each member of the board should openly identify potential problems from their perspective, and these should be evaluated with a cohesive strategy being determined and approved by the full board (COSO, 2004; IIF, 2009; BCBS, 2010; FRC, 2011; Group of Thirty, 2012).

Where the chairman and the chief executive officer do not grasp the fundamentals of the required change, failure will inevitably result, as has been experienced within the NHS in those failing trusts identified in both the Francis (2013) and Keogh (2013) reports. This weakness manifests itself through numerous indicators of underperformance, culminating in a failure to meet overarching fundamental objectives.

Ensuring the non-executive directors are independent and actively engaged

In December 2011, the FSA held a conference for non-executive directors (NEDs), where the regulator made it perfectly clear that NEDs needed to be much more actively engaged in implementation of the conduct agenda.[18] The fundamental role of NEDs is to take both an internal and an external perspective, with the aim of gaining assurance that:

❏ the organisation has a "positive culture", which is embedded throughout the organisation;
❏ a clear customer-focused strategic plan exists and is being implemented in a timely and effective manner;
❏ the quality of the products/services being provided to customers is appropriate and will remain so throughout their life;
❏ the organisation is profitable and its competitive position is being maintained and enhanced; and
❏ the reputational standing of the organisation is being safeguarded and enhanced – ie, the NEDs are fully aware of all significant risks faced; that these are being adequately monitored, mitigated and managed; and the potential threats to reputation are being minimised; importantly, in addition, positive actions are being taken to further enhance the firm's reputation and standing.

Establishment and continuous review of the top priorities of the board

Under the conduct agenda, the top priority for the board must be to ensure that the firm better serves customers and therefore develops the right customer base. This will require a firm to be more selective in choosing which customers to seek and retain. Where an existing customer poses a potential reputational threat, possibly because the firm does not have the required level of skills to properly service that customer throughout the life of the product, then the firm should consider disengagement.

While the cost/profit objective remains important, it should be regarded as necessary but not sufficient. Instead of simply reviewing efficiency and effectiveness with a view to reducing costs, the firm needs to consider which activities are failing to add value to the customer and therefore need to be discontinued (ie, a marginal contribution, value-added exercise needs to be undertaken).

Appointment of a C-level senior executive with specific responsibility for customer-services

While a significant number of firms are still in the early stages of implementation, within the insurance sector there is emerging recognition of the need to appoint an executive at board level with specific responsibility for customer services. This has resulted in creation of a new C-level position (ie, director of customer services). Alternatively, some firms have chosen to combine the responsibility for conduct either with those of the chief compliance officer or the chief risk officer.

Establishment of a conduct sub-committee, reporting to the full board

Some banks are establishing a conduct committee as a direct sub-committee of the board, with responsibility for seeking assurance of good conduct. Its composition may include board NEDs (with the senior independent director acting as chairman) and the C-level executive responsible for conduct, together with other C-level executives responsible for risk and compliance, marketing and communications, and finance. For example, Barclays has established a board conduct, reputation and operational risk committee, which considers conduct risk and the effectiveness of processes to ensure fair customer outcomes. The majority of members have to be independent non-executives and it will be chaired by the chairman of the board (Barclays, 2013).

Given that the primary responsibility of a conduct committee is to seek assurance, it must constantly review evidence with a view to justifying the firm's current approach and its stance with regard to the conduct risk appetite. Given the regulator's holistic view of conduct, the committee should adopt both an inward- and outward-looking perspective – the inward perspective being concerned with the firm's plans and actions, while the outward perspective needs to involve reviewing the actual outcomes achieved, taking a customer and regulatory interpretation and possibly including direct external inputs. The primary areas for consideration by the conduct committee are likely to include:

❏ conduct risk appetite;
❏ the new product approval process;
❏ objectives, key indicators and reporting; and
❏ remediation.

Business standards committee

Another approach is to establish a senior business standards committee. For example, in 2010 Goldman Sachs created a business standards committee to conduct an extensive review of its business standards and practices. The focus was on client relationships and responsibilities, conflicts of interest, structured products, transparency and disclosure, committee governance, training and professional development. In response, they established a firmwide client and business standards committee and enhanced the suitability framework to assess if clients had the background, experience and capacity to understand complex or strategic transactions. The firmwide client and business standards committee, chaired by the president and chief operating officer, sought to place clients at the centre of the firm's decision-making.

This also led to identification of categories of strategic transaction that might require heightened oversight and approval. For example where losses or gains could materially impact the client's financial position, and where the transaction could have a material effect on the market.

These issues are subject to review and approval by the firmwide suitability committee, which was formed as part of an "integrated and comprehensive firmwide framework for reputation risk monitoring and management". Suitability of products for different types of investor is a core issue in the conduct area. The committee reviews a range of products with characteristics that mean that they could be unsuitable for some types of investor. These include products classified as complex, as well as assessing the market in which the product is to be sold. This might include products that are non-linear or leveraged, illiquid, lacking price transparency or representing a significant potential for loss.

CONCLUSION

The banking and financial services sector has suffered substantial reputational damage following a range of conduct failures. This has severely eroded trust, changing the competitive environment and threatening the longer-term performance of the industry. This has meant that conduct has become a growing area of focus, with increased attention globally on the need for improvements. In the UK, the FCA is pursuing the conduct agenda, which aims to make firms more customer-centric, thereby improving trust, facilitating competition and enhancing overall financial stability. Several countries have responded similarly, increasing the likelihood of the conduct agenda gradually becoming a global regulatory focus.

Fundamentally, the conduct agenda is concerned with culture and ethics, which change constantly, being moulded by the socio-economic environment. However, there appears to exist a significant gap between the culture of firms within the financial services sector and the ethical standards expected by society. A firm needs to clearly determine its *raison d'être* (ie, asking why does it exist, how does it serve society?), then reset its conduct agenda accordingly. While cultural change happens naturally, managing that change is notoriously difficult; the path to change is not linear. It has been said by some that changing conduct as proposed by the FCA may take five to 10 years to achieve, or may even take a generation in some cases.

Unfortunately, there is a danger that regulation may have unexpected consequences, leading to ossification, standardisation of products and lower margins. Indeed, the previous "treating customers fairly" initiative became heavily reliant on management information systems in a rather servile way. It should be recognised that the conduct agenda is not about meeting narrow regulatory objectives but about achieving "good", "sustainable" profits.

With regard to regulation, it seems contradictory for the FCA to actively promote the conduct agenda while appearing not to adopt it themselves, continuing rather to rely mainly upon a policing style of enforcement. Indeed, a more engaged and transparent approach would have been expected, particularly as cultural change develops and matures. It should be realised that the regulators do not sit outside the financial services sector but are central to it, being protectors of the customer. If it is the intention to create firms that are responsive, resilient, customer-centric, learning organisations, a change in regulatory approach is required.

While many firms are already actively engaged in the conduct agenda, each is at a different stage of transition; there being no recognised "best practice". Indeed, each firm must develop its own solution determined by its particular objectives and conduct risk appetite. In general, the board of directors needs to consider how it is structured and what changes may be required to address the conduct agenda. In particular, it may be necessary to consider issues such as the need to establish a conduct sub-committee chaired by the senior independent non-executive director, the composition of that committee (possibly including external and union representation) and whether a C-level executive should be appointed with specific responsibility for conduct.

In order to create an honest and transparent culture throughout an organisation, consideration needs to be given to incentivise systems that encourage oversight by all. This, combined with staff development, is a key element in the creation of a high-reliability, flexible learning organisation.

It should be recognised that culture is not necessarily homogeneous throughout an organisation. Culture constantly changes over time due to numerous socio-economic and technological factors. Therefore, it is necessary constantly to assess the adequacy of culture and the appropriateness of the conduct agenda within each business unit, considering objectives, outcomes and reputational standing. This requires consideration of a multiple range of factors and perspectives. Therefore, existing risk management approaches may not prove entirely adequate and may need reassessing and enhancing. Assurance requires a forward-looking perspective, something at which risk management systems are poor.

ANNEX A – ROGUE TRADING

Rogue trading is an example of another form of conduct risk. It is a financial crime that is well understood and for which regulators such as the Office of the Comptroller of the Currency (OCC) have developed well-proven preventative policies and procedures. However, there exists a litany of such events. Why is this and what can be done? Financial crime in its various guises is considered to represent a serious risk to all businesses. In the UK, for example, the National Criminal Intelligence Service has identified fraud as one of the most serious risks that companies face, and has said it may represent between 2% and 5% of turnover for most organisations. In the EU, corruption costs approximately 120 billion euros annually. "Corruption undermines citizens' confidence in democratic institutions and the rule of law" according to Cecilia Malmström, EU Commissioner for Home Affairs. The Basel Committee identified seven key risks faced by banks, two of which were internal and external fraud. Unfortunately, fraud is notoriously difficult to detect and around 75% of fraudulent acts are only discovered by chance. The primary defences against financial crime are considered to be an ethical culture and vigilant management. To understand the reasons for specific events such as rogue trading, it is necessary to look at individual cases.

AIB–Rusnak (2002): US$691 million loss

John Rusnak was a currency trader with Allfirst Bank in Baltimore, which at the time was part of the AIB Group. Rusnak was a well-respected family man, religious and regarded as a pillar of the local community. On January 17, 2003, he was convicted of misappropriating US$691 million after a series of bad bets resulted in losses that at the time were the largest due to bank fraud. Rusnak faced up to 30 years in prison, although he actually served less than six. He remains liable for repayment of the full losses of US$691 million, although the actual amount eventually repaid will depend upon his future, relatively meagre, earnings. Rusnak covered up his activities by fear, bullying and deceit, as well as misuse of computer technology. Rusnak was not motivated by power and greed but by maintaining his social standing. The risk of imprisonment and personal financial penalties were not a deterrent. Unfortunately, he was failed by his firm due to poor and remote management oversight (Ludwig Report, 2002). Indeed, within the firm there was no form of supportive culture or confessional system available for him to escape the position in which he found himself.

Barings-Leeson (1995): £827 million (US$1.4 billion) loss

Possibly the most famous rogue trading episode in history was committed by Nick Leeson, which brought about the downfall of Britain's oldest investment bank, Barings. Leeson undertook unauthorised speculative trading in the futures markets on the Singapore International Monetary Exchange (Simex). Initially, Leeson made significant profits (£10 million in the first year, 1992) but losses were soon incurred and grew rapidly to £208 million by the end of 1994. In a desperate attempt to recover the situation, Leeson placed a short-straddle bet on the Singapore and Tokyo stock exchanges, which due to the Kobe earthquake proved to be disastrous. A flurry of further trades propelled losses to approximately £827 million. Leeson claimed that high stress levels over prolonged periods of time affected his mental and physical health. In 1995, he was sentenced to six and a half years prison in Singapore but was released in 1999 due to ill health. Leeson seems to have been more driven by fear of loss of status if he admitted to losses than a desire to gain financially.

It is surprising that a person like Leeson, who had previously been refused a UK broker's licence because of his fraudulent application, was then allowed virtually complete freedom of action in Singapore. Some, including the Singaporean authorities, have attributed a significant amount of blame to the management of Barings as well as the bank's deficient internal auditing and risk control systems (Choo San *et al.*, 1995).

1   http://www.ft.com/cms/s/0/b64c756e-d727–11e1–8e7d-00144feabdc0.html#axzz24xyFqQET
2   Dancing in the New Decade Generation Next and the Future of Nordic Financial Unions, Reykjavík, 14 April 2010. http://english.forseti.is/media/PDF/10_04_14_nfu.pdf
3   From "Journey to the FCA": http://www.fca.org.uk/static/documents/fsa-journey-to-the-fca.pdf
4   "UBS Securities Japan Co. Ltd Sentenced for Long-running Manipulation of Libor" http://geyergorey.com/ubs-securities-japan-co-ltd-sentenced-long-running-manipulation-libor
5   "Can Culture Be Regulated?" http://www.fsa.gov.uk/library/communication/speeches/2010/1004_hs.shtml

6 High Quality Care For All – NHS Next Stage Review Final Report https://www.gov.uk/government/uploads/system/uploads/attachment_data/file/228836/7432.pdf

7 "The Importance of Culture in Driving Behaviours of Firms…" http://www.fca.org.uk/news/regulation-professionalism

8 http://www.financial-ombudsman.org.uk/publications/technical_notes/ppi/PPI-case-studies.html

9 UK banks' PPI mis-selling bill swells to 20 billion pounds, http://uk.reuters.com/article/2014/02/03/uk-britain-banks-misselling-factbox-idUKBREA120K820140203

10 SEC Charges Merrill Lynch With Misleading Investors in CDOs, http://www.investorprotection.com/blog/2013/12/13/sec-charges-merrill-lynch-misleading-investors-cdos/

11 More Investors Burned by Structured Products, http://www.investorprotection.com/blog/2012/03/19/more-investors-burned-by-structured-products/

12 Senate Accuses Swiss Bank of Helping Americans Evade Taxes, http://business.time.com/2014/02/26/senate-accuses-swiss-bank-of-helping-americans-evade-taxes/#ixzz2wQnu8Uli

13 "FCA Fines Lloyds", December 2013: http://www.fca.org.uk/news/press-releases/fca-fines-lloyds-banking-group-firms-for-serious-sales-incentive-failings

14 STOP PRESS – Whistleblowing and the Parliamentary Commission on Banking Standards (PCBS) (http://www.pcaw.org.uk/files/Changing%20Banking%20For%20Good%20PR%2019%20June%202013FINAL.docx)

15 1) http://www.cqc.org.uk/public/hospital-intelligent-monitoring; 2) http://www.cqc.org.uk/sites/default/files/media/documents/20140312_intelligent_monitoring_indicators_and_methodology_for_publication_v4.pdf

16 "Knowing that the world they face is complex, unstable, unknowable and unpredictable […] they] position themselves to see as much as possible" (Weick and Sutcliffe).

17 http://www.federalreserve.gov/boarddocs/srletters/2008/SR0808.htm

18 FCA (December, 2011) Non-Executive directors conference; Delivering fair treatment for consumers of financial services, http://www.fca.org.uk/static/FsaWeb/Shared/Documents/pubs/guidance/gc11_30.pdf

REFERENCES

Adamson, Clive, 2013, "The Importance of Culture in Driving Behaviours of Firms and How the FCA Will Assess This", speech to the CFA Society UK Professionalism Conference, London (available at http://www.fca.org.uk/news/regulation-professionalism).

Barclays, 2013, "Board Conduct, Reputation and Operational Risk Committee", January.

BCBS, 2010, "Principles for Enhancing Corporate Governance – BCBS 176", Bank for International Settlements.

Boring, R. L., and H. S. Blackman, 2007, "The Origins of the SPAR-H Method's Performance Shaping Factor Multipliers", Idaho National Laboratory, April.

Bremmer, Ian, 2009, State Capitalism and the Crisis", *McKinsey Quarterly,* July (available at http://www.mckinsey.com/insights/public_sector/state_capitalism_and_the_crisis).

Choo San, Michael Lim, Nicky Tan and Ng Kuang, 1995, "Barings–Leeson, Baring Futures (Singapore) Pte Ltd: The Report of the Inspectors Appointed by the Minister for Finance: Investigation Pursuant to Section 231 of the Companies Act (Chapter 50)" (see also http://www.independent.co.uk/news/business/coverup-sealed-the-fate-of-barings-1578217.html).

CIPD, 2012, "Written Evidence – Submission from Chartered Institute of Personnel and Development (S008)", Parliamentary Commission on Banking Standards, London, September (available at http://www.publications.parliament.uk/pa/jt201213/jtselect/jtpcbs/writev/banking/contents.htm).

COSO, 2004, "Enterprise Risk Management – Integrated Framework", Committee of Sponsoring Organizations of the Treadway Commission. Altamonte Springs, Florida.

Darzi, A., 2008, High Quality Care For All – NHS Next Stage Review Final Report" June (available at http://www.official-documents.gov.uk/document/cm74/7432/7432.pdf).

FCA, 2013, "Lloyds Fined £28million", December (available at http://www.fca.org.uk/news/press-releases/fca-fines-lloyds-banking-group-firms-for-serious-sales-incentive-failings).

FCA, 2013, "Risk Outlook 2013" (available at http://www.fca.org.uk/static/fca/documents/fca-risk-outlook-2013.pdf).

Francis Report, 2013, "Report on the Mid Staffordshire NHS Foundation Trust: Public Enquiry", The Stationary Office, London.

FRC, 2011, "Guidance on Board Effectiveness", London (available at http://www.frc.org.uk/Our-Work/Publications/Corporate-Governance/Guidance-on-Board-Effectiveness.aspx).

FSA, 2007, "Treating Customers Fairly – Culture", July (available at http://www.fca.org.uk/your-fca/documents/-fsa-treating-customers-fairly—culture).

FSA, 2010, "Remuneration Code" (available at http://www.fsa.gov.uk/pages/Library/Communication/PR/2010/180.shtml).

FSA/FCA, 2012, "Journey to the FCA", October (available at http://www.fca.org.uk/static/documents/fsa-journey-to-the-fca.pdf).

FSB, 2013, "Guidance on Supervisory Interaction with Financial Institutions in Risk Culture", November (available at http://www.financialstabilityboard.org/publications/c_131223.pdf).

Fussell, J. B., 1975, "How to Calculate System Reliability and Safety Characteristics," *IEEE Transactions on Reliability,* 24(3), pp 169–74.

Goff, Sharlene and Emily Cadman, 2014, "UK Banks Count Climbing Cost of PPI Mis-selling", *Financial Times,* February 3.

Group of Thirty, 2012, "Toward Effective Governance of Financial Institutions", Washington DC (available at http://www.group30.org/rpt_64.shtml).

Goldman Sachs, 2013, "Business Standards Committee Impact Report", May (available at http://www.goldmansachs.com/a/pgs/bsc/files/GS-BSC-Impact-Report-May-2013-II.pdf).

Hollnagel, E., 1998, *Cognitive Reliability and Error Analysis Method – CREAM* (Oxford: Elsevier Science).

Idaho National Library, 2004, "The SPAR-H Human Reliability Analysis Method", September.

IIF, 2008, "Final Report of the IIF Committee on Market Best Practices: Principles of Conduct and Best Practice Recommendations Financial Services Industry Response to the Market Turmoil of 2007–2008", Washington DC (available at ww.iif.com/download.php?id=Osk8Cwl08yw=_).

IIF, 2009, "Reform in the Financial Services Industry: Strengthening Practices for a More Stable System", Washington DC, December (available at www.iif.com/download. php?id=ukBoiNBO8UE).

Instefjord, N., Patricia Jackson and William Perraudin, 1998, "Securities Fraud", *Economic Policy*.

Keogh, Bruce, 2013, "The Keogh Mortality Review", NHS (available at http://www.nhs.uk/NHSEngland/bruce-keogh-review/Pages/published-reports.aspx).

Lloyds Bank, 2012, "Banking Standards: Written Evidence from Lloyds Banking Group" (available at http://www.publications.parliament.uk/pa/jt201314/jtselect/jtpcbs/27/27v_we09.htm).

Ludwig Report, 2002, "Allied Irish Bank Allfirst Investigation into the Rusnak Affair", prepared by Promontory Financial Group and Wachtell, Lipton, Rosen & Katz, March (available at http://www.aibgroup.com/servlet/BlobServer/document.pdf?blobkey= id&blobwhere=1015597173380&blobcol=urlfile&blobtable=AIB_Download&blobheader=ap plication/pdf&blobheadername1=Content-Disposition&blobheadervalue1=document.pdf).

McConnell, Patrick J., 2013, "A Risk Culture Framework for Systemically Important Banks". *Journal of Risk and Governance*, Vol. 3, No. 1, 2013. Available at SSRN: http://ssrn.com/ abstract=2345542

Maddox Hargett & Caruso, 2013, "Structured Products: SEC Charges Merrill Lynch with Misleading Investors in CDOs", December (available at http://www.investorprotection. com/blog/2013/12/13/sec-charges-merrill-lynch-misleading-investors-cdos/).

Monaco Thomas J. and Andrew Haskins, 2014, "HSBC Review", Forensic Asia Bloomberg, company report number 14, January14.

Moody's Investor Services, 2003, "Moody's Analytical Framework for Operational Risk Management of Banks", January.

Parliamentary Commission on Banking Standards, 2013–14, "Changing Banking for Good, First Report of Session 2013–14, Volume II: Chapters 1 to 11 and Annexes, Together with Formal Minutes" (available at http://www.publications.parliament.uk/pa/ jt201314/jtselect/jtpcbs/27/27ii.pdf).

Quinn, R E. and K S. Cameron, 2011, *Diagnosing and Changing Organizational Culture: Based on the Competing Values Framework* (San Francisco, CA: John Wiley).

Reason, J., 1985, "Predicting Human Error in High-risk Technology", lecture to BPS Annual Conference, Swansea, March.

Reason J., 1990, *Human Error* (New York, NY: Cambridge University Press).

Reason, J., 1997, *Managing the Risk of Organisational Accidents* (Surrey, UK: Ashgate Publishing).

Reuters, 2012, "RBS CEO says Banks Need Culture Change to Regain Trust" (available at http://uk.reuters.com/article/2012/10/01/uk-rbs-hester-idUKBRE89013I20121001).

Sants, H., 2010a, "Do Regulators have a Role to Play in Judging Culture and Ethics?", speech to Chartered Institute of Securities and Investments Conference, London.

Sants, H., 2010b, "Can Culture be Regulated?", speech to Mansion House Conference on Values and Trust, London.

Sants, H., 2012, "Developing a Strong Risk Culture" (available at http://www.pwc.com/en_GX/gx/financial-services/pdf/developing-strong-risk-culture.pdf).

Schein E. J., 1990, "Organizational Culture", *American Psychologist*, 45(2), February.

Stiglitz, Joseph, 2010 *Freefall: America, Free Markets and the Sinking of the World Economy* (New York, NY: W. W. Norton).

The Guardian, 2013, "Barclays Close Controversial Tax Avoidance Unit", February (available at http://www.theguardian.com/business/2013/feb/09/barclays-closes-tax-avoidance-unit).

UN–PRI, Principles for Responsible Investment, (available at http://www.unpri.org/about-pri/about-pri/).

Weick, K. and K. Sutcliffe, 2001, *Managing the Unexpected: Assuring High Performance in an Age of Complexity* (San Francisco, CA: Jossey-Bass).

Young, B., 2011, "Leadership and High Reliability Organizations – Why Banks Fail", *Journal of Operational Risk*, 6(4), September, pp 1–20.

Young, B., 2013, "The Future of Operational Risk Management in Banking: From Deterministics Towards Heuristics and Holistics?", in Shahin Shojai and George Feiger (Eds), *Risk Management in Financial Institutions* (London: Euromoney Books).

Young, B. and R. Coleman, 2009, *Operational Risk Assessment: The Commercial Imperative of a More Forensic and Transparent Approach* (Chichester, England: Wiley).

9

Internal Audit and Risk Culture

Stephen Gregory

EY

Internal audit functions have a critical role to play in assessing the risk governance framework, including the risk culture of the organisation, and informing executive management and boards of directors of the results of their work. For many internal audit functions, this role represents a major change to their mandate and to the nature of work they have traditionally carried out. Delivering on the new mandate carries with it important implications for the skills and capabilities of the internal audit function itself.

This chapter looks more closely at the role that internal audit functions should play in assessing, reporting upon and improving risk culture within a complex firm, drawing on practical experience with firms across the financial services sector. It explains the unique position that internal audit occupies, and how performing such a role is a fundamental part of delivering on the internal audit function remit. The chapter examines the expectations of regulators globally regarding the role of internal audit in assessing risk governance in financial firms, and how internal audit functions are increasingly assessing risk culture across the firm as well as in particular business units. It also explains the methods being used by internal audit functions to assess risk culture and test conformance with expected standards. Finally, the chapter explores the ways in which highly effective internal audit functions are changing their staffing models and ways of working to deliver trustworthy assessments and support improvement where required.

UNDERSTANDING THE ACTUAL RISK CULTURE OF AN ORGANISATION

The risk culture of an organisation is reflected in the behaviours and actions of people within it. Establishing a risk culture that is consistent with risk appetite and consistently applied across the organisation is challenging. The quality of understanding of the firm's policies and procedures by individuals, their personal motivations and how they react, the quality of information they receive upon which to take decisions, the space/freedom they have to influence change and the ways they go about decision-taking are among the many factors that reflect the actual risk culture as distinct from that designed or targeted.

A large organisation operating across national boundaries and with different lines of business is likely to have a variable risk culture. Change the individuals who form part of a business and the nature of risk culture is also likely to change. Delegated authorities determine the degree to which any one individual or team should be able to impact the organisation as a whole. Determining whether such variability in risk culture has had an adverse impact on the risk profile of the organisation, or is likely to in the future, is a critical matter for boards and their risk and audit committees.

A major challenge facing the boards of directors, especially of large and complex organisations, is how to understand risk culture in the various parts of the business for which they are responsible. In an interview, one non-executive director of a multinational spoke of the difficulty he has to understand the cultural aspects of the organisation given its sheer size and diversity. He also highlighted a tendency for directors to be "fed the party line" when showing concern about what was "really happening" and how people were "really feeling".

Some mechanisms can make issues more apparent. A director of another multinational firm, who sits on the board-level risk committee, said that he highly values seeing the results of the group's annual people survey. This is because the survey has been tailored with questions that address aspects of risk culture. He uses the survey results as a source of information to focus his risk thinking on specific hot spots, be they geographies or teams.

A common theme among board directors has been the desire for trustworthy information about the actual risk culture and its impact on the quality of risk governance of the organisation in all its locations. Directors especially want to know in which areas of the business risk culture increases the likelihood of inappropriate risks being present. They also want to know whether actions being taken are resulting in positive change. Furthermore, while they use a range of data sources to focus their attention, the lack of reliable sources, independent from management influence, is a common concern.

The internal audit function did not used to be often cited as a source of information concerning the actual, observed risk culture. Change is occurring, however, as internal audit functions are being directed to address matters of risk governance by their stakeholders, including external regulators. Meanwhile, internal audit functions themselves are changing to better equip themselves to meet these needs.

THE ROLE OF INTERNAL AUDIT IN RISK GOVERNANCE

The "International Standards for the Professional Practice of Internal Auditing (the Standards)"[1] have been in force for many years, and require the "purpose, authority and responsibility of the audit function" to be formally documented in an audit charter approved by the board of directors. The charter must be consistent with the definition of internal auditing as follows:

> Internal auditing is an independent, objective assurance and consulting activity designed to add value and improve an organisation's operations. It helps an organisation accomplish its objectives by bringing a systematic, disciplined approach to evaluate and improve the effectiveness of risk management, control and governance processes.[2]

In the context of financial services firms, the need for a clearer and expanded role of the internal audit function is being promulgated by regulators across the globe. The central banks and regulators in the G20 set out their expectations in various Financial Stability Board (FSB) papers, including their "Thematic Review on Risk Governance",[3] as follows:

> An assessment that is independent from the business unit and the risk management control function can assist the board in judging whether the risk governance framework, internal controls and oversight processes are operating as intended. This may be performed by internal audit or by third parties such as audit firms or consultants. Regardless of the approach, it is critical that the assessment results in

an overall opinion on the design and effectiveness of the risk governance framework and be performed by individuals with the skills needed to produce a reliable assessment. Currently, audit functions at only a few firms provide overall opinions regarding the risk governance framework.

Consistent with the FSB's requirements, certain country regulators (such as the Office of the Comptroller of the Currency, OCC)[4] as well as professional bodies such as the Institute of Internal Auditors, the body responsible for professional standards globally, have produced guidance and, in some instances, rules that set out an internal audit responsibility for assessing the risk governance framework. The UK Chartered Institute of Internal Auditors (CIIA) issued guidance in July 2013[5] that further clarifies the role and mandate of internal audit functions that operate in this sector.

> The primary role of internal audit should be to help the board and executive management protect the assets, reputation and sustainability of the organisation. It does this by assessing whether all significant risks are identified and appropriately reported by management and the risk function to the board and executive management; assessing whether they are adequately controlled; and by challenging executive management to improve governance, risk management and internal controls.

In the US, the Federal Reserve issued in January 2013 a supplemental policy statement on the internal audit function.[6] This statement requires each institution to have an internal audit charter that explains, among other matters, the "objectives and scope" of the function and its "responsibility to evaluate the effectiveness of the institution's risk management, internal controls and governance processes".

The expectations of regulators go far beyond current practice. The OCC has proposed rules requiring internal audit to evaluate reputation and strategic risk, as well as assessing the appropriateness of risk levels and trends. The FSB sees an annual opinion on the risk governance framework as good practice.

A central part of risk governance and achieving an appropriate risk culture in the eyes of the regulators is adherence to a risk appetite statement set by the board. This is a major shift for banks because the risk appetite will have to be set in both qualitative and quantitative terms (covering traditional financial risks such as credit and market, as well as non-financial risks such as compliance, legal

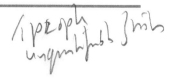

and IT), and then embedded down through the organisation, ensuring that business decisions right down to a business unit and product level are tied back to the risk appetite. This is clearly set out in the FSB's paper on risk appetite.[7] Internal audit is seen as having a core role to play in ensuring that the risk appetite framework (RAF) is adequate and effectively deployed. The FSB makes the point that:

> An effective RAF ... should allow the risk appetite statement to be used to promote robust discussions on risk and as a basis upon which the board, risk management and internal audit functions can effectively and credibly debate and challenge management recommendations and decisions.

Internal audit (or another independent assessor) is given a wide role in terms of assessments required and judgement that has to be exercised, including:

❏ routinely assessing the RAF on an institution-wide and individual business line, and legal entity basis;
❏ reporting to the board on the implementation of the RAF, as well as adherence to limits;
❏ independently assessing the design and effectiveness of the RAF, including the link to organisation culture, strategic planning, compensation and business planning; and
❏ assessing the design effectiveness of risk management techniques and management information systems (MIS) in relation to risk appetite.

This marks a major shift for many audit functions that had become boxed into a more limited mandate, where the focus was reviewing whether policies and procedures were being complied with rather than considering the adequacy and operating effectiveness of the entire risk governance framework, and particular aspects of it such as risk appetite. It also pulls internal audit into areas such as the impact of compensation, and strategic and business planning on the effectiveness of the RAF.

AUTHORITY AND STATURE
To fulfill their mandate, internal audit functions must be positioned within an organisation so that they are wholly independent from line management. They must have a direct reporting line to the board

audit committee (or equivalent), and unrestricted access to information and individuals within the firm. The audit committee is there to ensure the function directs its time to appropriate areas of the business without undue influence of management, and is able to report findings to those with ultimate responsibility for governance and the firm's systems of control. A secondary reporting line usually exists to an executive director, with the best practice being the chief executive officer. The purpose of the secondary reporting line is twofold: to ensure internal audit has access to the information it requires on a timely basis; and to ensure proper business engagement with the function and the results of their work.

Nothing in the role and remit of internal audit replaces the responsibility of management to establish effective governance, risk management and internal control. As Louise Redmond discussed in Chapter 3, most firms describe the role of internal audit as equivalent to a third line of defence independent from management (first line) and the business-supporting risk and compliance functions (second line).

Taken together these requirements of independence, authority and positioning mean that the internal audit function is uniquely placed to test and report on risk culture. Furthermore, the role of internal audit to evaluate governance, risk management and internal control means that risk culture should be central to their programme of work.

THE ROLE OF INTERNAL AUDIT IN RISK CULTURE

There is a long-standing practice for internal audit work to be risk-based, and indeed this is a requirement of the professional standards. Higher-risk activities should be subject to more extensive and more frequent testing to determine whether the systems of governance, risk management and internal control are operating effectively and in line with risk appetite. Risk is inherently higher in those areas of business that have a weaker risk culture, and so internal audit have always had a bias towards more frequent and in-depth auditing of areas with weaker risk cultures. However, with few exceptions, audit work has not tended to focus on culture as a key component of the systems of governance and control, and therefore has not often been a target for audit itself.

In the course of their normal activities, internal audit must consider the organisation as a whole, understand and validate its risk profile, determine the critical systems of control and perform testing to assess the operating effectiveness. This gives the internal audit function a genuinely global coverage responsibility and, through their day-to-day work, an insight into business operations that other functions within the firm do not have.

However, it is only latterly that many internal audit functions have specifically recognised the importance of risk culture as a critical component of the governance infrastructure of the firm and begun to target audit work in this area. In the context of financial services firms, the UK's CIIA are clear about the need for internal audit to address risk culture going forward:

> Internal audit should include within its scope the risk and control culture of the organisation. This should include assessing the processes (eg, appraisal and remuneration), actions (eg, decision-making) and "tone at the top" are in line with the values, ethics, risk appetite and policies of the organisation.
> Internal audit should consider the attitude and approach taken by all levels of management to risk management and internal control. This should include management's actions in addressing known control deficiencies as well as their regular assessment of controls within their areas.[8]

This requirement is the most explicit statement of responsibility for the audit of culture issued with the support of standards setters and regulators. It is increasingly common to find these matters reflected in changes to the internal audit charters as firms beyond the group directly regulated see this as a global best practice.

The challenge for internal audit functions has therefore been set; it is likely that internal audit having a specific responsibility for assessing and testing risk culture will become the new practice norm. The question then is how should internal audit respond?

INTERNAL AUDIT RESPONSE

Few internal audit functions have a specific mandate for auditing risk culture and fewer still have a track record in this area. For the majority of internal audit functions, this represents a significant change to remit. The starting point for many functions therefore is a board-level mandate for internal audit to assess and report upon risk governance, including culture aspects and an associated change to the internal audit charter. Effective communication of this new responsibility to executive management is required so as to legitimise internal audit working on these matters.

Incorporating risk culture as a key part of internal audit work requires change to internal audit planning, the execution of audit work (including testing) and the reporting of findings/follow up of remediation. Cultural considerations are therefore incorporated into all the major aspects of audit work. In this way, internal audit can ensure that cultural issues that lie behind risk exposure across the business as a whole are fully addressed.

Early adopters of an extended responsibility for risk culture auditing have tended to focus on specific audits that address risk culture, either as an independent system of control or through auditing particular components (such as compensation audits). While such audits have provided valuable insights, the wider challenge for internal audit functions is how to explicitly reflect risk culture across the broad body of work they carry out so as to give a robust assessment based on evidential observations.

An effective internal audit response to auditing risk culture has four key components:

❑ board-level sponsorship for the internal audit function to address risk culture;
❑ an organisation-wide risk culture framework and performance standard against which actual practice can be measured;
❑ changes to the internal audit function's approach to planning, execution and reporting the results of internal audit work; and
❑ the deployment of suitably skilled and experienced internal audit staff.

BOARD-LEVEL SPONSORSHIP FOR INTERNAL AUDIT TO REPORT ON RISK CULTURE

One aspect where change is needed is alignment of expectations between the role that internal audit functions set out to deliver, the requirements of board committees and the requirements of executive management. Sometimes these expectation gaps can be fundamental, driven by the experience and background of individuals in executive or non-executive roles. While the audit charter, and therefore the overall remit of internal audit, is reviewed annually, there also needs to be agreement about the practical ramifications of their remit and how that manifests itself in the work the function performs. The most common gaps relate to internal audit's role in improvement or advisory work, their role in auditing the firm's systems of risk management and control, and the balance of their duties in checking operational control are working as intended, including in lower risk areas. Furthermore, expectation gaps usually come to prominence when dealing with board-level issues such as strategy, governance and culture, so it is critical that a clear and detailed mandate is set for the internal audit function.

The existence of new internal audit requirements presents financial services firms operating in the jurisdictions affected with the opportunity to redefine the role and remit of the internal audit function. The new standards mark a significant shift in the role of internal audit that requires board-level adoption and sponsorship, as well as effective communication across the organisation. This is particularly the case given the fundamental nature of the changes to remit and in terms of internal audit's proposed wider access to decision-making bodies. This includes internal audit's attendance as an observer at risk management committees and other decision-making bodies (FSB),[9] and their involvement in policy development, new product and strategy discussions (OCC).[10] In addition, BaFin[11] requires that internal audit should be given information on changes to risk management in a timely fashion.

Traditionally, internal audit functions have focused their work on the design of internal control over business process and testing compliance with those internal controls that address significant business risks. For many years, internal audit work has focused on higher risk business processes or business areas. However, aspects of risk culture have tended not to be addressed unless there are gaps identified in the design or operation of internal controls. Even in those circumstances, culture was addressed as a root cause of control issues rather than a deficiency in itself. Until latterly, the majority of internal audit functions would not explicitly target audit work to uncover instances of weak risk culture.

As internal audit functions broaden their scope and address higher level governance matters in a more complete fashion, it is not unusual for them to meet resistance from management. Such resistance tends to stem from one or more of the following three concerns:

❑ Concerns about the extension of scope of internal audit into new areas that are sometimes deemed to be the responsibility of others. Typically, such expectation gaps are closed through effective communication of the precise role of internal audit that is being executed with board sponsorship.

❑ Concerns about the basis for assessing risk culture in the specific area of business in which the particular executive has responsibility. The concern is heightened by the fact that internal audit reports go to the highest levels within the firm. The use of an organisation-wide risk culture assessment model is key to addressing such concerns.

❑ Concerns about the experience and capability of the internal audit team. This concern may be coloured by previous experience of internal audit and is, in practice, a key constraint on the ability of internal audit to operate in this area.

Addressing each of these concerns is a pre-requisite for effective internal audit in the risk culture area.

RISK CULTURE ASSESSMENT FRAMEWORK

Internal audit needs to be equipped with a robust assessment framework against which actual practice can be measured and for which management has responsibility. As organisations develop their own risk culture framework, specific standards are being defined against which actual practice can be compared. The framework represents the board's view of "what good looks like" or "what is acceptable and what is not". Where such a framework exists and is deemed to be robust, internal audit plays a key role in testing actual performance against the standard and following up corrective actions.

An example of a risk culture assessment framework is EY's ICOM (individual, capability, organisational and motivation) model (see Figure 9.1). Other risk culture assessment models are available, and indeed many firms are developing specific models of their own.

From Figure 9.1, the first segment of the ICOM model includes factors related to leadership, such as tone from the top but also behaviours. Leaders in the business need to "walk the walk". If there is a course of action that could boost profits, but going down that route would cut across values, what decision should be made? The question of leadership reaches right down into middle management.

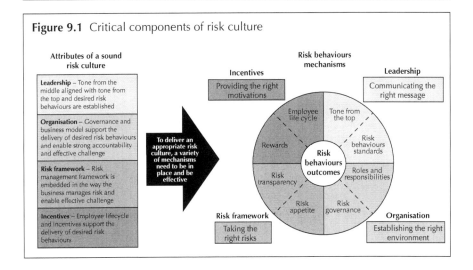

Figure 9.1 Critical components of risk culture

How do middle managers react to behaviour that has cut across the desired culture but made a profit? How leadership communicate expectations is important.

The second segment includes factors that affect employee motivation, knowledge, beliefs and behaviours. This includes rewards, remuneration and promotion, but also aspects such as hiring and firing policies and training, including onboarding, professional training and leadership training.

The third covers organisation structure affecting risk governance, including clarity of roles and accountability. This gets into the heart of business ownership of risk, independent oversight functions and the role of internal audit itself. Proactivity, in the sense that risk-taking behaviour that breaches controls/expectations has consequences, is very important.

The fourth is the risk framework covering both financial risks and non-financial risks, such as conduct risk and, importantly, the embedding of risk appetite to ensure that all risks are managed in line with the overarching goals of the board. Another aspect is open communication of issues and concerns and acceptance of voices challenging the received wisdom. The whole area of risk transparency is fundamental. If senior management and the board are not aware of risks because management information is not clear, data is poor or methodologies inadequate, they cannot react.

The ICOM model is a mix of softer areas such as tone from the top and harder-edged areas such as risk appetite and risk governance. It therefore captures the elements in the round that are important to deliver an effective culture. This is in line with regulatory thinking. The FSB has made it clear that they see the indicators of a strong culture as the following:

❏ Tone from the top: The leadership of the organisation sets the core values and expectations, and promotes, monitors and assesses risk culture and considers the impact on soundness.
❏ Accountability: Employees understand core values and approach to risk, and are aware that they will be held accountable in relation to the institution's core values and approach to risk, and any risk-related goals and values.
❏ Effective communication and challenge: Open communication and effective challenge to decision-making processes.
❏ Incentives: Performance and talent management reinforce the risk culture; financial and non-financial incentives support core values at all levels.

In terms of the ICOM model, these elements are contained within the four segments. The model also includes the areas that the FSB regards as necessary foundations for a strong risk culture: effective risk governance and risk transparency, and embedded risk appetite.[12] Underpinning the model are maturity models describing the characteristics of practice – from standard or expected through to leading practice.

Using a model like this, which covers all the necessary elements for a strong risk culture, provides a framework for gathering and assessing the evidence. Actual assessments can be plotted and reported against the framework in terms of maturity or conformity. Furthermore, specific matters that come to the attention of the internal audit function can be mapped back against the model to facilitate improved understanding of their significance, and hence the priority attached to improvement.

The existence of such a framework permits internal audit functions to:

❏ adopt a comprehensive approach to the audit of risk culture through a formal consideration of risk culture drivers, at least at the planning stage of the audit;

❏ compare the risk culture in a specific area of the business subject to audit against a set of standards adopted by the organisation, thereby highlighting gaps;

❏ facilitate comparison across different parts of the business and thereby more readily highlight best and worst practices; and

❏ track changes over time on a consistent basis.

ENHANCEMENTS TO INTERNAL AUDIT APPROACH TO REFLECT RISK

Incorporating the consideration of risk culture has a pervasive impact on all aspects of work of the internal audit function, from deciding key risk areas on which to focus their detailed work, the execution of their testing and the reporting of conclusions throughout the organisation.

The majority of internal audit functions classify their work into the three main phases, as set out in Figure 9.2. Planning takes place at an organisation-wide level and involves selecting areas of the business in which detailed internal audits will be carried out. Testing involves the collection of evidence as to whether governance, risk management and internal controls have been properly designed and are functioning as intended. Reporting consists of the synthesis of the results of testing and the communication of assessments to senior stakeholders, notably the board's audit committee.

Internal audit planning

Internal audit planning is a fundamental activity of the internal audit function intended to ensure that the time and effort of the internal audit staff is focused onto higher-risk areas of the business. It needs to be an ongoing process that results in changes to planned activity due to new information and changes in the business. With limited resources at the disposal of the internal audit function, deciding where these resources are best deployed is critical.

The outcome of the planning activity is a schedule of internal audit assignments that the function will execute over a forthcoming time horizon. Planning also produces specific areas of detailed scope and underlying rationale that the audit staff taking up responsibility for execution must take account of in designing testing. Finally, audit planning needs to be robust because areas not selected for audit carry with them an inherent assertion that they are lower risk, and

Figure 9.2 Enhancements to internal audit work to address risk culture

Planning	Testing	Reporting
1. Collecting information pertinent to risk culture across the organisation 2. Identifying specific areas of focus based upon known risk drivers and their potential impact	1. Top-down culture audits 2. Broadly based risk culture diagnostic and impact assessment 3. Testing risk culture alongside all audit work	1. Aggregation of results 2. Assessing the significance of gaps 3. Consolidating audit results and thematic findings

the reasons for such an assessment is of value to stakeholders for both information and to facilitate their challenge.

Among the larger institutions, internal audit functions generally have a flexible audit plan. Priority is given to remaining up-to-date by responding to emerging risk. For this reason, internal audit functions are moving away from a discrete annual audit planning process that results in an annual plan, towards a more dynamic process whereby the plan changes more frequently than annually as new information and circumstances comes to light.

The challenge for internal audit functions is deciding on key risk areas that warrant specific in-depth internal audit work. To do this, the vast majority of internal audit functions maintain an audit universe that is intended to represent the entire organisation subdivided into meaningful business units, areas or processes. Increasingly, the firmwide risk universe is being adopted by internal audit as a basis for their own audit selection where they are confident that the firmwide universe is robust. Such universes provide a useful vehicle for reporting internal audit coverage decisions, as well as the results of internal audit work.

The impact of risk culture on business risk has not previously been rigorously assessed by internal audit functions. Specific adjustments were made to audit plans to reflect clear examples of weak risk culture, commonly as a result of specific control failings. Those audit functions using a quantitative approach to risk assessment incorporated some consideration of culture in inherent risk characteristics, such as experience of the management team and track record in fixing issues. However, the weighting attached to these matters rarely impacted the audits selected for the plan except through use of judgement override.

Formally incorporating risk culture considerations into internal audit's planning procedures can result in different areas of the business being flagged for more in-depth audit work, as well as clearer focus areas in selected audits. As internal audit functions take a more strategic approach that reflects the importance of the governance and control exercised from the board down, corporate governance and risk culture are certain to feature more prominently in audit plans. Certain internal audit functions of larger firms have already recognised this and plan to incorporate at least specific elements of risk governance and risk culture into their audit plans each year on a non-optional basis. Furthermore, as internal audit becomes increasing tuned into the key risk culture drivers, audits will be planned, promoted in priority or refined in scope as a result.

For example, internal audit work on the sales processes associated with products subsequently known to have been mis-sold rarely gave sufficient focus to the compliance risks. Risk culture drivers such as the top-down drive for sales growth, especially of highly profitable products and the bonus culture associated with meeting or exceeding sales quotas, either did not feature or were insufficiently weighted as factors affecting audit priority and scope.

While many internal audit functions are adapting their planning approach, important challenges remain. One particular challenge relates to obtaining pertinent data about risk culture and drivers across a large and complex organisation. Addressing this challenge requires internal audit to be involved closely with the mechanisms used to manage the business (such as leadership teams, executive/management committees and project steering committees) and to adopt a proactive approach to relationship management with key business executives. In addition, internal audit can access a wider range of information that is relevant to risk culture, some of which was accessed for planning in the past (including business strategies, risk assessments, performance reports), as well as new sources such as self-assessments and people/culture surveys.

Professional judgement is required for internal audit to distil the wide range of information they collect, and to assess the impact this has on risk culture and, consequently, audit priorities and scoping. Those internal audit functions that use traditional quantitative approaches to risk assessment will need to take particular care to ensure a true representation of the impact of culture is represented in their planning outputs.

Testing

Testing refers to the gathering of evidence by the internal audit function upon which to base an assessment and subsequent reporting. The objective of testing is to enable internal audit to produce a reliable assessment of the risk culture that actually exists across the business, as distinct from that the board and executive management have designed. Internal audit is accustomed to collecting evidence from multiple sources, and assessing the reliability of evidence and its sufficiency as a basis for assessment. This is particularly important in the area of risk culture where evidence can be less persuasive and more difficult to obtain.

In-depth audit work and testing by internal audit in the area of risk culture tends to consist of three complimentary activities:

❑ Detailed testing of the high-level governance and control environment, and addressing each of the systems of control that have been put in place to ensure promulgation of a sound risk culture across the organisation.
❑ Broadly based testing of risk culture from the bottom up, using surveys, workshops and interviews. Such techniques tend to concentrate on high-volume data collection and the execution of focused tests in specific areas of concern.
❑ Audits of the risk culture as an integral component of each and every piece of audit work. In these instances, particular drivers of risk culture are determined and assessed specific to the circumstances of the audit scope.

Regulators, in dialogue with particular firms, have encouraged internal audit functions to address risk culture and its impact, whether good or bad, as a critical component of each individual audit, as well as performing specific audits of components of the overall governance framework. Indeed, this is important for internal audit to report on how risk appetite is embedded in the risk governance framework, and how it is affected by approaches to compensation and business planning. It is therefore important that a balanced approach is taken incorporating aspects of all.

Furthermore, undertaking a broadly based work programme is important if internal audit is to produce group-wide thematic reporting that also highlights the improvements required.

Testing of governance and the control environment
Risk culture and risk governance are very closely intertwined; one cannot exist without the other. It is impossible to achieve a good risk culture without good risk governance, and risk governance will be undermined if there is poor risk culture. High-level governance audits are increasingly being conducted by internal audit as a regular part of their audit plan. Results are presented to the board, which incorporate the findings in their own self-assessments and improvement plans. Given that many firms have started to strengthen their governance arrangements, governance audits, when done well, are highly valued because they provide an early assessment as to whether the board's intentions are being achieved. As experience develops, internal audit is likely to perform at least a minimum level of coverage each year on governance matters, supplemented by in-depth work on specific components – such as those represented in the assessment framework. As with all audit work, the particular components of the risk culture framework subject to audit would be determined according to their importance.

Broadly based bottom-up testing
The second area of work for internal audit functions is the bottom-up assessments that are intended to determine the nature of risk culture on the ground; this is the actual culture existing at the time of the audit, not that designed or desired by the board. Robust evidence can be gathered during the execution of individual assignments, but such assessments can only ever impact a small proportion of the organisation as a whole in any one year. This approach is about the design of work to collect data from larger populations that the regular, routine audit work could not address.

The extent to which internal audit go into this second area of work is influenced rightly by the existence and reliability of other evidence sources operated by management. Where management have designed and implemented measures that collect information about the risk culture as first- or even second-line processes, internal audit will typically review and test the integrity of these processes. Where such measures do not exist, internal audit often works with management to design appropriate data gathering.

The most common technique being used to assess organisation-wide risk culture is staff questionnaires. Sometimes these questionnaires specifically focus on culture by containing questions that address both the levels of understanding and the specific behaviours in relation to risk culture. For example, questions can cover staff members' awareness of risk tolerances in their area of the business, as well as attitudes to compliance and reporting. Cultural questions are also added to broadly based staff surveys, which are managed typically by the human resources (HR) functions.

The benefit of questionnaires is the ability to reach large numbers of people at a point in time. The disadvantages relate to quality of completion and possible bias. It is therefore common for supplementary techniques to be adopted alongside questionnaires, such as telephone interviews, facilitated workshops that can drive completion of a questionnaire or assess and validate questionnaire results. Use of a question bank targeted at different roles and functions is important to give structure to the interviews. These can be used to "triangulate" towards an answer. For example, HR could be asked about the view taken of breaches in control in promotion/pay discussions, the risk function could be asked the same question as well as individuals in the business unit. It is also important that questions are evidence-based in relation to the HR question – for instance, how many examples can HR cite of individuals who had met or exceeded their sales targets but because of control or culture failures had received a lower bonus.

All the key players need to be brought into the interview process, with targeted interviews of key individuals:

❏ the board and board committees;
❏ executive management;
❏ business lines;
❏ human resources;
❏ risk management;
❏ other control functions, such as compliance and legal; and
❏ finance.

Testing culture in each audit assignment

Internal audit functions are also adapting their audit methodologies to ensure critical cultural factors are both identified and tested for each assignment they undertake. As explained earlier, this is in addition to the execution of particular risk culture audits triggered by the audit planning process and attributable to higher levels of risk.

Having decided upon the scope and boundaries of an audit during the planning process, the key considerations giving rise to the audit appearing on the plan are expanded upon in producing specific terms of reference. The most important components of the risk culture assessment framework can be identified by considering the seriousness of the implications of a weak culture. Those components are incorporated into scope, and management's procedures to ensure a target risk culture exists are then determined, and tests designed and executed to validate their existence in operation.

For example, in an audit of a sales process concerning complex financial products, the adherence to risk appetite, the basis of compensation paid to sales staff and the accuracy of risk reporting may be identified as key components of risk culture that require assessment. Specific audit procedures would therefore be designed to address these areas to the extent that significant business impacts may occur due to failure to meet the expected standards of performance and behaviour. Particular experience and expertise are required to determine the particular components of risk culture to assess in designing suitable tests and in interpreting the results and their implications for the effective management of risk.

Reporting

The purpose of internal audit's reporting is to provide stakeholders with an accurate assessment of the risk culture of the organisation or part of the organisation (for particular audits), and to report gaps and the measures that will be taken to address them. It is common that such reporting is against the assessment framework used to determine the nature and extent of audit work.

Effective reporting requires the ability to aggregate multiple data sources of variable reliability, identify relevant themes and obtain consensus for improvement actions. In practice, most reporting compares the auditor's assessment of current state to the desired state, commonly targeted by management. It also compares

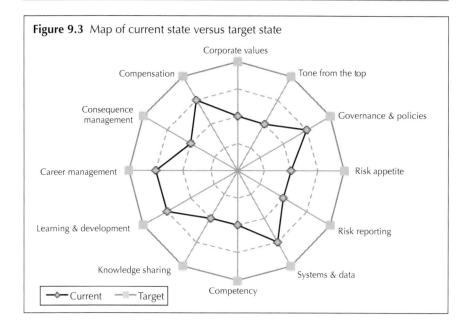

Figure 9.3 Map of current state versus target state

performance across the organisation so as to highlight specific hot spots.

Figure 9.3 provides an example of high-level reporting using the ICOM model as a basis. It compares the target state set by the board with the actual state assessed by the internal audit function from the multiple evidence sources available to it. The gaps between current and target state should be addressed by enhancements that become the subject of ongoing monitoring.

Increasingly, the reporting of actual risk culture is being taken on by the first and second lines of defence, in which case internal audit reporting focuses on an assessment of the reliability of such reporting and on the appropriateness of management actions.

ENHANCEMENTS TO INTERNAL AUDIT STAFFING

The single biggest challenge that internal audit functions face as they seek to meet higher performance standards is to improve the calibre of internal audit staff. The FSB, in their 2013 "Thematic Review on Risk Governance",[13] highlighted the need for the annual opinion on the design and effectiveness of the risk governance framework "to be performed by individuals with the skills needed to produce a reliable assessment". The report also highlighted the importance of internal audit having the stature to effectively carry out their role.

As internal audit work becomes more strategic and focused on matters of significance to the board, the implications for internal audit skills are massive. Addressing the audit of risk culture (as well as the risk appetite and overall risk governance framework) calls for people with sound professional judgement, able to operate at the highest levels in the organisation.

Addressing this resourcing challenge calls for radical change to the staffing models traditionally used by internal audit functions. In the past, internal audit functions have adopted pyramid-shaped staffing structures where a large number of junior staff perform the majority of fieldwork. Such staffing models were filled typically from the bottom, with more senior people rotating out of internal audit for career progression. Internal auditors were promoted as they gained experience, and learning was largely provided "on the job".

Generally, internal audit functions of major firms have understood this and are engaged in making significant change to their staffing models to make them both higher skilled, and more robust and sustainable. Pyramids are being flattened as internal audit becomes more senior and gains business experience.

Specialist skills are also required in specific risk areas to equip the internal audit functions with a better ability to challenge management in both first and second lines. Recruitment of subject matter specialists without an audit background directly into higher levels of the internal audit structure is often required. As a consequence, many internal audit functions envisage a more expensive staffing model with a greater proportion of senior and specialist staff than has been the case in the past.

Internal audit functions appear to have also started to invest more in the skills and capabilities of their team through better training, and wider learning and development initiatives. These include a wide range of technical and personal development training, as well as improved coaching, mentoring, staff appraisal and development schemes. This is much needed and long overdue, as internal audit functions commonly have invested no more than 5% of their budget in staff development.

A larger number of internal audit functions also plan to implement rotation arrangements with key areas of the business for

Risky idea of CRO ~ CKO

experienced people with development potential. For internal audit, this provides a steady stream of people with sound business and commercial experience who have credibility with the organisation's executive management (or who can quickly establish it).

Importantly, there has also been increasing use of external resourcing from third-party professional firms, especially for skilled specialists. Such arrangements can enhance independence and objectivity, improve point-in-time capability and provide ongoing confidence that staffing needs can be met, especially in areas where talent is in short supply.

All these initiatives are important if internal audit is to be able to access a richer talent pool of people to deploy, and thereby enhance capability and credibility in performing their work.

CONCLUSION

The lessons of the financial crisis in relation to risk culture are being addressed by wide-ranging initiatives undertaken through sponsorship from the board downwards. Many of these initiatives are the subject matter of other chapters in this book.

Internal audit now has a key role to assess and report upon risk culture as a key component of their reporting on governance, risk management and internal control. Regulators are converging towards the view of a heightened role and responsibility for the internal audit function that is consistent with assessing and reporting upon risk culture.

Nothing in the internal audit role replaces the responsibility of executive management to put in place effective systems of control that are implemented consistently across the organisation. Internal audit is, however, uniquely placed to report to the board on whether these objectives are being met and to highlight improvement areas. To fulfil this remit requires substantial change to internal audit procedures and personnel, a process that some functions have already begun.

1 Published by the Institute of Internal Auditors, and revised in October 2012 (available at https://na.theiia.org/standards-guidance/Public%20Documents/IPPF%202013%20English. pdf).

2 Institute of Internal Auditors, October 2012 (available at https://na.theiia.org/standards-guidance/Public%20Documents/IPPF%202013%20English.pdf).

3 FSB, 2013, "Thematic Review on Risk Governance", peer review report, February 12.

4 OCC, January 2014 (available at http://www.occ.gov/news-issuances/bulletins/2014/bulletin-2014–1a.pdf).

5 Chartered Institute of Internal Auditors, 2013, "Effective Internal Audit in the Financial Services Sector", July.

6 Board of Governors of the Federal Reserve System, 2013, "Supplementary Policy Statement on the Internal Audit Function and its Outsourcing", January.

7 FSB, November 2013, "Principles for an Effective Risk Appetite Framework".

8 Institute of Internal Auditors, October 2012 (available at https://na.theiia.org/standards-guidance/Public%20Documents/IPPF%202013%20English.pdf).

9 FSB, November 2013, "Principles for an Effective Risk Appetite Framework".

10 OCC, January 2014 (available at http://www.occ.gov/news-issuances/bulletins/2014/bulletin-2014–1a.pdf).

11 BaFin, "Minimum Requirements for Risk Management (available at http://www.bafin.de/SharedDocs/Downloads/EN/Rundschreiben/dl_rs_0915_ba_marisk.pdf?_blob=publicationFile).

12 FSB standards for effective risk governance are set out in the "Thematic Review of Risk Governance" (2013), and standards for risk appetite are set out in the "Principles for an Effective Risk Appetite" (2013).

13 FSB, 2013, "Thematic Review on Risk Governance", peer review report, February 12.

10

Compensation and Risk: Regulation and Design of Incentive Schemes

José Luis López del Olmo

Banco de España

One key area of regulatory focus with regard to risk culture has been the issue of the structure of compensation arrangements in banks. In this vein, the Financial Stability Board (FSB) considers compensation practices that promote appropriate risk-taking behaviour as one of the three foundational elements that support a sound risk culture in financial institutions,[1] the other two being effective risk governance – including the roles and responsibilities of the board – and an effective risk appetite framework. This chapter therefore looks at the changing regulatory environment regarding incentive structures that affect the nature of the arrangements and the governance around them. It also explores challenges related to the design of an incentive-compatible remuneration structure for risk-taking businesses such as banks but which is also relevant for other industries.

Up until 2007, policymakers in general and prudential regulators in particular paid only limited attention to remuneration policies in banks. Before that, the limited references were largely in relation to broad corporate governance perspectives focused on listed companies. From 2007, and increasing in intensity during and after the global financial crisis, there was a marked change in public policy. However, there has been considerable controversy regarding the path that policy should take and, indeed, whether the official sector should intervene at all. The debate was in effect a "battle" between two camps with very different views. On the one side were defenders of the freedom of shareholders to make decisions aimed to maximise the value of their companies, "confronted" on the other by those who wanted to impose radical changes to remuneration approaches for banks, even limiting total remuneration on the grounds of financial stability.

The global regulatory approach driven by the FSB has focused on reinforcing corporate governance and links to risk management, but implementation of this broad approach has differed across countries. There are two patterns: some countries have adopted a supervisory approach that has high-level principles and more flexibility (examples are the US and, more prominently, Canada), whereas other jurisdictions have been more dirigiste, particularly the EU and Switzerland (see FSB, 2011).

THE DEVELOPMENT OF A NEW REGULATORY APPROACH TO REMUNERATION

Remuneration: To intervene or not to intervene, that is the question

No one questions that compensation policy is an extremely useful instrument that managers have in their toolkits to help them achieve their objectives by reinforcing or encouraging particular behaviour (in general, not only in financial services). Incentives need to be considered broadly, not just in terms of compensation. Individuals will also be incentivised by promotion prospects and status, and not only money. Much of the focus regarding the debate on incentives is centred, however, on variable performance or target-linked pay, and in particular bonuses.

It is also widely accepted, at least in free market economies, that "compensation arrangements are the result of arm's length bargaining between executives and boards seeking to serve shareholders' interests".[2] This principle applies to all types of business and industry. Bebchuk and Fried (2010) argue that directors have various incentives to "support or go along with arrangements favourable to the company's top executives", undermining the arm's length nature of the negotiation. Investors may find it difficult to coordinate action (a collective action problem), and Bebchuk and Fried support this by suggesting that executive pay is lower and more linked to performance when there is a large outside shareholder or a greater concentration of institutional shareholders. Nonetheless, the focus of policy in the area of remuneration in general is on disclosure, to aid investor action, and reinforcement of director independence, as well as on general improvements in corporate governance. Few would support the general regulation of remuneration. This goes hand in hand with a belief in the free market economy and a reluctance to intervene in corporate decisions.

On the other hand, it is accepted that public intervention in the financial services sector is necessary to preserve financial stability. With regard to banks, market discipline is undermined by expectations that some banks are too big to fail, although work on resolution mechanisms is trying to deal with this. In addition, the cost of banking sector fragility is high. Financial stability is dependent on the banking system continuing to function, and the costs of bank crises in terms of lost GDP are substantial. During the crisis, repeated injections of public money into the banking industry were necessary to limit its extent, and this reinforced the perceived need for public intervention. Indeed, this was actually considered by some as the main reason for public intervention, including in remuneration.

In the battle between these two contrasting principles, the status quo before the crisis that began in 2007 was that prudential regulators did not try to influence remuneration in the banking industry. They limited most of their "intrusiveness" to capital needs, and latterly also to liquidity requirements. However, there is a broad consensus that poor remuneration arrangements were at the root of the crisis, which helps to explain the change of this status quo. A Federal Reserve Bank of Kansas research paper noted in 2010 that "the massive taxpayer assistance to large financial firms in 2008 and 2009 has generated substantial popular support for government intervention to control and/or punish 'recklessness and greed'".[3] Moreover, 98% of industry participants in a survey conducted by the Institute of International Finance (IIF) considered that "… compensation structures were a factor underlying the crisis …"[4]

The initial pillars of public policy in remuneration practices: Transparency and governance to protect shareholders

Up until 2007, regulators did not intervene in compensation in the financial services industry. The industry was therefore affected by the general measures to enhance the position of shareholders. The European Commission made two sets of recommendations in this area. The first issued in December 2004[5] and the second published two months later.[6] The first recommendation highlights the conflict of interest between directors of listed companies and their share-holders, and in response sets out a number of principles to ease this natural tension. These mainly refer to enhanced governance and transparency.

❏ Disclosure of the policy on director's remuneration where, for example, it includes the need to provide sufficient information on the linkage between remuneration and performance.
❏ To enhance the capacity for shareholder action, remuneration policy should be an explicit item on the agenda of the annual general meeting of shareholders.
❏ Disclosure of the remuneration of individual directors.
❏ Share-based remuneration should be subject to the prior approval of shareholders.
❏ Information requirements on share-based remuneration schemes.

The second set of recommendations was also designed to deal with the potential for conflict of interest between management and share-holders, and sets out the importance of three committees: the nomination of directors committee, the audit committee and the remuneration of directors committee.

This focus on shareholder power supported by disclosure and enhanced corporate governance had various limitations that have influenced the willingness to regulate remuneration in banks. First, there was the issue of weak legal enforceability. It required pressure from shareholders to ensure that these recommendations were fully adopted because, as recommendations, they were not usually mandatory. Second, the scope of application was restricted because disclosure and other provisions were limited to remuneration of members of the board. The provisions did not cover other influential individuals. Third, the focus was on companies with shareholders, thus excluding organisations such as mutual, which are important in the financial services industry, with cooperatives and savings banks in some countries having this structure. Policymakers could have made the rules mandatory, but they would still have been concentrated on shareholder action and therefore not applicable to all financial institutions.

The main issue, however, was that the shareholder-focused

approach of the policy to date did not deal with incentives in those organisations whose business was taking financial risk.

The "intrusion" of legislators and regulators

First steps: 2007 to 2009

As the financial crisis unfolded, the international financial community was increasingly convinced that inadequate remuneration policies in the banking sector had contributed to excessive risk taking that, ultimately, was jeopardising financial stability in the main financial centres.

Although a direct link between risk taking and remuneration is hard to prove, there were a number of aspects where banks' approaches to remuneration had weaknesses.

❏ Deficiencies in governance – greater involvement of the board (and shareholders) would have been desirable in the establishment of the remuneration policy down through the organisation.

❏ Remuneration geared to the achievement of short-term profit targets – a focus on longer-term profitability of activities would have been desirable.

❏ Metrics used to measure performance were not adjusted to reflect risks or, if there was a risk adjustment, it did not necessarily reflect medium- to longer-term risks, in part because of the difficulty of measurement. On top of that, "tail" (or extreme) risk was not factored in.

❏ Many firms did not have processes to reflect wider risk culture behaviour in decisions on bonuses, let alone promotion or other incentives.

In October 2007, with losses mounting in the banking industry and bonuses still being paid, the ministers of finance and governors of the G7 countries mandated the FSB (at that time still called the Financial Stability Forum) to design a set of recommendations to strengthen institutions and financial markets. As a result, in April 2008 the FSB published a report[7] that contained almost 70 recommendations, one of which was that: "The financial industry should align compensation models with long-term, firmwide profitability. Regulators and supervisors should work with market participants to mitigate the risks arising from remuneration policies". The FSB accordingly initiated work on the link between risk and compensation policies that eventually led to the publication of its "Principles for Sound Compensation Practices"[8] (on April 2, 2009) and their related implementation standards[9] (on September 25, 2009).

These principles and standards are still the most comprehensive documents covering compensation practices in the financial sector.

Principles and standards of the FSB: Enhancement of the old paradigm

The decisions on the principles and standards of the FSB[10] took place against the backdrop of a political debate engendered by the magnitude of public sector bail-outs required by the industry. One of the most significant manifestations of this debate came with the publication of a letter in the *Financial Times* and *Le Figaro* on September 4, 2009, jointly signed by European Ministers of Finance from France, Germany, Italy, the Netherlands, Luxembourg, Spain and Sweden.[11] This letter stated that it was their duty to "put an end to destructive irresponsibility by certain financial players". It condemned some banking practices as "dangerous, improper, cynical and unacceptable". The letter also said that "risks associated with compensation schemes must be supervised very strictly", and made a call for a "strict compensation policy to be put in place". It referred to the prohibition of guaranteed bonuses and the need to spread bonuses over a few years. It also said that bonuses should reflect true performance, and went as far as saying that some of the bonuses raised moral questions and that bonuses should be capped.

The FSB principles and standards[12] embraced to some extent these ambitious political goals. In part, the emphasis was on increased governance and transparency, going beyond earlier recommendations. The FSB required a deeper involvement by the board of directors in the setting of remuneration policy, and called for greater transparency coupled with a supervisory review of remuneration policies. The principles and standards concerning these two aspects can be grouped into the following areas.

Effective governance of compensation:

❏ Principle 1. The board of directors must oversee the compensation system's design, and should not be controlled by the CEO and management team.

❏ Principle 2. The board of directors must monitor and review periodically the operation of the compensation system.
❏ Principle 3. Staff in the risk control department must be independent and compensated in an independent manner from the business areas that they oversee.
❏ Standard 1. Financial institutions should have a board remuneration committee.
❏ Standard 2. For employees in the risk department, remuneration should be determined independently of other business areas and performance measures should be based on the accomplishment of their objectives.

Transparency (supervisory oversight and engagement by stakeholders):

❏ Principle 8. Supervisory review of compensation practices.
❏ Principle 9. Firms must disclose comprehensive and timely information about compensation practices.

These principles and standards were in the tradition of previous transparency and governance-focused standards applied to listed companies.

Principles and standards of the FSB: Development of a new paradigm

In mid-2009, the most divisive issue between different members of the G20 (in line with the above-mentioned letter signed by European Ministers) was the debate over whether the continental approach calling for limitations to variable compensation should be adopted, or whether the Anglo–US approach of no caps would prevail. The solution was to adopt an approach that did not include a blanket limit on variable remuneration, but did provide for it to be limited "as a percentage of total revenues when it is inconsistent with the maintenance of a sound capital base".[13]

At the time, the Basel Committee was working on enhancement of the quality of bank capital and an increase in the quantity of capital held by banks by imposing various buffers. One buffer would be countercyclical – a capital conservation buffer designed to be built up in good times and drawn down in periods of stress. This enabled capital and discretionary bonuses to be linked. Depending on how far the conservation buffer had been reduced when a bank was under pressure, the payout of earnings in the form of dividends, share buy-backs and bonuses would be limited.

Additionally, this political solution was accompanied by a change in the approach of supervisors to remuneration policies. International regulators went one step further and transformed the traditional approach (governance + transparency) into a new paradigm: a requirement to align remuneration with risk, and in particular long-term risks. The principles and standards of the FSB[14] that deal with this alignment are as follows.

❏ Principle 4. Compensation must be adjusted for all types of risk.
❏ Principle 5. Compensation outcomes must be symmetric with risk outcomes.
❏ Principle 6. Compensation must be sensitive to the time horizon of risks.
❏ Principle 7. The mix of cash and equity must be consistent with risk alignment.
❏ Standard 3. Variable compensation should not limit the capital base of banks.
❏ Standard 4. Compensation should take into account the full range of potential risks.
❏ Standard 6. A substantial portion of variable compensation (eg, 40–60%) should be deferred.
❏ Standard 7. The deferral period should not be less than three years.
❏ Standard 8. More than 50% of variable compensation should be in shares.
❏ Standard 11. Guaranteed bonuses are not consistent with sound risk management.

Finally, there were some other standards whose nature is related to this risk alignment concept but also more akin to governance improvements.

❏ Standard 12. Existing contractual payments related to terminations should be re-examined.
❏ Standard 14. Banks should require that employees do not use

personal hedging strategies to undermine the risk alignment effects embedded in compensation arrangements.

The risk alignment of compensation practices is mainly built around two ideas: payment is made part in cash and part shares; and payments are deferred. These ideas were not completely new and were already being used by a number of companies. What was completely new is that these principles became binding for the banking industry, and that supervisors would explicitly review adherence in their examination activities. The setting of minimum percentages of shares to cash was also an innovation.

However, the FSB is going further than this and moving into the area of non-financial rewards. They have suggested that "other incentives, including performance reviews and promotions, should be supported by clearly formulated and well-documented processes".[15]

We will now look at the both the scope for institutions and the scope for employees. For the former, the FSB (and the Basel Committee on Banking Supervision, BCBS) generally address their recommendations to large, internationally active banks. However, no one should dispute that all banks, irrespective of their size, nature, business model or complexity, should have in place prudent compensation policies.

When these international standards are transposed into domestic legislation, it is usual for regulators to accept the principle of proportionality and recognise that, for some very small institutions or limited licence firms, some provisions – for example, a standalone remuneration committee – would not be appropriate.

In large banks, especially if they are dedicated to businesses where the risk of the operations is difficult to assess, a much more robust structure is needed in order to manage the risks stemming from compensation policies.

In terms of the scope for employees, one issue is how many employees should be covered by some of the provisions envisaged by regulators and, in particular, by the provisions of deferral. Although all banks should have prudent compensation practices for all employees, the more specific FSB requirements are focused more on key players in the firm. For example, it would not be practical to require deferral of variable compensation for all employees. The key to identifying employees subject to some requirements on their compensation packages, and the concept everyone agrees on, is that the provisions should be applied to material risk takers.

However, the boundaries of this concept are not unambiguous and some jurisdictions have tried to clarify and harmonise them. In particular, in the European Union, the European Commission issued rules on March 4, 2014 (Commission Delegated Regulation N° 604/2014) based on a draft standard submitted by the European Banking Authority to standardise this definition. This regulation sets out that some common qualitative and quantitative criteria will be applied to determine those staff considered as material risk takers – for example, all members of the board, both executives and non-executives, staff earning above a predefined threshold (500,000 euros) or the top 0.3% of highest earning staff in a bank will (with some exceptions) be considered material risk takers.

In the EU, there is also the concept of "high earners", which is the term used in its legislation to refer to people earning more than a million euros. For this set of people (normally, although not auto-matically, identified as material risk takers), the European legislator requires some additional transparency at the country level, not individually on remuneration. The EBA has published figures of country-by-country high earners in the period 2010–12.[16]

In line with the FSB's principles, the US approach[17] underscores the importance of including employees who, as part of a group, have the ability to expose the bank to material risks – for example, a branch manager in a retail or commercial bank. This is an area of focus because lending decisions at a branch level contributed to the crisis, although it is not always clear whether it was poor bank credit policies that were at fault or whether remuneration practice played a role. Also, these employees have quite limited powers to grant loans above a certain amount and without approval from a group/senior committee.

Going forward, supervisors will not identify risk takers but will have a say in the appropriateness of the identification.

Steps taken by national authorities: The European approach versus the US approach

The FSB began a regular programme of peer reviews in 2010 to look at implementation of their recommendations. Two different approaches have been used to implement the FSB recommendations in the remuneration area: regulatory or supervisory.

The US approach is supervisory, and is based on the use of high-level principles that give flexibility to firms. This approach works if it is accompanied by supervisory assessments. According to the FSB's 2011 peer review, countries such as Canada and Japan have followed a similar supervisory stance, while others (such as Spain) also used a similar approach in the early days of implementing the FSB principles and standards.

On the other hand, some countries – notably the European Union plus Switzerland – have pursued a regulatory approach where higher reliance is placed on prescriptive requirements. In the case of the European Union, a cap on the size of bonus payments has been imposed by Directive 2013/36/EU,[18] setting a maximum variable portion as a multiple of the base salary. It is important to note two characteristics of this limit: (i) it is not based on the financial situation of the bank; and the multiple can be increased from one to two with the explicit approval of shareholders. In any case, the total amount of remuneration is not limited, only the variable part as a multiple of the fixed part is capped.

Some supervisors have suggested that "a consequence of the cap may well turn out to be an increase in fixed pay. This would in turn have a negative effect on stability by locking in costs."[19] The different approaches adopted in different jurisdictions may also create strains to the extent that there is an international market for some bank staff, especially staff related to capital markets activities. Hence, firms headquartered in jurisdictions affected by hard caps on bonuses may end up losing staff "bid out" by banks operating from softer legislative regimes, or some businesses may move out of these jurisdictions. Legislators adopting this approach are aware of this implication. As in any other topic related to international competition, it is desirable that a global approach is pursued to level the playing field.

The particular case of public state aid

The main objective of the global changes developing in the prudential regulation of banks, including the orientation to compensation practices, is to minimise the likelihood of banking crises in the future. However, these changes will take some years to be fully implemented (more capital, additional liquidity ratios, improvements in quality of capital, better risk management, etc), and in the meantime public resources have been injected in the banking industry.

Therefore, although the approach to remuneration policies should not be different in banks that have received public funds, it is widely accepted that in cases of exceptional government intervention supervisors should have the ability to directly restructure the compensation scheme of banks. The justification for this stronger "intrusiveness" of public powers is not based on the grounds of protecting investors (as was the paradigm until 2009) or safeguarding financial stability (the new paradigm after 2009). The rationale for this strengthened control mechanism is to facilitate an appropriate use of public resources.

DESIGNING AN INCENTIVE-COMPATIBLE REMUNERATION STRUCTURE

The principles and standards of the FSB were a remarkable step forward, especially the development of a clear conceptual framework with the goal of strengthening the financial system. For remuneration, the approach needed to be put into practice quickly and in an internationally coordinated way. Talent is highly mobile and if implementation rules differed across countries, then some jurisdictions could find themselves on an unlevel playing field. It is at this juncture that the BCBS was called upon to act, and to act quickly, and they produced an assessment methodology for compensation principles and standards in a very short period.[20] Just a few months later, in October 2010, a further document was released setting out methodologies for risk and performance alignment of remuneration. This document[21] is, for the time being, one of the most comprehensive public policy papers focusing on the alignment between risk and remuneration.

The US regulatory agencies carried out an "incentive compensation horizontal review", and a report[22] was published in October 2011 after conducting this activity. The report contains a very interesting categorisation of the methods observed to make incentive compensation more sensitive to risk: (i) risk adjustment of performance; (ii) deferral mechanisms; (iii) using longer periods to assess employee performance; and (iv) reducing the sensitivity of awards to short-term performance.

Alignment of risk and compensation: The corporate framework

The goal of risk-adjusted performance is to align employee incentives with shareholder interests, including longer-term profitability, and reduce incentives for excessive risk taking to boost short-term profits. With increasingly explicit risk appetites being set by firms, financial compensation also needs to reflect whether risks taken are consistent with that risk appetite. This whole area of risk-adjusted performance remains a work in progress in the industry.

Achievement of an appropriate compensation approach requires strong corporate governance supported by senior management and the board of directors. It is also necessary to embed the remuneration policy in the general risk management framework of the bank. The industry agreed that "In order to implement change, senior management, including the CEO, CFO and CRO, need to be fully involved … and closely engaged with Human Resources on compensation." (IIF, 2009)

Performance measurements

Most firms have performance measurement frameworks in place to assess whether the goals of the company, the business unit and the individual are being met. However, a wide range of financial and non-financial metrics is usually used to assess employees' remuneration. Supervisors accept this approach (BCBS, 2010a and 2010b) and the industry emphasises this concept: "… Incentive compensation schemes based solely on financial performance measures cannot fully capture shareholder interests, and as such, firms should pay strategically to shape employee behavior" (see IIF, 2009).

With regard to financial targets, metrics such as revenue, profit or income, cashflow or return on equity, are frequently used. They are often accounting-based and usually backward looking. The share price is particularly used in relation to senior management. These metrics pose certain challenges with regard to remunerating employees of financial services firms because an intrinsic part of the activity of many employees is risk taking. The BCBS have pointed out that "such measures rarely capture the full range (or any) of the risk that employee's activities pose for the firm."[23] This is no doubt a consideration in other businesses as well, because profits could be boosted by reducing safety margins, for example, or risking future reputation by paring back quality or selling unsuitable products, but it is starker in the case of banks and other types of financial services firm.

Even the baseline for profit or results is not a given. To begin with, what kind of results should be considered: accounting results or management results? It seems that there is widespread acceptance that management results should be used because they can be linked more easily to the individual performance of employees, which was one of the goals of the FSB. This does raise the question of potential double counting if a number of individuals claim that they have contributed to the results. Furthermore, it can be argued that the value of the franchise should be deducted when computing the performance of a particular business line or unit.

From a prudential supervisors' perspective, accounting results could be more suitable for several reasons. First, they are the standard metric used by many agents (tax authorities, analysts, investors, shareholders, etc). Second, they are prepared according to audit standards and probably use more prudent assumptions than management accounts. Nevertheless, there are still some additional complications. For instance, what should be done with extraordinary items? Generally, most people would agree that extraordinary profits should be removed, but what about an extraordinary loss? Furthermore, it is not always straightforward to agree on this concept. Many will argue that carry trade profits stemming from long-term monetary policy transactions should be included as extraordinary items, while others disagree.

Finally, there are potential pitfalls in expressing targets in relative terms compared to the market. For example, if a bonus were to be paid if the market value of the bank performed better than the average of its competitors, how would a fall in value be treated? If the peer group has reduced its market value by, say, 50% while the particular bank had experienced a reduction of "only" 30%, would that warrant a bonus and how would the supervisors view a payout in such circumstances?

This analysis has focused on the financial aspects of performance, but the challenges are potentially even greater in terms of inclusion of softer risk factors such as general adherence to risk controls, and to risk culture and non-risk factors such as improvements in the quality of service for customer-facing activities. Many functions are cost centres rather than profit centres (for example, back office, compliance and risk functions), which raises the question of how to performance-link these functions. It is easier to look at costs and efficiency rather than actions that reduce risks elsewhere in the organisation. However, it is widely accepted that risk functions should not benefit from the performance targets of the business units.

Size of the pool

The BCBS identified two different approaches being used to size the total bonus pool: top down and bottom up. Under the top-down approach, the pool is set according to criteria tied to the firm's overall performance. This is then distributed to business units according to their own performance relative to targets. The process cascades down to the individual employee level. The BCBS sees one advantage as the link this provides between the available bonus pot at all levels with the firms overall performance and risks, and also the firm's overall goals.

In contrast, the bottom-up approach starts at the level of the individual and depends on the criteria set for that employee. The remuneration pool of a business unit depends on the sum of the awards to individuals in that unit. The BCBS set out two key weaknesses. First, the bonus is based solely on an individual's achievements and ignores overall firmwide performance. Second, an individual's contribution can be difficult to measure, which makes the discussion focus more on the pay level of competitors. The BCBS also thought that this approach could lead to cross-subsidisation between business lines. In practice, many banks use a mix between the two approaches.

The incorporation of risk measures

The FSB and the BCBS (and eventually supervisors and banks around the world) have highlighted the importance of appropriately including risk in remuneration policies. The BCBS[24] stressed the importance of risk-adjusted performance, but also identified a number of factors that could weaken the link between performance measurement and appropriate incentives:

❏ measures such as the share price may be influenced by factors such as market sentiment and the economy unrelated to the actions of the firm;

❑ relative performance measures may encourage more risk taking;
❑ to increase incentive effects, variables used to measure risk and performance should relate closely to decisions made by the employee; however, allocation of performance to business lines may be a challenge; and
❑ discretion and judgement is necessary to measure risks taken.

Adjusting performance for risk is not straightforward. To begin with, risks associated with current activities and transactions are not known with any certainty in advance. In short-term straightforward transactions, an accurate estimate of risk may be possible but it becomes much harder with regard to complex and longer-term transactions. Even basic risk adjustment of performance is not straightforward. For a moment, let us consider that a bank before engaging in a financial operation knows the returns that will be made, less likely losses. For example, if 50,000 mortgage loans are granted or 50,000 credit cards sold to customers, it is known how much money is going to be earned from these activities and how much the bank would lose from customers being unable repay after one year has elapsed, after two years, and so on until the end of the operation. In such a case, it would be quite straightforward to incorporate risk in the performance calculation made for the employees extending the loans. The forward revenue from the loans could be calculated net of likely losses. In other words, performance could be adjusted *ex ante*. In this world, immediate payout of performance-related bonuses would not create incentive difficulties.

In fact, many parts of this calculation would be uncertain even for a simple product such as a mortgage. The revenue would not be certain because, on some products, returns could be affected by a change in funding costs or margin, the number of borrowers defaulting changes with the economic climate and mortgages are prepaid at different rates, as well as depending on interest rate developments and the economic climate.

In practice, *ex ante* adjustments are made using return on regulatory capital employed (where regulatory capital is proxying the risk), or return on economic capital or return on capital needed to cover pre-set stress tests. The three measures of capital all reflect (to a greater or lesser extent) the risk of future losses caused by the risks incurred by taking on the business.

There are other elements and uncertainties that need to be adjusted for as well. Many banks did not charge business units fully for the cost of funds, which has led to a focus on improving funds transfer pricing post-crisis, and certainly did not charge business units for the liquidity risks their activities posed. This can be included now in performance metrics by allocating to business units the cost of the liquid assets buffer held to protect the banks from liquidity pressure in the future. This buffer has now been imposed globally under Basel III, which provides a standard metric that captures off-balance-sheet items such as undrawn lines, as well as on balance-sheet funding and asset structure.

Real life is also more complex in other ways. Many financial activities run operational risks that can be difficult to measure *ex ante* (although improvements are needed in this regard); and there are also potential reputation risks from some types of activity. This is why additional adjustments are needed to assess true performance even *ex post* after adverse outcomes (losses) have materialised. This has created pressure to defer at least a portion of remuneration until the outcomes can more clearly be seen. Even some straightforward risks such as credit outcomes can prove very different from those expected or allowed for in economic capital or regulatory capital models. *Ex post* performance adjustment should reflect this. Practices across the industry to deal with these issues are still under development.

It is paramount that the incorporation of risk metrics in compensation calculations is cautious and consistent with the whole risk management framework of the organisation. For example, if a bank that uses internal models for computing regulatory capital (built to a more prudent standard) but adjusts performance for compensation decisions using less prudent metrics (eg, economic capital), the risk-adjusted compensation may be closer to the bank's own assessment of risk but could ignore more prudent assumptions of possible future default rates.

By and large, it is not common for the metrics that capture concentration risk to be included in risk adjustment for compensation. These are stress-test results and capital is required for concentrations. Under Pillar 2 of Basel II, banks were required to calculate both and supervisors add extra Pillar 2 capital buffers to cover the risks. However, these are not reflected in the Pillar 1 regulatory capital measures or for compensation calculations. Economic capital measures may reflect concentrations, but could understate them. This means that individual incentives probably ignore an individual's contribution to growing concentration risk for the bank.

Both of these issues could mean that more losses arise after the compensation has been paid than was expected and for which compensation had been adjusted. One way of dealing with this drawback is to evaluate performance over longer periods, and a simple approach could be to use risk factors from prior-year actions when calculating incentives.[25]

Deferral and clawback

Ex post adjustments can be built in by using deferral periods or clawbacks. Malus arrangements enable deferred awards, prior to payment, to be reduced or cancelled. The awards can be reduced if actual attained performance does not reach pre-set levels. The BCBS found that by mid-2010 most large international banks featured a deferral period and vesting schedule.

Deferral in payments can also act as a lever to retain employees, which is paramount for talent management in companies. However, from a prudential perspective, the importance of time is that it helps to implement *ex post* risk alignment. The FSB standards provided an indicative time of three years for deferred payments that in fact has become the norm. The FSB standards suggested that 40–60% of compensation should be deferred.

Whereas malus clauses work before the conclusion of the deferral period, clawback provisions are put into contracts to reclaim compensation already paid. Clawbacks can be triggered when the employee is found to have provided misleading information or breached controls. There are more issues with clawback than deferral, and cases tend to be focused on mismanagement, fraud or negligence.

Deferred compensation is complicated by employees leaving before the end of the performance measurement period. The BCBS[26] has pointed out that golden handshakes (ie, provided by the hiring firm) could have the effect of reducing the effectiveness of deferral arrangements in improving risk-taking incentives.

They also indicated that, in the case of employees exposing the firm to long-term risks, deferral simply would not be protracted enough to counteract the effect of initial profits but much later risk of loss. In terms of profits versus losses in the deferral period, their strong view was that there should only be reduction to bonuses due to achieved performance, not any upward adjustment.

Instruments for the payment

Linked to the concept of deferral, banks are required to award part of the variable (and even the base) salary in shares. Stock options and share-based schemes are a potent instrument to incentivise employees and to focus them on long-term objectives, as long as there are vesting periods that provide the necessary time dimension. A vesting schedule determines when the employee receives full ownership of the shares or options.

These forms of variable remuneration meet the test that the EBA set out, that "the price or value of instruments awarded as variable remuneration should reflect changes in the credit quality of the firm, in particular if it deteriorates".[27]

On the issue of shares and cash, the FSB initially (in April 2009) just made the point that the risk should be consistent with risk alignment. In September 2009, the FSB implementation standards suggested that a substantial proportion (at least 50%) of bonuses should be awarded in shares or share-linked instruments. The BCBS provided additional guidance by defining both "share transfer restrictions" and "transfer restriction period" (or retention period), and clarifying that the latter is different from deferral period.

Latterly, and in the context of other discussions, regulators have started to consider the use of other instruments for non-cash payments. Paul Tucker, at the time deputy governor of the Bank of England, opined that "the authorities need to consider whether to require management to be paid to a significant extent in subordinated debt".[28] Subordinated debt would give no profit upside, and therefore would not encourage short-term profit-seeking while giving downside risk. Another non-cash instrument that can be used is bail-in-able debt. The concept of bail-in (first formulated by Paul Calello and Wilson Ervin, at the time employees of Credit Suisse, in an article published in 2010)[29] has become a cornerstone of the search for a way to enable large banks to be resolved and avoid the bail-out approach that had hitherto been used. The proposal now is that specially designated debt would have contractual terms to enable it to absorb losses (either imposing haircuts to some debtholders or converting debt into equity) if bail-in had been triggered by the authorities. Bail-in-able debt has yet to be fully defined, but Credit Suisse is using "wipe out" bonds for some bonus payments, which have a similar characteristic. They pay a floating interest rate, but if the Credit Suisse position weakens at a certain point the bonds are written down to zero.[30]

Banks have used other forms of instrument as well. In 2009, Credit Suisse used commercial mortgage-backed securities already on the balance sheet to pay bonuses.[31] These types of security had performed particularly badly in the crisis. Perhaps a new form of "skin in the game" for some markets would be using the securities created by some desks to pay bonuses to reign in excesses in boom times.

INDUSTRY PROGRESS

In October 2011, the FSB published a thematic peer review on compensation practices[32] that had a chapter dedicated to banks' progress in implementing the FSB principles and standards. The report covered a sample of around 60 large international banks, and found that:

❑ remuneration committees had been created in virtually all large banks;
❑ quantitative *ex ante* risk adjustments, normally linked to Basel II computation methodologies, are widespread; in some cases, backtesting or other techniques were used to analyse the effectiveness of adjustments;
❑ some firms also use qualitative indicators;
❑ revenues for calculating compensation are normally in line with accounting standards;
❑ procedures for identifying material risk takers differ across banks;
❑ variable compensation is normally higher than 60%, and in some cases is in the range 75–90%;
❑ deferral periods are normally three years, and in some cases have reached four or five years;
❑ malus and clawback clauses are still to be implemented by many firms; and

❑ disclosure of compensation practices, normally as part of the annual reports, has improved.

The IIF also released a report in October 2011 to provide an overview of the steps taken by the industry in applying the FSB principles and standards. This report encompassed 50 large international banks, and its conclusions, albeit rather more optimistic, were in line with the results of the FSB peer review.

As has been pointed out, an unlevel playing field could have some on progress in implementing sounder compensation structures. Nonetheless, a time of moderate growth (of markets and profits) is an opportune moment to try to change compensation practices.

CRITICAL APPRAISAL

The Chinese leader Zhou Enlai once famously claimed that "it was too early to say", referring to the significance of the French Revolution of 1789, because only 200 years had passed. In the field of compensation practices in the financial services industry, perhaps it will not be necessary to wait that long to assess critically the pros and cons of the steps taken by the industry, bank regulators and other authorities, but it will certainly take some time.

One of the most visible limitations of public policy in this area is that more radical *ex post* performance measures such as clawback may clash with labour laws. Another weakness is that developments have been very much focused on bonuses, forgetting other aspects of remuneration that can be relevant – for example, pension commitments or termination payments. On the other hand, it is clear that transparency has improved as is shown by the average number of pages dedicated to pay structures in annual reports compared with the early 2000s. One reason for these increasingly lengthy documents is that incentives schemes have become more complex, which is not a positive development, as a result of incorporating risk into remuneration policies.

In quantitative terms, there seems to be no apparent impact on credit growth or market liquidity because of the changing practices in incentives. Some other measures (leverage ratios, increased capital ratios, stress tests, liquidity buffers, etc) have much greater impact on credit and liquidity.

Also, in quantitative terms it seems that things are diverging. The number of people receiving very large compensation packages has reduced in many countries (at least this is the conclusion stemming from the EBA reports on high earners), while at the same time pay for non-executives directors has risen notably.

In conclusion, let us propose a final comment on the caps that have been imposed on variable remuneration in the EU legislation. If these limits are not accompanied by other actions, such as enhanced scrutiny by shareholders and regulators, they could have the undesirable effect of increasing base salaries to offset the limitations imposed to variable remuneration. This underlines the complexity of achieving change in the remuneration area.

This chapter represents solely the views of the author and does not reflect those of the Banco de España. Nevertheless, the chapter has benefited from many previous discussions with some colleagues at the Banco de España, especially Fernando Vargas, Esther Palomeque and Eva Catarineu. I would particularly like to thank Patricia Jackson, a former supervisor, whose insights and valuable comments have contributed to broadening the chapter from too supervisory an approach.

1 FSB (2014).
2 See Bebchuk and Fried (2010).
3 De Young *et al.* (2010).
4 IIF (2009).
5 European Commission (2004).
6 European Commission (2005).
7 FSF (2008).
8 FSF (2009).
9 FSB (2009).
10 At this point it is important to bear in mind that the majority of FSB members belong to central banks (normally including financial regulators) and ministries of finance.
11 Available at http://www.ft.com/cms/s/0/896628cc-97b2–11de-a927–00144feabdc0.html
12 FSB (2009).
13 ibid.
14 ibid.
15 FSB (2014).
16 EBA (2013a).
17 FRB (2011).
18 Article 94 (1)(g)(i) and (ii).
19 See "The Changing Face of Prudential Policy", speech given by Katharine Braddick (Director for Prudential Policy, Prudential Regulation Authority, Bank of England) on March 11, 2014.
20 BCBS (2010a).
21 BCBS (2010b).
22 FRB (2010).
23 BCBS (2010a).
24 ibid.

25 FRB (2010).

26 BCBS (2010a).

27 EBA (2014).

28 See "Competition, the pressure for returns, and stability", speech given by Paul Tucker on October 17, 2012 at the British Bankers' Association Annual Banking Conference, London.

29 Available at http://www.economist.com/node/15392186.

30 Lex column, *The Financial Times*, February 11, 2014.

31 ibid.

32 FSB (2011).

REFERENCES

Basel Committee on Banking Supervision, 2010a, "Compensation Principles and Standards: Assessment Methodology", January.

Basel Committee on Banking Supervision, 2010b, "Range of Methodologies for Risk and Performance Alignment of Remuneration", consultative document, October.

Basel Committee on Banking Supervision, 2010c, "Basel III: A Global Regulatory Framework for More Resilient Banks and Banking Systems", December.

Bebchuk, Lucian and Jesse Fried, 2010, "Tackling the Managerial Power Problem: The Key to Improving Executive Compensation ", *Pathways Magazine*, Harvard.

European Commission, 2004, "Commission Recommendation of 14 December 2004 Fostering an Appropriate Regime for the Remuneration of Directors of Listed Companies (2004/913/EC)", December.

European Commission, 2005, "Commission Recommendation of 15 February 2005 on the Role of Non-executive or Supervisory Directors of Listed Companies and on the Committees of the (Supervisory) Board (2005/162/EC)", February.

De Young, Robert, Emma Peng and Meng Yan, 2010, "Executive Compensation and Business Policy Choices at US Commercial Banks", The Federal Reserve Bank of Kansas City, January.

European Banking Authority, 2013a, "Report: High Earners – 2010 and 2011 Data", July.

European Banking Authority, 2013b, "Report. High Earners. 2012 Data", November.

European Banking Authority, 2014, "Final Draft Regulatory Technical Standards on Classes of Instruments that are Appropriate to be Used for the Purpose of Variable Remuneration", February.

European Commission, 2004, "Fostering an Appropriate Regime for the Remuneration of Directors of Listed Companies".

European Parliament and European Council, 2013, "Directive 2013/36/EU of 26 June 2013 on Access to the Activity of Credit Institutions and the Prudential Supervision of Credit Institutions and Investment Firms".

European Parliament and European Council, 2013, "Regulation (EU) No 575/2013 of 26 June 2013 on Prudential Requirements for Credit Institutions and Investment Firms".

Federal Reserve Board, 2010, "Incentive Compensation Practices: A Report on the Horizontal Review of Practices at Large Banking Organisations", Board of Governors of the Federal Reserve System, October.

Financial Stability Board, 2009, "Principles for Sound Compensation Practices: Implementation Standards", September.

Financial Stability Board, 2011, "Thematic Review on Compensation: Peer Review Report", October.

Financial Stability Board, 2012, "Implementing the FSB Principles for Sound Compensation and their Implementation Standards. Progress Report", June.

Financial Stability Board, 2013, "Implementing the FSB Principles for Sound Compensation and their Implementation Standards: Second Progress Report", August.

Financial Stability Board, 2014, "Guidance on Supervisory Interaction with Financial Institutions on Risk Culture" A Framework for Assessing Risk Culture", April.

Financial Stability Forum, 2008, "Report of the Financial Stability Forum on Enhancing Market and Institutional Resilience", April.

Financial Stability Forum, 2009, "Principles for Sound Compensation Practices", April.

Institute for International Finance, 2009, "Compensation in Financial Services", in collaboration with Oliver Wyman, March.

Institute for International Finance, 2011, "Compensation Report on Wholesale Banking 2011: Assessing Three Years of Progress", in collaboration with Oliver Wyman, October.

11

A View from the Remuneration Committee: Emerging Good Practice in the UK

Alan M. Judes

Strategic Remuneration

Some of the largest collapses in firms and share prices during the financial crash of 2007–08 took place in organisations where top management held very significant shareholdings. A simple mantra of paying executives in the form of deferred shares would not have prevented the problems from occurring. The remuneration committee needs to take into account the link between culture and remuneration policies in designing the reward strategy. Risk is on the agenda for the remuneration committee more than at any other time. This chapter therefore considers the formation of the remuneration committee in the UK, its responsibilities to set policy for the company as a whole and the actual pay of the executive directors, how the Association of British Insurers (ABI) and Financial Reporting Council (FRC) have extended the requirement to consider risk in remuneration policy from the financial services sector to industry generally, how remuneration committees are dealing with their responsibilities and challenges, and how the concept of clawback is being significantly extended.

THE HISTORY AND ROLE OF THE REMUNERATION COMMITTEE

The remuneration committee is a sub-committee of the board of a publicly listed company in the UK. In the US, the equivalent committee is called the compensation committee. There are typically three to five members, and they are usually all independent non-executive directors of the company. The structure is similar across all industries. The remuneration committee is not a creation of company law; indeed, the Companies Acts of 1985 and 2006 do not contain any reference to remuneration committees. Rather, the remuneration committee has developed from the requirements of corporate governance guidelines that started with the creation of ProNed in 1982, which was sponsored by the Bank of England, the Stock Exchange, the Confederation of British Industry (CBI) and others. In 1991–92, Sir Adrian Cadbury, the chairman of ProNed, chaired a committee that produced a report on the financial aspects of corporate governance. This report contained the following:

> We also recommend that boards should appoint remuneration committees, consisting wholly or mainly of non-executive directors and chaired by a non-executive director, to recommend to the board the remuneration of the executive directors in all its forms, drawing on outside advice as necessary. Executive directors should play no part in decisions on their own remuneration. Membership of the remuneration committee should appear in the Directors' Report. Best practice in this field is set out in ProNed's Remuneration Committee guidelines, published in 1992.[1]

This recommendation was accepted and successive reports have been issued, leading to the UK Corporate Governance Code[2] that sets out standards of good practice in relation to board leadership and effectiveness, remuneration, accountability and relations with shareholders. All companies with a premium listing of equity shares in the UK are required under the listing rules to report on how they have applied the Code in their annual report and accounts.

RESPONSIBILITIES OF THE REMUNERATION COMMITTEE

The remuneration committee determines the pay of the executive directors of the company, and has responsibility for specifying the remuneration policy of the company. The Cadbury Committee struggled with the concept of giving shareholders a binding vote on executive remuneration. It is not surprising, there was a concern as to how to deal with a negative vote in respect of payments that had been made contractually. However, developments in corporate governance since then have seen shareholders being given an advisory (non-binding) vote on the remuneration report in 2002 and a binding vote on remuneration policy in 2013. The responsibility of the remuneration committee in 2014 is to set the remuneration policy for the company, to obtain shareholder approval for the remuneration policy and to ensure that payments made to directors are in accordance with this policy. Any payments made that are not in accordance with the policy are null and void, and if the company incurs any loss the directors authorising the payment can be personally liable to make good the losses.

CORPORATE GOVERNANCE: THE LINK BETWEEN REMUNERATION POLICIES AND RISK MANAGEMENT

Following the financial crisis of 2007–08, the "Review of Corporate Governance in UK Banks and Other Financial Industry Entities" (the Walker Report)[3] was commissioned by the Prime Minister in February 2009 to examine board practices at UK banks, which was later extended to other financial institutions. This report perceived an imbalance between shareholders' limited liability for institutional debts and the effectively unlimited liability of the taxpayer when obliged to bail them out. "Serious deficiencies in prudential oversight" were noted, along with "major governance failures within banks", but still promotion of best practice rather than formal regulation was identified as the best means to ensure ownership of good corporate governance.

The review comprised five key themes, with two affecting risk and remuneration:

❏ greater dedicated non-executive directorial focus on risk management is required, supported by a dedicated chief risk officer (CRO); and

❏ substantial enhancement is necessary of board-level oversight of remuneration of all senior employees (not just board level), to be more closely aligned with medium- and long-term risk and performance.

Initially, the Walker Report was relevant only for financial businesses, but some of the recommendations are being applied to all UK listed companies. In particular, the obligation for the remuneration committee of a listed UK company to factor risk into their workload has moved from the finance sector to industry generally. These obligations are spelled out in the "Principles of Remuneration" of the ABI. The ABI represents the insurance industry and its interests in the UK, Europe and around the world, and has 440 members who own approximately 20% of the FTSE All-Share Index along with over £1.5 trillion of assets, according to their website. The ABI has been giving guidance to its members on voting on share plans and remuneration matters since 1987 in a low key, proactive but non-confrontational approach to corporate governance, and its recommendations have great weight.

The ABI principles of remuneration have included references to risk and remuneration since September 2011, and its latest guidance issued in November 2013 contained a number of provisions covering the link between risk-adjusted performance and remuneration. In particular, they make clear that "Shareholders look to the remuneration committee to protect and promote their interests in setting executive remuneration". The guidance included the following recommendations.

❏ Non-executive directors should scrutinise the performance of the executives, and ensure that risk management systems are robust.
❏ Remuneration committee members are accountable to shareholders for the structure and quantum of remuneration.
❏ Remuneration committees should set remuneration within the context of overall corporate performance. Structure should be aligned with strategy and agreed risk appetite, reward success fairly and avoid paying more than is necessary.

In addition, remuneration policies should:

❏ be set to promote value creation through transparent alignment with the agreed corporate strategy; and
❏ support performance, encourage the underlying sustainable financial health of the business and promote sound risk management for the benefit of all investors, including shareholders and creditors.

Remuneration committees have been working hard since 2011 to take into account the guidelines of the ABI at the remuneration committee and remuneration policy level. The need to do this has been reinforced by proposed changes[4] to the UK Corporate Governance Code published by the FRC. In November 2013, the FRC published a consultation paper entitled "Risk Management, Internal Control and the Going Concern Basis of Accounting", in which it sought views on both proposed changes to the UK Corporate Governance Code and related draft guidance on risk management. The proposed changes to the UK Corporate Governance Code are mainly to C.2.1 and C.2.2 on risk management and internal control. However, from a remuneration committee perspective, it is important to note the changes proposed to Schedule A: "The design of performance-related remuneration for executive directors", which now includes the wording "Remuneration incentives should be compatible with risk policies and systems" in the first paragraph.

It is fair to say that most UK listed companies have carried out extensive analysis and reporting of the risk management systems of the company, together with detailed reporting of the risks facing the organisation and how they are being managed. The challenge is to factor in the work being done in risk management into the remuneration committee's work stream and the company's remuneration policies.

REPORTING RISK TO THE REMUNERATION COMMITTEE

In terms of consideration of the links between the remuneration policies and the risk objectives of the firm, the financial services sector has led the way and other industrial companies are beginning to follow. One relatively easy way to bring an understanding of the wider risk objectives of the company into the remuneration committee is to have a formal presentation to the committee at least once a year. This would cover the company's risk appetite and the actual risk exposures, and be given by the CRO. This can lead to the setting of clear requirements for risk and risk appetite being considered in the remuneration policy agreed by shareholders. For example, one company's remuneration policy has the following requirement:

> The Committee considers a report on risk exposures each year, in relation to the agreed risk appetite of the Group, and has the discretion to reduce the outcome of the annual incentive plan based on that report.

In the case of this company, the committee considers the level of profit achieved and whether more risk was taken to achieve it. The CRO gives a presentation on the risks taken and is asked to confirm whether or not in their opinion any adjustments to the payout are required to reflect greater risk being taken. In other words, was the disclosed level of profit reported only achieved by taking excessive risks or positions outside the company's stated risk appetite? This would mean that risk-adjusted performance would in fact be lower than the stated figures.

Old Mutual, for instance, disclosed in their 2013 annual report and accounts that their remuneration committee received a paper from the CRO to confirm that targets had been fulfilled within the risk appetite of the company. Some companies disclose considerable detail on the role of risk and the risk management process in remuneration setting. Legal & General, for example, made clear in their 2012 accounts[6] that the bonus steering committee (BSC), the CRO and the group director of regulatory risk and compliance all played central roles with regards to the setting of "reward structures and evaluating whether achievement of objectives and any payment from plans have taken into account the overall risk profile of the Company".

They say that the BSC, which reports to the remuneration committee, has "continued to review and challenge" all bespoke bonus schemes on a regular basis. They ensure they support business strategy while delivering within risk appetite. Further, another area of focus of the BSC is to reduce the number and complexity of bonus plans, and it should always considers whether a general discretionary bonus plan would be more appropriate. The BSC must approve bonus schemes before submission to the remuneration committee.

Legal & General also set out the role of the CRO and group director of regulatory risk and compliance, both of whom work closely with the remuneration committee. The group director of regulatory risk and compliance "reports to the Committee on an annual basis regarding payments of bonus schemes for the year and provides input into how those schemes operate for the following year. In addition, the group director of regulatory risk and compliance confirms whether any risks have been taken outside of pre-agreed parameters that may lead the Committee to consider whether it should impact the payment of bonus schemes and confirms that all plans for the following year meet business objectives without encouraging undue risk." The CRO looks specifically at the overall risk profile of the company and whether executive directors have achieved objectives within the company's accepted risk appetite. The CRO also reviews the executive directors' objectives for the forthcoming year to ensure they are in line with the risk parameters.

The remuneration committee also needs to decide how best to design the total remuneration package of the CRO, and those individuals who are charged with ensuring the accurate measurement of risk and the truth and fairness of the reporting in the financial statements. For these roles, it is important to balance the basic salary and benefits, and short- and long-term incentives that are the components of the total remuneration package. Giving such roles a pure profit-based performance measure for annual incentives can create an uncomfortable conflict of interest for the individuals occupying them. Remuneration committees are including specific bonusable objectives for those roles that are required to deliver high-quality governance and control framework, and the remuneration committee can look at specific measurable outcomes to assess performance in setting variable pay for those roles. For example, the delivery of an annual incentive can be dependent upon the satisfactory delivery of risk reviews, compliance plans and the reports from internal and external audit. Outside the financial services sector, the role may fall into job titles reporting to the finance director, including the head of internal audit.

An example taken from one firm's policies regarding the additional governance weighting that is given to a finance director, in contrast with the chief executive and other members of the top management team, is as follows:

> Short-term incentives: The split in financial and scorecard objectives remain 75%/25% for the Group Chief Executive and 50%/50% for the Group Finance Director. As the Group Finance Director is responsible to the Board for all financial matters, including management control over the Group Internal Audit, Compliance and Risk functions, his scorecard elements (which emphasise financial risk, governance and capital management objectives) have a significantly higher weight than the Group Chief Executive and line management executives.[7]

In addition, there is typically a discretionary override such that the entire annual incentive scheme can be "disapplied" for a year if, during that year, an individual occupying a regulatory role breaches risk appetite. Such a breach should be visible to the remuneration committee, and indeed the board as a whole, within the existing reporting and governance structures.

EMERGING GOOD PRACTICE ON PERFORMANCE MEASUREMENT: FACTORING RISK INTO PERFORMANCE MEASURES AND TARGETS

Many companies are building risk measurement and assessment into the measures and targets that are being used for annual and long-term incentive plans (LTIPs). Although these plans are most visible in the disclosure of the directors' emoluments, the design of the plans is relevant for all participants in these incentive arrangements. In this way, the concept of risk management can be cascaded and communicated down the company to all participants.

It has become increasingly common to use economic profit as a measure for incentive and reward purposes, instead of a simple profit before tax or an earnings per share measure. The key difference is that in calculating economic profit there is an additional charge for the provision of equity capital that is needed to back the risks in the business. This equity capital is not shown as having any charge in conventional accounts. Shareholders expect a higher return on their equity investments than providers of debt – equity is frequently scarce and expensive, and carries more risk if the firm fails. Economic profit, which deducts a charge for the weighted average cost of capital (including equity as well as debt), allows for an incentive design that recognises risk. If the economic capital measures are accurate, the charge will be higher the more risk is taken. In simple proportionate terms, if risk exceeds risk appetite, the economic capital charge will be higher than it would otherwise have been. For example, a property investment company can specify the maximum loan to value ratio that the board has authorised. If it emerges that management wishes to have a higher level of gearing, then the additional risk borne will result in a greater charge for the provision of capital beyond the specified risk appetite. This will reduce the economic profit arising and reflects the additional risk taken.

Large groups often initiate economic profit measures by using the weighted average cost of capital for the group as a whole for this purpose. Increasingly, groups are stratifying their subsidiaries into different risk groups and then applying appropriate cost of capital charges for the business that is undertaken by each subsidiary. It is to be expected that some businesses in the group will have very different risk profiles and therefore should have different charges for the capital required to run them.

Another way of including risk measurement in the performance measures involves reducing the share of profit that goes into an annual incentive pool when risk measures are breached. Most executives will be familiar with geared incentive plans where, after threshold profit levels are achieved, each incremental unit of profit funds a proportionately greater contribution to the pool. Similar approaches could be used to reduce the share of profit that goes into the pool if risk measures indicate that risk has exceeded threshold metrics. An alternative approach to include risk in the annual incentive structure is to use a balanced scorecard approach to setting performance measures and targets for annual, and indeed for long-term, incentive arrangements. In its filings with the Financial Services Authority (FSA),[8] the Royal Bank of Scotland set out how it would use balanced scorecards that include risk metrics to adjust incentive arrangements for risk. They made clear that this is a two-way street. The board risk committee is made aware of the implications of remuneration decisions for risk management and the process ensures that the risk aspects of remuneration policy are managed.

This consists of several elements.

❑ The balanced scorecard of performance metrics for both the annual and the long-term incentive arrangements incorporate risk measures.
❑ Awards will only vest if the remuneration committee is satisfied that the risk management during the performance period has been effective. The remuneration committee is advised independently on this by the board risk committee.
❑ The remuneration committee receives advice from the head of restructuring and risk on the risk adjustment of measures for bonus pool funding, and a risk review of individual performance evaluations is carried out for the management committee.

❏ The chairman of the board risk committee may attend remuneration committee meetings to advise on matters relating to risk adjustment.

EMERGING GOOD PRACTICE ON PERFORMANCE MEASUREMENT: DEFERRING REMUNERATION AND PAYING REMUNERATION IN THE FORM OF SHARES

For many years, it has been commonplace for the remuneration committee to defer part of the annual incentive for all executives participating in the annual incentive plan, so that it is paid up to three years later rather than immediately when determined. This is not new: it was first introduced in the early 1990s by the UK stockbroker Smith New Court, and was shortly followed by other firms, including UBS. Typically, bonuses are locked in for three years, and if a person leaves before then they forfeit the money. In some ways, it seemed that investment banks were hankering after their old partnership status. Salomon Brothers admitted as much in 1990 when it set up its equity partnership plan, which paid the bank's high rollers partly in Salomon shares.

Therefore, the concept of deferring annual incentives and paying what otherwise would have been immediate cash in the form of company shares is not new. However, what is new, and is a direct response to factoring risk into the remuneration package, is introducing malus or clawback over the shares and cash bonus. In the 1990s, the purpose of the deferral was simply to lock in the employee receiving the deferred incentive, or more likely to increase the cost to a competitor for talent who would have to buy out the entitlement as an inducement for the employee to take up the new employment. Malus and clawback are methods used by the company to enable them to recover the incentives that had been deferred or paid out earlier if it later emerges that excessive risk was taken to earn the profits that fuelled the incentive payment in the first place. Malus describes the withholding of sums to be paid, and clawback refers to the recovery of sums that have been paid.

Malus, the opposite of bonus, is used in the context of the forfeiture of a number of shares (or other securities or cash) representing a deferred incentive that has not yet vested – that is, the employee has not yet become entitled to the assets. Typically, the shares or other assets are held on behalf of the employee by an employee share trust and, in the event of serious irregularities (including excessive risk that leads to the restatement of previously published accounts), the shares are forfeited by the employee.

DISCLOSURE OF MALUS/CLAWBACK

Following the promulgation of the new disclosure regulations by Statutory Instrument 2013 No. 1981, the new UK directors' remuneration report regulations came into force on October 1, 2013. The next day, the FRC issued a directors' remuneration consultation document as it was considering whether to amend the UK Corporate Governance Code. One of the questions asked in the consultation was should the Code adopt the terminology used in the regulations and refer to "recovery of sums paid" and "withholding of sums to be paid". It is expected that the UK Corporate Governance Code will be amended by the FRC to use the same descriptions that are contained in the regulations.

The directors' remuneration policy, subject to a binding vote from shareholders of UK listed companies, requires every company to set out a future policy table. Part of the disclosure that is required in the table is for an explanation to be given as to whether there are any provisions for the recovery of sums paid or the withholding of the payment of any sum. As a result, general industrial companies are following the trail initially blazed by financial services companies and introducing both malus and clawback policies. Imperial Tobacco has, for example, put clawback provisions in place for the three years following payment of its annual bonus, and also has clawback provisions for its share matching scheme and LTIP. EasyJet has clawback for its annual bonus, LTIP matching share award and LTIP performance share award. The policy describes the provision for the recovery of sums paid for annual bonus as follows.

> The cash and deferred elements of bonuses are subject to clawback at the discretion of the Committee in the event of misstatement of results for the year to which the bonus relates or an error in determining the cash bonus or the number of shares comprising a deferred share award within three years of the payment of the cash bonus.[9]

ENFORCING MALUS AND CLAWBACK

Malus is relatively easy for a remuneration committee to enforce as trustees typically hold the shares, and the employee will not yet have received any benefit from the shares. Clawback can be much more challenging to enforce, particularly as the employee may have spent the proceeds after receiving them on vesting and so recovering the assets may not be possible. Remuneration committees that have introduced clawback policies have commonly also introduced a method of ensuring that, for the period during which clawback can apply, there are provisions for the recovery of the shares from the employee. One method used requires the employee to place the proceeds of the share vesting after tax in a certificated form with the company secretary. The employee then signs a blank transfer form and gives a power of attorney to the company secretary to transfer the shares in the event of a clawback arising. HM Revenue & Customs (HMRC) have been consulted on the income tax implications of such a clawback, and have helpfully given guidance that the discovery of a mistake, which would result in clawback of an amount paid subject to the deduction of income tax and NIC under PAYE, can lead to a refund of the tax withheld by the employer if it is clear that the payment of the incentive was made in error. In this way, the net of tax clawback on the employee can lead to a complete recovery of the incorrectly paid bonus by the employer. In 2014, there have not been any legal actions over malus and clawback where it was argued they had not been used reasonably (or there was no sufficient evidence of it).

The application of deferral and clawback have been further endorsed by the Prudential Regulation Authority (PRA) of the Bank of England. In March 2014, it issued a consultation paper entitled "Clawback",[10] where it proposed an amendment to its remuneration code[11] requiring firms to amend employment contracts to enable them to apply clawback to vested variable remuneration. Panel 11.1 shows the main premises of this consultation paper, and shows how far-reaching the proposals are:

Initially, these proposals for extending clawback for a six-year period will apply only to those large financial institutions regulated by the PRA. However there has been speculation that the Financial Conduct Authority may apply a similar proposal to larger asset management firms. Although these proposals can be clearly seen as being only applicable to and relevant for large financial institutions where failure leads to systemic risk for the economy as a whole, there is concern that what is initially proposed for financial firms could become the norm for industrial companies as well.

PANEL 11.1: CLAWBACK CONSULTATION

A firm should as a minimum be able to clawback vested variable remuneration when:

❑ there is reasonable evidence of employee misbehaviour or material error; or
❑ the firm or the relevant business unit suffers a material downturn in its financial performance; or
❑ the firm or the relevant business unit suffers a material failure of risk management.

The PRA expects firms to amend employment contracts to allow for the application of clawback to all vested awards up to six years after vesting.

As in the case for malus, clawback should not be limited to employees directly culpable of malfeasance. For example, in cases involving a material failure of risk management or misconduct, firms should consider applying clawback to those employees who:

❑ could have been reasonably expected to be aware of the failure or misconduct at the time but failed to take adequate steps to promptly identify, assess, report, escalate or address it; or
❑ by virtue of their role or seniority, could be deemed indirectly responsible or accountable for the failure or misconduct, including senior staff in charge of setting the firm's culture and strategy.

DEFERRALS INTO SHARES ARE NOT SUFFICIENT

Although it is accepted that deferral of the vesting of shares that have been part of the bonus is a key part of a remuneration policy that is supportive of risk management, it is clear that simple deferral is not sufficient to ensure that incentives and the risk culture are appropriate. Clearly, there needs to be a focus on the risk environment and culture, and the board is responsible for this. The ABI guidelines state that risk management starts at the top of the company with board responsibilities and that the remuneration committee, and that remuneration policy has a supporting role regarding alignment of remuneration policies with these goals. Even if the structure of remuneration is such that senior executives would lose out significantly if the firm failed, this is not a guarantee that an appropriate risk culture and risk control environment will prevail. Three examples of US financial organisations show this very clearly. At Lehman Brothers, the chief executive officer (CEO) held onto 10 million shares of Lehman stock until the end and lost almost US$1 billion. The value of the CEO's holdings in Bear Stearns declined from US$993 million to less than US$15 million, removing him from the list of the wealthiest individuals in the US. The exiting CEO of Citibank owned 1.61 million shares that decreased from US$50 to US$5 a share between 2007 and 2009.

Unfortunately, remuneration policies themselves are no substitute for leadership and control of the company by a knowledgeable board that understands the businesses in which the company operates and the risks incurred.

CONCLUSION

Remuneration committees face a number of challenges in terms of fulfilling their role and responsibilities, as will now be discussed.

Quantification of risk in an appropriate format

The challenge for a remuneration committee facing this issue for the first time is to receive reports quantifying risks being taken in an appropriate format for regular monitoring and review. Clearly, the risks taken must be consistent with the risk appetite, and measurement must reflect the risk profile given the business strategy and objectives of the company, and must be appropriate in the context of the company. A useful exercise is to look at the failure of competitor companies and analyse what the risk issues were and how they could have been avoided. Salutary lessons can be learned in this way, and the management team can see the advantages of avoiding problems that have caused failure elsewhere.

Risk appetite

It is important that the board has agreed a risk appetite. One of the challenges is to recognise that any new activity or, indeed, the expansion of an existing business into a new territory carries a risk. The objective of specifying the risk appetite is not to stifle expansion or entrepreneurial spirit, but rather to ensure that any risk taken will be within the specified risk appetite, and therefore any failure would not be sufficient to risk the existence of the entire company or group.

Funds at risk

The remuneration committee should receive reports on the magnitude of exposures not just at year-end or month-end, but also at high points during the year. It is not uncommon for traders to close many positions as the year-end approaches, but risk is incurred every day, not just when the annual financial statements are drawn up.

Dealing with breaches

Remuneration committees need to be firm in dealing with breaches of risk appetite even if the results of the positions taken were profitable. It will not take long for the whole risk management process to fall into disrepute if deliberate breaches are not sanctioned because the results were favourable. If unauthorised but profitable risk positions are tolerated, then the whole risk management system breaks down.

It is always a challenge to manage risk in a company, but with the publication of the 2013 disclosure regulations giving shareholders a binding vote on remuneration policy, there is a real opportunity for remuneration committees to address the issue and to factor risk into the remuneration structure and remuneration policies.

1 Paragraph 4.42 of "The Report of the Committee on the Financial Aspects of Corporate Governance 1992" (available at http://www.jbs.cam.ac.uk/cadbury/report/index.html).
2 Available at https://www.frc.org.uk/Our-Work/Codes-Standards/Corporate-governance/UK-Corporate-Governance-Code.aspx
3 Available at http://webarchive.nationalarchives.gov.uk/+/http:/www.hm-treasury.gov.uk/walker_review_information.htm
4 https://www.frc.org.uk/News-and-Events/FRC-Press/Press/2014/April/Consultation-on-the-UK-Corporate-Governance-Code-p.aspx
5 "Annual Report and Accounts 2012: Considering Risk" (available at http://reports.legalandgeneralgroup.com/2012/ara/governance/directorsreportonremuneration/governanceandapproach/consideringrisk/print.html).
6 ibid.
7 This has been paraphrased from page 104 of Old Mutual's 2012 annual report (available at www.oldmutual.com/download/20054/2012).
8 http://www.investors.rbs.com/~/media/Files/R/RBS-IR/annual-reports/fsa-remuneration-disclosure.pdf
9 From the EasyJet annual report for year ending September 30, 2013 (available at http://corporate.easyjet.com/~/media/Files/E/Easyjet-Plc-V2/pdf/investors/result-center-investor/annual-report-2013.pdf).
10 Bank of England, Prudential Regulation Authority, "CP6/14 Clawback".
11 PRA Handbook, "The Senior Management Arrangements, Systems and Controls (SYSC) 19A: The Remuneration Code", sets out the standards that banks, building societies and designated investment firms have to meet when setting pay and bonus awards for their staff. It aims to ensure that firms' remuneration practices are consistent with effective risk management (available at www.bankofengland.co.uk/publications/Documents/other/pra/policy/2013/remunerationstanda).

12

Risk Transparency and Risk Culture for Financial Institutions

Sylvie Mathérat

Banque de France

Risk is at the very heart of banking activities; therefore, a key success factor for any financial institution is its ability to effectively pool, manage and diversify its risk in order to achieve an optimal balance between risks and returns. This risk management requires institutions to have clear knowledge of their individual risk exposures so that they can provide meaningful information to both internal and external stakeholders. Risk transparency therefore has two aspects: transparency with regard to the risks within a financial institution, and transparency with regard to its external stakeholders.

Internal risk transparency is a prerequisite for creating a more robust risk culture within financial institutions. It allows boards and senior management to hold the front-office business units accountable if the risks taken exceed the institution's risk appetite. This is an essential factor in changing the existing risk culture and leaning against risk creep in good times.

External transparency is also vital in order to increase the market discipline of financial institutions whose risk culture leads to high risk-taking. The lack of visibility surrounding risks in financial services firms tends to prevent external stakeholders from separating sound financial institutions from those that are overly risky. This reduces the incentive for risky financial institutions to exercise market discipline in good times and, during a crisis, tends to exacerbate liquidity pressures as all financial institutions are treated with equal suspicion.[1] Better disclosure of risks to the market is thus essential to help investors and counterparties judge the risk culture of individual firms and react accordingly.

This chapter focuses on both these aspects of risk transparency and on their importance for establishing a robust risk culture. The first section highlights some of the lessons of the crisis, before there is an exploration of why internal and external risk transparency are essential to a sound risk culture, and what financial institutions have done since the crisis to improve their internal risk management. The next section looks at the areas where there is room for improvement in external disclosure, both on a mandatory and voluntary basis, in order to achieve the goal of improved market discipline.

BACKGROUND

As the financial crisis showed, risk transparency is first and foremost an internal exercise that has to be based on meaningful information and consistent analyses. Transparency implies that financial institutions and their management boards are able to understand and endorse the risks they are taking. Furthermore, it implies giving sufficient information to external stakeholders (such as depositors, shareholders, senior creditors and clients) to enable them to assess properly the risks the financial institution is willing to take. External transparency can thus be split into two aspects: transparency with regard to the risks that the financial institution itself incurs; and transparency with regard to the risks that the financial institution transfers when selling its products.

The issue of opacity was brought to the fore during the crisis. The limited amount of disclosure in certain unregulated markets resulted at times in a mismeasurement of risks and fuelled market uncertainty, as counterparties lacked sufficient information about each other's exposures. The absence of sound information also prevented regulators and market participants from realising that certain counterparties had built up systemic exposures. The textbook example is the case of AIG in the credit default swap market. This should change with implementation of European Market Infrastructure Regulation (EMIR) in Europe and the Dodd–Frank Act (DFA) in the US.[2]

Furthermore, as has been argued,[3] the heightened perception of counterparty credit risk in 2007 and the consequent freezing of the interbank market in 2008 meant that lack of transparency may have intensified the crisis by driving up funding costs across the market, not just for weaker financial institutions. Another feature of the run-up to the crisis was the attempt by investors to simplify risk identification and information processing by mechanistically relying on credit ratings, often resulting in a form of blind faith. One example here is the US subprime mortgage market and the securitisation of these products, which demonstrated that financial institutions acting as investors and other institutional investors had poorly assessed the risks and potential losses.[4] Here, a lack of readily available information on the loans in the pools and the sheer complexity of the products led many organisations to rely excessively on credit rating agencies. The complexity and opacity of the securitisation market made it difficult for investors to carry out proper due diligence on purchases, which in turn led to risk mismeasurement and mispricing by many market participants.

RISK TRANSPARENCY IS ESSENTIAL TO SUPPORT A ROBUST AND SOUND RISK CULTURE

Internally: Risk transparency within financial institutions

In order to adequately monitor the risks stemming from banking activities and thus provide the basis for a strong risk culture, improved techniques and accurate data are needed to actually identify the risks. In particular, financial institutions need to make a clear assessment of their specific risk profile, taking into account characteristics such as: (i) their risk appetite; (ii) their business model; and (iii) the features of the market and their specific positioning within these markets. Internal models are useful for making sure that risk calculations actually fit with specific risk profiles. However, meaningful information on the risk evaluation methodologies used (including the parameters of the internal models, where relevant) should be clearly communicated and understood by the senior management in order to avoid "black box" effects.

Greater use of internal stress testing, in addition to internal models, could strengthen risk analyses. Indeed, stress tests are an essential tool for evaluating potential losses in the event of major stress. Relying only on indicators such as the value-at-risk (VaR) for risks in trading positions is not satisfactory since this measure does not provide information about the potential impacts of extreme risk events. Of course, financial institutions also use other indicators to complement VaR information and to trigger corrective measures when necessary. However, using stress tests allows internal action plans aimed at addressing the materialisation of risks to be refined and made more adequate.

A particular focus should also be placed on risk concentrations. For this purpose, internal risk management could take advantage of the "large exposures" supervisory reporting tool, developed by the Basel Committee, to assess the sources of risk. This tool is designed to allow banks to measure and limit individual exposures that are large compared with their level of capital.[5] It could be used as a readable support that could be easily and widely circulated internally to support a strong risk culture.

Once risks are identified and measured, a clear internal reporting process, based on economic capital models and stress tests, should be developed to keep boards and senior management informed on whether the institution's banking activities are consistent with its risk appetite and resilience. Indeed, internal risk transparency is particularly important for boards and senior management; if neither of them is aware of the risks undertaken, they cannot hold business heads accountable[6] and cannot ensure that activities fit both with the financial institution's risk appetite and its strategy. In this respect, reporting appears to be an essential tool in an institution's risk culture for supporting the board's approved risk appetite.

Reporting will only prove efficient if it requires the participation of the board and management as well as that of operational staff at all levels. A strong risk culture implies ongoing and constructive dialogue between the board, the management and staff. To this end, the risk department should be vested with sufficient authority in the hierarchy to be taken into account by senior management as well as by the business lines.[7] Staff should also be held directly accountable for identifying and reporting risk. As the Financial Stability Board (FSB) suggested, this implies, among other things: setting clear expectations for employees in terms of transparency; implementing mechanisms enabling staff to share information on risks; effectively holding employees accountable for any failure to meet expectations; promoting whistleblowing; and including incentives such as remuneration metrics that take account of the employee's compliance with the transparency requirements. These practices could incentivise the dissemination of an efficient risk culture, including risk transparency, across all business lines. In addition, transparency and visibility with regard to internal risks could be enhanced by mobilising internal audit departments. Financial institutions have already taken steps to enhance their risk management; for instance, the job of chief risk officer (CRO) has become a cornerstone of the organisational chart, while the headcount of risk management teams has been increased and business heads are taking more account of risks in their decision-making.

However, implementing an effective risk culture may require in-depth organisational changes that can only be achieved over the long term for large organisations such as banking groups. It may be necessary, for example, to modify the management system from a top-down to a more bottom-up approach, incentivising risk identification, management, mitigation and reporting by employees themselves,[8] although the impulse in terms of risk management/risk governance can also come from the top ("tone from the top").

External transparency is key to enhancing market discipline

This section focuses on the second aspect of risk transparency: external disclosure. As stated, in the case of financial institutions, external transparency can be divided into two different types: (i) the disclosure of information concerning risks that the financial institution may transfer to clients; and (ii) the disclosure of information concerning risks to which the financial institution is itself exposed, and which may impact other stakeholders (depositors, senior creditors/bondholders and shareholders).

Although external disclosure regarding products may appear a challenge, it carries essential benefits

The main challenge associated with the first aspect of external transparency is linked to asymmetric information and conflicts of interest. The subprime crisis in 2007–08 is a striking example, as banks did not inform their clients appropriately about the quality of the products they sold. The problem does not so much lie in the complexity of the financial products but rather in their opacity. In the run-up to the crisis, the prospectuses communicated to investors grew increasingly long, sometimes up to 500 pages, and each organised the information in a different way. Moreover, the structure of the securitisation market was such that the information on default rates in residential mortgage-backed security (RMBS) pools was only available to investors in a particular structure. As default rates rose, structures became more highly tranched and their organisation became less intelligible to stakeholders.[9] Clients need to to able to construct their own risk analysis and not have to rely only on external assessments (such as credit rating agencies' views), and product opacity makes this impossible.

There are at least three requisites for external stakeholders to be able to perform this analysis, and thus for transparency to be efficient. First, investors need to have sufficient information about all aspects of the products they are buying (underlying assets, cashflows, etc). Second, this information needs to be easily accessible – ie, the search costs should not be too high, particularly for investors buying a large number of financial products within a short space of time. Third, stakeholders must be able to process the information properly. These requirements apply both to institutional investors and retail customers buying savings products with complex features; in the latter case, jurisdictions have attempted to address the problem by establishing regulations on consumer protection and the provision of information to customers of financial institutions.

It is key for market discipline that financial institutions overcome the challenges related to the external disclosure of the risks to which they themselves are exposed

The second aspect of external transparency – ie, the disclosure of information on the risks incurred by the financial institution – is quite difficult to achieve. Although it is important for external stakeholders to understand the risk appetite of a financial institution and the quality of its risk management, the institution itself may be reluctant to disclose strategic information about its core businesses. As for shareholders, although they are supposed to have access to strategic information and can in theory dismiss the top management, they might face a situation of asymmetric information in a principal–agent configuration. Meanwhile, bondholders and depositors do not get the same level of information as they do not bear the same amount of risk.

With the introduction of bail-in measures, however, it seems more necessary to enhance the level of information given to all types of stakeholder; ideally, external stakeholders should be able to react to signals about risk culture, not to problems when they arise. Shareholders or market analysts, for instance, should be able to price financial institutions' equity taking proper consideration of the financial institutions' respective risk profiles. Indeed, in times of stress, this is key in order to be able to distinguish financial institutions that efficiently control their risks from those that do not. If this distinction is not possible, it can trigger a general climate of mistrust that penalises the entire banking system; this can in turn cause the interbank market to freeze up, and lead to a drying up of banks' bond markets or even a run on deposits. If uncertainty about the risks borne by a financial institution can drive up the cost of funding, then greater transparency, all other things being equal, should reduce the cost of external funding for healthy financial institutions. For all these reasons, external transparency is vital to reduce the information asymmetry[10] between stakeholders and financial institutions.

Greater transparency can actually help restore confidence in financial institutions at a time of great uncertainty. In less stressed periods, a lack of transparency allows financial institutions to take on more risks and to increase their leverage, and can therefore undermine financial stability. As a corollary, high-quality disclosure practices minimise uncertainty and therefore the risk of a gap between market expectations and the actual occurrence of events. Hence, by disclosing regular and reliable information, a financial institution can help analysts to set their anchor[11] at a level close to what may really happen. Indeed, behavioural economics shows that the larger the gap between anchors and occurrences, the larger the risk of overreaction. Consequently, financial stability would be enhanced by regular high-quality disclosure.

Moreover, when they are obliged to disclose information about their risk management, financial institutions are strongly incentivised to enhance their actual system of risk management. In this respect, improved disclosure of stress scenarios could help external transparency and internal risk management. The Enhanced Disclosure Task Force (EDTF)[12] has identified best practices in terms of stress-testing disclosures. Although disclosing information about stress tests does not imply that the stress tests themselves constitute a best practice, it does reveal which financial institutions pay special attention to communicating their stress-test results, and are thus more likely to rely on internal stress testing as a management tool. According to the EDTF, the 2011 annual reports of Santander and BNP Paribas stand out from those of other financial institutions: Santander provides a detailed analysis of adverse scenarios and BNP Paribas provides key features of different stress scenarios, as well as the results of these stress tests in terms of the decrease in revenues from market activities and trading portfolios.

A good way for a financial institution to improve both internal and external transparency is to extend the application of their stress testing and enhance its features, which implies that it should be signed off by the board. The EDTF suggests that "stress testing disclosures should provide a narrative overview of the bank's internal stress-testing process and governance".[13] For example, Barclays' 2012 annual report indicates that its board approves the range of scenarios to be tested by an independent "group risk" team. The results are reviewed and signed off by business CROs, then reviewed and challenged by the head office functions, and reviewed by the executive committee and the board risk committee, before being shared with the board and the supervisory authority. Disclosure is thus a way of putting pressure on financial institutions to maintain good management practices and achieve market discipline. In addition, better disclosure will help markets to distinguish sound financial institutions from overly risky ones, which could prevent or mitigate contagion effects in the event of stress.

Nonetheless, there are a number of obstacles to improving own-risk transparency, as outlined below.

❏ Risk is quite an abstract concept that does not materialise only in quantitative measures. Risk management relies heavily on the effectiveness of internal communication, management methods, the quality and relevance of internal controls, etc, which are elements that are not straightforward to communicate about.

❏ There are multiple addressees to take into account, both from internal and external points of view. For instance, shareholders are interested in information about the viability of the business model and profitability, while short-term debtholders (such as money market funds) might focus more on liquidity. Customers and other counterparties also have different focuses of interest.

❏ The scope of information expected by stakeholders is broad and requires significant resources for financial institutions. In particular, the content of reporting requirements has been extended under the Basel III framework implemented in Europe through the Capital Requirement Directive (CRD) and the Capital Requirements Regulation (CRR), which were published on June 26, 2013. By way of example, regulators now require comprehensive internal rating-based models and risk weights, as well as detailed information on product categories and on types of counterparties. This may appear quite demanding to financial institutions.

❏ Supervisory rules are not fully harmonised across jurisdictions (although significant efforts have been made under the Basel III process to harmonise disclosure templates), which may hinder comparability.

❏ It can be difficult to find an appropriate timing for disclosing information, especially to the public. Indeed, in the event a financial institution encounters difficulties, there is a trade-off to be made between informing the different stakeholders immediately and the potential procyclical reactions that might worsen the situation.

❏ Banking activities are also quite complex, especially for large banks. It might be a challenge to show simply and clearly the risks stemming from complicated financial products.

❏ There is another trade-off to be made for financial institutions concerning the disclosure of information that might be strategic or sensitive.

In spite of these difficulties, which were taken into account by regulators and by members of the industry, several public and private initiatives have been launched to promote better risk transparency. The Vickers and Liikanen reports, for example, suggested ringfencing core banking activities from more speculative ones in order, among other things, to clarify the different business lines and organisational charts, and make bank structures easier to read from the outside.

Other examples of initiatives to enhance risk transparency relate to the securitisation market.

❏ The credit claims securitisation project supported by Banque de France:[14] in March 2014, several major banks active in France set up a special purpose vehicle called Euro Secured Notes Issuer (ESNI) that issues notes backed by underlying loans to small and medium enterprises (SMEs). This new instrument is designed to be much simpler, more transparent (relying on a portfolio look-through approach) and less risky than other forms of securitisations.

❑ In June 2012, market participants launched the Prime Collateralised Securities (PCS) initiative in conjunction with the Association for Financial Markets in Europe (AFME) and the European Financial Services Round Table (EFR), to create a high quality asset-backed securities (ABS) label. With the ECB's sponsorship, market participants also created the European DataWarehouse to provide access to loan-level data and facilitate transparency for both investors and originators. Investors and/or credit risk analysts can thereby enhance their analysis of the ABS market using a loan-by-loan approach.

THERE IS STILL ROOM FOR IMPROVEMENT IN EXTERNAL DISCLOSURE
The objective of transparency relies on mandatory disclosure set by the regulator …
As shown above, disclosure often leaves financial institutions facing a dilemma as to the scope and granularity of the information needed. Therefore, in addition to relying on the initiative of individual financial institutions, supervisors and regulators may need to take action to foster risk transparency.

Regulatory disclosure requirements and limits
The Basel Committee on Banking Supervision (BCBS) included some "Pillar 3 disclosure requirements" in the Basel II framework, which were integrated into the CRD and CRR in the European Union. The Basel Pillar 3 rules require banks to draft a disclosure policy at group level that should be approved by the board of directors. Banks should also assess the appropriateness, validation and frequency of information disclosure. More specifically, banks are required to communicate on the credit, market and interest rate in the banking book, equity in the banking book and operational risks in their banking book, from both a qualitative and quantitative point of view. As an example, they are expected to disclose the amount of impaired

loans, broken down by geographical area, carried in their balance sheet.

However, these requirements have significant limitations. To begin with, since the Pillar 3 rules primarily apply at group level, not all entities in a group are required to meet them, which can be a source of opacity. Moreover, the disclosure requirements differ for banks using the standardised or the internal ratings-based approaches, which may impair comparability. Indeed, 25% of the variability in risk-weight calculations in relation to credit risk in the banking book can be explained by differences in internal model calibrations from one bank to another, or by supervisory choices at the national level,[15] which limits comparability. Furthermore, standardisation is limited, as the Basel rules leave a significant margin of discretion to supervisors and banks on the content and form of the expected disclosure. By way of example, although banks use VaR metrics for some exposures, the parameters such as the level of risk likelihood (1% or 5%) and the time horizon (one day or two weeks) may vary from institution to institution. This makes these metrics difficult for stakeholders to compare and interpret. The lack of standardisation and transparency in the Pillar 3 rules thus undermines the mandatory dimension of the disclosure requirements.

Ways of improving disclosure requirements

One obvious way to ensure proper disclosure is to make it mandatory and to ensure that requirements are complied with, including by applying sanctions to financial institutions where needed. It might prove useful for stakeholders to require financial institutions to indicate which elements they disclose on a mandatory, harmonised basis, and which ones they communicate as a result of their own internal decision.

In addition, as improving the quality of disclosure is an ongoing process, the Basel Committee is conducting a review of Pillar 3 disclosure requirements, with a particular focus on comparability between banks.[16]

The next step could be for supervisors to develop the use of stress testing further, and to vary the communication of the results according to the addressee (financial institution, supervisor, market investors or the general public). The experience of the US and EU stress-test exercises suggests that public disclosure of supervisory stress-test results can have a beneficial impact on external transparency through the following two channels.

❑ The disclosure itself reduces the opacity of financial institutions by providing valuable information to market participants.[17]
❑ The disclosure of supervisory information tends to provide incentives for financial institutions to increase their subsequent voluntary disclosure.[18] Despite potential negative effects such as *ex post* inefficient or speculative reactions, it appears to improve transparency, and therefore market discipline.

Another tool that supervisors could use to promote greater transparency consists of encouraging internal and/or external auditing in order to verify the reliability of the information disclosed. Regulators could also consider encouraging more focused, targeted and comparable data reporting in order to enhance the quality of the information disclosed.[19]

As a partial conclusion, it is possible to say that, to date, standardised reporting and disclosure – common reporting (COREP), financial reporting (FINREP), stress tests based on common scenarios – remain essential because of the lack of a spontaneous transparency culture among financial institutions. However, the objective should be to incentivise financial institutions to disclose more and better information voluntarily so that they adequately reflect their individual risks. This would be a way of preserving a diversity of risk approaches and enhancing risk transparency.

... and voluntary disclosure by financial institutions

As early as 1998, the BCBS issued a report providing general guidance and recommendations to banks and supervisors for enhanced transparency.[20] In terms of content, the report identified six useful categories of information:

❑ financial performance (as this gives an insight into, for example, a bank's potential to repay deposits and liabilities, and to contribute to capital growth);
❑ financial position (including capital, solvency and liquidity);
❑ risk management strategies and practices (philosophy, overall policy and methodologies, risk measurement and monitoring, etc);

❏ risk exposures (including credit risk, market risk, liquidity risk, and operational, legal and other risks);
❏ accounting policies; and
❏ basic business, management and corporate governance information.

In terms of quality, the report called for comparability, relevance, reliability and timeliness of disclosure. Although these recommendations were designed for supervisors, it is still reasonable to expect the banking industry to come up with its own, self-initiated proposals for better disclosure, given that external risk transparency directly benefits financial institutions by making them more trustworthy for investors.

On October 29, 2012, the EDTF issued a report entitled "Enhancing the Risk Disclosure of Banks", identifying seven fundamental principles for disclosure and setting out 32 recommendations. The seven principles are:

❏ disclosures should be clear, balanced and understandable;
❏ disclosures should be comprehensive and include all of the bank's key activities and risks;
❏ disclosures should present relevant information;
❏ disclosures should reflect how the bank manages its risks;
❏ disclosures should be consistent over time;
❏ disclosures should be comparable among banks; and
❏ disclosures should be provided on a timely basis.

The recommendations include, for example, presenting "a flow statement of movements since the prior reporting date in regulatory capital" (number 11), or summarising "encumbered and unencumbered assets in a tabular format by balance-sheet categories" (number 19).

The principles, which relate to the content of the information disclosed as well as to the means of communication used, do not differ to any significant extent from the proposals put forward by the BCBS. Therefore, there appears to be some agreement between public institutions and the private sector on what should be disclosed in order to ensure risk transparency.

In fact, the most decisive factor for risk transparency is the quality rather than the quantity of information disclosed; disclosure alone does not necessarily result in transparency if the information issued is not meaningful.[21] In that sense, external communication should be thorough, accurate and comprehensive in order to enable stakeholders to "assess the expected risks and returns of investing in, lending to, or having other exposures to a bank", and to limit misinterpretations. In particular, it should be complete, as any omission could cause information to be false or misleading.[22]

As regards the format of disclosure, information should be presented to stakeholders in an intelligible manner. Risk disclosures are often very long and not presented in a comparable way across firms and over time. Thus, for comparability purposes, harmonised communication formats should be favoured. This certainly does not mean that the contents of disclosures by financial institutions should be homogenised; a diversity of risk assessments across financial institutions (as well as across market participants) should be favoured in order to: (i) maintain the smooth functioning of markets (different market participants have different expectations); (ii) be able to detect the majority of risks; and (iii) avoid herding effects. As an example, financial institutions could be given incentives to publish their own stress tests, comprising different hypotheses and scenarios specifically suited to their individual risk profile. Better coordination could lead to more comprehensible disclosure.

In this respect, Sanjay Sharma[23] has suggested a disclosure framework that every financial institution could rely on. In his view, the structure of financial disclosure could consist of an overview of the state of the institution, including a selected set of indicators and contextual commentary, followed by more consistent developments, including quantitative information on every aspect of mandated or voluntary areas of disclosure.

The tenets of disclosure could consist of:

❏ providing information on the context, explaining the situation of the institution, such as:
  ○ the risk–return balance of the bank (eg, returns of business segments versus risk indicators);
  ○ a historical perspective;
  ○ cross-business and industry comparisons; and
  ○ measurement limitations of the models and methodologies for quantifying and estimating underlying risks.

❏ ensuring completeness, ie, comprehensiveness, timeliness (on a quarterly and an annual basis) and relevance.

Lastly, disclosure could include information on:

❏ the current state of the institution (business performance and strategy, capital position, risks);
❏ its future prospects (macroeconomic environment, regulatory changes, business unit strategies); and
❏ its functional attributes (organisational structure, culture, decision-making mechanisms, compensation structure).

This framework would provide financial institutions with useful guidance. Although financial institutions might be reluctant to provide information they deem sensitive or too strategic, the suggested framework could be a relevant objective for disclosure purposes.

Financial institutions have already taken steps to improve risk disclosure practices

Financial institutions have undeniably improved their communication practices with regard to their risk profile. The EDTF has monitored the progress made by banks between 2011 and 2013. Before 2012, only 34% of banks in the sample[24] had fully implemented the EDTF recommendations. This proportion grew to 50% at the end of 2012, and 72% of banks planned to comply with the set of recommendations in their 2013 annual reports.

Those banks identified as best-in-class disclose quantitative information in accordance with the EDTF recommended figures, which facilitates comparison between institutions. In particular, they manage to provide complex information such as funding and market risks, encumbered and unencumbered assets, and off-balance-sheet commitments on a quantitative and robust basis. They tend to publish Pillar 3 disclosure and their annual report simultaneously, or to merge both documents. Conversely, some banks still tend to limit themselves to disclosure of qualitative, less comparable, information.

The recommendations that get the highest planned compliance rate are mostly qualitative. They concern the following elements: definition of risk; description of major risks; explanation of the risk organisation and key functions; and description of non-performing assets policies. Conversely, implementation plans are much lower for certain quantitative aspects, such as describing the link between market risk and the balance sheet, presenting a risk-weighted asset (RWA) flow chart, publishing the amount of encumbered and unencumbered assets, and providing maturity tables for balance-sheet and off-balance-sheet items.

All risks do not benefit from the same level of transparency. In the 2012 annual reports, most of the banks in the EDTF sample (63%) disclosed information on the recommended standard concerning risk governance and risk management strategies.[25] In descending order, banks tend to communicate efficiently on credit risk (51%), liquidity risk (47%) and market risk (31%). There are several reasons that could explain this result; obviously, credit risk is the most familiar of all banking risks and is the first to be taken into account in the prudential rules with solvency ratios. It is also relatively easy to provide simple information about credit risks since the metrics are numerous and quite well known (non-performing assets, probability of default, loss given default, exposure at default, etc).

Liquidity risk is more challenging because, although it is inherent to banking activities, it has only been highlighted relatively recently. Therefore, there might be a learning process involved in communicating efficiently about this risk. Also, the very nature of liquidity means that it fluctuates, so financial institutions would need to be able to explain why their short-term liquidity coverage ratio (LCR) changes significantly on an ongoing basis. Moreover, the pool of liquid assets acts as a buffer and should be usable in the event of stress; although this is the very purpose of the ratio, banks facing difficulties might trigger a market overreaction if they presented a ratio below 100%. As for market risk, the challenge may come from the need to find simple but comprehensive metrics to give a faithful picture of the risk profile. An additional challenge is to be able to connect market risks with balance-sheet and income statement items.

According to the report, in 2012 there were significant gaps between regions in disclosure practices. UK banks had the highest rates of compliance for all types of risk, while European and US banks had the same level of compliance on the whole, although they differed with regard to specific risk categories (US banks were more advanced in terms of liquidity risk disclosure, while European banks disclosed better information about capital adequacy and RWAs).

In the European Union, the European Banking authority (EBA) has also noted that banks significantly improved the quality of their Pillar 3 reports in 2012. According to the EBA, consistency and comparability of disclosures are possible areas for improvement. This would be easier to achieve if common disclosure templates were published (for liquidity and leverage ratios, for example). The EBA also identified room for improvement in disclosures concerning capital deductions, credit exposures under the IRB approach, and securitisation and market risks.

CONCLUSION

Better risk transparency on the part of financial institutions could lead to a better understanding of risk by the management board and, externally, by all market participants. Internally, improved techniques to assess risk concentrations are essential, as is stress testing. Externally, although much progress has been made, challenges still remain over which data should be disclosed and how it could be used by market participants. Initiatives launched by private sector representatives as well as supervisors are necessary to achieve meaningful and reliable risk transparency practices. Banks should pursue their efforts in that direction.

In the face of enhanced disclosure, outside observers may themselves find they need to develop a better risk culture in order to properly use and interpret the information disclosed, especially concerning new types of information (such as liquidity ratios). With regard to this point, there could be grounds for improving market education. Greater market maturity could, in turn, allow for more transparency from supervisors and financial institutions, as information would be better absorbed by analysts.

As the IMF stated in its Global Financial Stability Report (GFSR) in 2009: "In the long term, … pricing discipline, stronger risk management, and increased focus on simpler and more stable businesses, combined with robust disclosure, should be supportive of bank profitability". If necessary, this last statement should provide the ultimate incentive for financial institutions to enhance their internal and external transparency policies.

The author would like to thank Camille L'Hermitte and Garance Prouillac for their helpful contributions, and Patricia Jackson for her careful reading.

1 Bank of England (2009).
2 These regulations are aimed at improving the transparency and stability of OTC derivatives markets by incentivising central clearing and making registration with trade repositories compulsory.
3 Sowerbutts and Zimmerman (2013).
4 Jackson (2013).
5 According to Article 322 of the Capital Requirement Regulation (Regulation (EU) No. 575/2013 of the European Parliament and of the Council of June 26, 2013, on prudential requirements for credit institutions and investment firms and Amending Regulation (EU) No. 648/2012), "an institution's exposure to a client or group of connected clients shall be considered a large exposure where its value is equal to or exceeds 10% of its eligible capital".
6 Financial Stability Board (2014).
7 Financial Stability Board (2013).
8 Financial Stability Board (2014).
9 Jackson (2013).
10 Sowerbutts and Zimmerman (2013).
11 See papers by Amos Tversky and Daniel Kahneman.
12 "The EDTF was formed in 2012 at the initiative of the FSB. The task force represents a unique private sector initiative to develop recommendations for enhancing risk disclosure practices by major banks starting with end-year 2012 annual risk disclosures and continuing into 2013 and beyond", according to the FSB website.
13 EDTF (2013).
14 The first two objectives are to encourage SME loans and to increase the amount of collateral available on the interbank market.
15 Basel Committee on Banking Supervision (2013), Regulatory Consistency Assessment Programme (RCAP), "Analysis of risk-weighted assets for credit risk in the banking book".
16 As stated by Stefan Ingves, chairman of the BCBS, in his keynote address to the 15th Annual Convention of the Global Association of Risk Professionals in New York on March 4, 2014.
17 See, for instance, Morgan, Peristiani and Savino (2010) for the US stress tests, and Petrella and Resti (2013) for the EU stress tests.
18 See Bischof and Daske (2013).
19 ibid.
20 Basel Committee on Banking Supervision (1998).
21 ibid.
22 ibid.
23 Sharma (2013).
24 31 banks in Europe, North America and Asia: Canada (Scotiabank, BMO, National Bank of Canada, RBC, CIBC, TD Bank); US (State Street, Wells Fargo, Citi, Goldman Sachs, JPMorgan, Morgan Stanley, BofA); Europe (Santander, BPCE, BNP Paribas, Crédit Agricole, Société Générale, IntesaSanPaolo, KfW, ING, Danske Bank, Deutsche Bank, UBS); UK (Barclays, HSBC, Standard Chartered, RBS); Russia (Sberbank); Asia (MUFG, DBS).
25 ibid.

REFERENCES

Bank of England, 2009, "Financial Stability Report", December.

Basel Committee on Banking Supervision, 1998, "Enhancing Bank Transparency", September.

Bischof, J. and H. Daske, 2013, "Mandatory Supervisory Disclosure, Voluntary Disclosure, and Risk-taking of Financial Institutions: Evidence from the EU-wide Stress-testing Exercises", *Journal of Accounting Research*, 51(5).

Bouvard, M., P. Chaigneau and A. de Motta, 2013, "Transparency in the Financial System: Rollover Risk and Crises".

Enhanced Disclosure Task Force, 2012, "Enhancing the Risk Disclosures of Banks".

Enhanced Disclosure Task Force, 2013, "Progress Report on Implementation of Disclosure Recommendations".

European Banking Authority, 2013, "Follow-up Review of Banks' Transparency in their 2012 Pillar 3 Reports", December.

Financial Stability Board, 2013, "Consultative Document: Guidance on Supervisory Interaction with Financial Institutions on Risk Culture".

Financial Stability Board, 2014, "Consultative Document: Guidance on Supervisory Interaction with Financial Institutions on Risk Culture – A Framework for Assessing Risk Culture".

Fraisse, H., 2013, "Discussion of S. Peristiani, D. Morgan, and V. Savino, (2010), "The Information Value of the Stress Test and Bank Opacity", *Federal Reserve Bank of New York Staff Reports*, No. 460.

Gorton, G., 2008, "The Panic of 2007", papers and proceedings for the Federal Reserve Bank of Kansas City, Jackson Hole Conference.

International Monetary Fund, 2009, "Global Financial Stability Report".

Jackson, P., 2013, "Causes of the Global Financial Crisis, Fact and Myth : Lessons for Regulators and Bank Management" (available at http://www.kraka.org/sites/default/files/causes_of_the_global_financial_crisis_latest.pdf).

Morgan, D., S. Peristiani and V. Savino, 2010, "The Information Value of the Stress Test and Bank Opacity", *Federal Reserve Bank of New York Staff Reports*, No. 460.

Petrella, G. and A. Resti, 2013, "Supervisors as Information Producers: Do Stress Tests Reduce Bank Opaqueness?", *Journal of Banking & Finance*, 37(12).

Sharma, S., 2013, *Risk Transparency* (London: Risk Books).

Sowerbutts, R., P. Zimmerman and I. Zer, 2013, "Banks' Disclosure and Financial Stability", *Quarterly Bulletin of the Bank of England*, Q4.

13

The Importance of Data and IT for a Strong Risk Culture

Darren Smith and Andrew Cross

Royal Bank of Scotland

To support effective risk governance and a strong risk culture, good information on the amount of risk being taken is essential. Without good data and supporting IT, risk transparency would not be sufficient to enable senior management to manage risk effectively and react appropriately to risk-taking behaviour. It will also mean that incentives are not adjusted properly. However, this is also a two-way street; in cultures where risk is not given much weight, the pressure for internal transparency of risks is also less.

The 2007–08 financial crisis highlighted serious shortcomings and variations in capabilities across the banking industry.

> One of the most significant lessons learned from the global financial crisis that began in 2007 was that banks' information technology (IT) and data architectures were inadequate to support the broad management of financial risks. Many banks lacked the ability to aggregate risk exposures and identify concentrations quickly and accurately at the bank group level, across business lines and between legal entities. Some banks were unable to manage their risks properly because of weak risk data aggregation capabilities and risk reporting practices. This had severe consequences to the banks themselves and to the stability of the financial system as a whole (Basel Committee on Banking Supervision, 2013).

This led to growing interest and activity by both the industry and regulators. The Senior Supervisors Group (SSG) was a key forum for senior representatives of supervisory authorities to engage in dialogue on risk management practices, governance and other issues concerning complex, globally active financial institutions, and to work collectively on selected risk management weaknesses exposed during the crisis. Its activities tied in with the work of the Financial Stability Board (FSB) on "too big to fail" banks, or systemically important financial institutions (SIFIs). It assessed the risk management practices that helped make some firms better able than others to withstand market stresses (Senior Supervisors Group, 2008) and reviewed risk management lessons from the global banking crisis (Senior Supervisors Group, 2009).

The FSB reports, in turn, led to the creation of specific working groups on risk appetite frameworks and IT infrastructure (Senior Supervisors Group, 2010). Lack of agreement on IT strategy between business and IT, short-term financial decisions, weak data governance, and mergers and acquisitions were identified by the 2010 report as the key causes of fragmented risk IT. Similarly, the SSG focused on the importance of IT governance in strategic planning, the existence of automated risk data aggregation capabilities, integration of new/acquired IT systems and appropriate systems capacity as key features necessary to support effective risk IT. The working groups also highlighted the close interdependency between setting an effective risk appetite framework and a robust risk data infrastructure to underpin risk measurement, and the criticality of these for both strategic planning and tactical decision-making.

The recognition of IT and data inadequacies, their critical impacts and the significant resource commitments firms would need to make to address them led to the development of the Basel Committee's "Principles for Effective Risk Data Aggregation and Risk Reporting", which created specific standards for SIFIs. The principles were timed to come into effect for global systemically important banks (G-SIBs) at the beginning of 2016 to coincide with the introduction of the added loss-absorbency requirement for regulatory capital. However, although the principles provide a useful framework and industry driver, they require significant interpretation and judgement – firms must ensure their capabilities reflect their business models and risk management strategies.

In order to increase risk transparency, regulators have also increased the volume and granularity of data, regulatory reporting and public disclosures they require. This, in turn, has increased the demand for risk data and IT, and further exposed the data and IT limitations of banks. Key initiatives have included the Enhanced Disclosure Task Force (EDTF) report on risk disclosures, the FSB common data templates and the introduction of regulator-led stress-testing regimes in many jurisdictions, such as the Comprehensive Capital Analysis and Review (CCAR) in the US. The volume and pace of change has led to an increased need for tactical solutions in many firms, pending delivery of enhanced strategic capabilities.

This chapter looks at why good risk data and IT aggregation capabilities are essential for effective risk governance and a strong risk culture, their key characteristics and the challenges in achieving them.

LINK BETWEEN RISK DATA AND IT, AND RISK GOVERNANCE AND CULTURE

> Measurement is the first step that leads to control and eventually to improvement. If you can't measure something, you can't understand it. If you can't understand it, you can't control it. If you can't control it, you can't improve it.[1]

Data and IT are the tools that enable risk measurement, which itself is a key enabler for effective risk governance and culture. The old business adage, "What gets measured gets managed", underlines the fact that measurement focuses management attention and facilitates incentives that drive appropriate behaviour. However, deciding what to measure is crucial. Senior management and risk governance bodies must define the information they need to fulfil their roles effectively, and should be done based on need rather than dictated by current capabilities or historical practices. This ranges from governance of the firm's aggregate risks to monitoring the risk-taking behaviour of key individuals in order to influence remuneration and risk culture. Such information needs should be informed by the firm's business model, risk appetite and risk frameworks. These needs should then inform IT strategy and investments (although systems should be designed with adaptability and the ability to identify emerging risks in mind).

There are a number of common measurement pitfalls that must be avoided.

❏ There can be a tendency to focus on what is easy to measure, rather than what is important. For example, while it is relatively easy to measure current risk positions, it is more complicated to forecast them or translate them into financial impacts such as their effect on profitability or capital. This is why clearly articulated demand from data consumers is so important.

❑ Reports may be overloaded with too much data and too little insight. Executive reports do not need to include all available data, but should be focused on key areas – including risk appetite breaches, top and emerging risks, and forward-looking risk profile – that require awareness and action. Too much information can distract from communication of the most important messages. Metrics are only part of the story; action plans and qualitative insights are critical.

❑ Measurement choices can have unintended consequences, such as deterioration of those activities that are not measured. As an example, in the UK there has been significant debate about the unintended impact of the introduction of new targets for hospital waiting times in the 1990s. A number of studies highlighted correlations between the improvements in waiting times and deterioration in other areas, such as emergency treatment for heart attack patients, because these were not tracked and therefore not managed (Propper *et al.*, 2008). Making sure the organisation is equipped with an appropriate range of measures is important, but it is also crucial to ensure that those measures do not replace good judgement or drive behaviour that is at odds with broader strategy.

Risk management performance should be a major consideration in the firm's overall performance assessment and remuneration-setting process – for both individual business units and key personnel – in order to properly incentivise effective risk management. Best practice is for a holistic and standardised scorecard covering key risk considerations, underpinned by objective risk metrics where possible and subjective assessments where not. Key considerations would include:

❑ risk review of business strategy and performance;
❑ risk appetite;
❑ impact of risk decisions on customers (including conduct risk);
❑ risk insights from stress testing;

❏ risk control effectiveness; and
❏ risk culture.

There should be close alignment between the metrics used for performance assessment and the metrics used for ongoing risk oversight in the organisation's senior executive committees and at board level: "What gets measured gets done, what gets measured and fed back gets done well, what gets rewarded gets repeated."[2]

Risk culture is also a key influencer on the quality of risk data and IT capabilities. The culture shapes demand, including identifying who wants to see risk data (only risk professionals, or business representatives as well) and influences both investment appetite and execution commitment. Good data and IT require significant resource and financial investment. Much of the necessary work takes place outside of the risk function (eg, enabling process and system activity in core businesses) or competes for shared scarce resources, such as IT. Therefore, this requires firms, not just the risk function, to recognise the value that risk information brings to the organisation. Accordingly, the risk function needs to engage with key decision-makers throughout the broader firm, and explain its data and IT requirements, how these support the business, and the costs and risks of not addressing these. Otherwise, making the financial business case for investment in risk IT is often challenging (which surprises many regulators), because it can be difficult to quantify the financial impact of improved risk management and savings may be long term in nature. By way of example, by how much would improved credit risk data aggregation reduce impairments? Given the cyclical nature of banking, could any such saving be meaningful tracked? As a result, much of the risk investment undertaken by firms to date has been driven by regulatory initiatives, with variable levels of benefit for risk management itself depending on how firms have leveraged the investment for broader risk management purposes.

Embedding a more structured and standardised approach across the risk management function (eg, common risk metrics) is a test of the coherence of the risk culture within a firm. Embedding risk-related requirements in the relevant business processes (for example, new business approval or the strategic planning process) and investment initiatives is a test of the recognition and commitment by the business to risk management and the value it brings to the firm. Also, the level of effort invested in ensuring high standards around risk data reflects the importance attached to accurate risk information. With overall responsibility for approval and oversight of risk strategy implementation, a bank's board plays a critical role in setting the tone for the organisation, ensuring expectations are clear as well as supporting investment and execution initiatives.

CHARACTERISTICS OF GOOD RISK DATA AND IT

The Basel Committee set out 14 principles grouped under four themes (see Table 13.1), which are a useful way of framing the key characteristics of good risk data and IT. The themes are: (i) overarching governance; (ii) risk data aggregation capabilities; (iii) risk reporting practices; and (iv) supervisory review tools and cooperation.

Overarching governance

Good governance is critical for success. Firms need to take a systematic and formalised approach to managing risk data and IT to avoid fragmented solutions and inconsistent approaches to reporting. The key feature of strong governance is a documented framework that articulates clearly the key capabilities required, the architectural strategy to meet these, the data quality risks and minimum acceptable standards, and the risk reporting process. Producing such a framework should prompt discussion within firms, with regulators and between peers. As a result of that discussion, a clear and considered view of the capabilities required should be developed that reflects the business model of the firm, and the expectations of the board and senior management. This can then be implemented across the organisation. The risk reporting process should be directly linked to the firm's risk appetite and risk management frameworks, since data and IT are simply enablers of effective risk management. For that reason, governance should be closely aligned with the firm's general risk management governance arrangements, and should be agreed with the firm's senior management and the board. The engagement of senior management and the board is critical to give the framework legitimacy, generate support for investment funding and ensure support for implementation throughout the firm.

The framework should be a living (although controlled) document, reviewed regularly and continuously updated to reflect material developments in the firm's business models, risk frameworks and the wider risk environment. New initiatives such as corporate actions, new product development and internal projects should be reviewed to assess how they comply with, or affect, the firm's data and reporting framework. Compliance with the framework should be regularly monitored and the results reported to the senior management and the board, so that they are aware of any limitations and resulting remediation plans. An assurance programme, conducted by the internal audit function – or another independent party with suitable skills – is appropriate to provide senior management, the board and regulators with confidence in the framework. These ongoing activities require firms to develop sufficient skilled resources and dedicate them to these activities. Over time, the additional cost of this proactive engagement in new initiatives should be offset by the less visible costs arising from a less actively engaged risk function (eg, workarounds, duplication of activity, re-working to meet risk requirements).

Risk data aggregation capabilities

Risk data aggregation capabilities should be driven by the business requirements defined in the framework. Firms should be able to measure each risk type identified in line with the defined frequency, timeliness and accuracy standards, taking into account the dynamics of risk and reporting needs in a crisis situation, as well as routine reporting. This perspective, together with the wider industry trends in the increasing digitalisation of banking interactions (driven by both customer demand and the drive to reduce costs) should lead to a step change in frequency and timeliness. As a general rule, data aggregation processes should be highly automated in order to meet the relevant requirements of frequency, timeliness, accuracy and adaptability. Manual aggregation processes and data cleansing slow down the reporting process, reduce the frequency of reporting, increase the associated operational risk and reduce reporting flexibility because, normally, only targeted data is scrubbed. Capabilities should be broad and adaptable enough to meet a wide range of reasonably foreseeable risk information needs. In practice, this means firms need a small number of granular risk data stores, likely one for each risk type identified, containing a broad range of risk

Table 13.1 Basel data and reporting principles overview

Overarching governance and infrastructure	1	Governance	A bank's risk data aggregation capabilities and risk reporting practices should be subject to strong governance consistent with other principles and guidance established by the Basel Committee.
	2	Data architecture and IT infrastructure	Data architecture and IT infrastructure – a bank should design, build and maintain data architecture and IT infrastructure which fully supports its risk data aggregation capabilities and risk reporting practices not only in normal times.
Risk data aggregation capabilities	3	Accuracy and integrity	A bank should be able to generate accurate and reliable risk data to meet normal and stress/crisis reporting accuracy requirements. Data should be aggregated on a largely automated basis so as to minimise the probability of errors.
	4	Completeness	A bank should be able to capture and aggregate all material risk data across the banking group. Data should be available by business line, legal entity, asset type, industry, region and other groupings that permit identifying and reporting risk exposures, concentrations and emerging risks.
	5	Timeliness	A bank should be able to generate aggregate and up to date risk data in a timely manner while also meeting the principles relating to accuracy and integrity, completeness and adaptability. The precise timing will depend on the nature and potential volatility of the risk being measured as well as its criticality to the overall risk profile of the bank. This timeliness should meet bank-established frequency requirements for normal and stress/crisis risk management reporting.
	6	Adaptability	A bank should be able to generate aggregate risk data to meet a broad range of on-demand, ad hoc crisis management reporting requests, including requests during crisis situations, requests due to changing internal needs and requests to meet supervisory queries.

	7	Accuracy	Risk management reports should accurately and precisely convey aggregated risk data and reflect risk in an exact manner. Reports should be reconciled and validated.
Risk reporting practices	8	Comprehensiveness	Risk management reports should cover all material risk areas within the organisation. The depth and scope of these reports should be consistent with the size and complexity of the bank's operations and risk profile, as well as the requirements of the recipients.
	9	Clarity	Risk management reports should communicate information in a clear and concise manner. Reports should be easy to understand yet comprehensive enough to facilitate informed decision-making. Reports should include an appropriate balance between risk data, analysis and interpretation, and qualitative explanations.
	10	Frequency	The board and senior management (or other recipients as appropriate) should set the frequency of risk management report production and distribution. Frequency requirements should reflect the needs of the recipients, the nature of the risk reported, and the speed at which the risk can change, as well as the importance of reports in contributing to sound risk management and effective/efficient decision-making across the bank. The frequency of reports should be increased during times of crisis.
	11	Distribution	Risk management reports should be distributed to the relevant parties and include meaningful information tailored to the needs of the recipients, while ensuring confidentiality is maintained.
Supervisory review tools and cooperation	12	Review	Supervisors should periodically review and evaluate a bank's compliance with the eleven principles.
	13	Remedial actions and supervisory measures	Supervisors should have and use the appropriate tools and resources to require effective and timely remedial action by a bank to address deficiencies in its risk data aggregation capabilities and risk reporting practices. Supervisors should have the ability to use a range of tools, including Pillar 2.
	14	Home/host cooperation	Supervisors should cooperate with relevant supervisors in other jurisdictions regarding the supervision and review of the principles, and the implementation of any remedial action if necessary.

Source: RBS

measures and attributes, which enable firms to "slice and dice" information along multiple dimensions and measures (see Figure 13.1).

Risk management processes and information needs include supporting many day-to-day activities – such as risk approval for new lending – that are closely aligned with core business processes, not just periodic reporting processes. The view of risk should be consistent throughout the entire process to facilitate a common understanding of risk across the organisation, and at transactional, portfolio/business unit, legal entity and group levels. However, the broad spectrum of activity makes developing an appropriate architecture challenging. As technology advances, the technical options for aggregating data across systems increases – yet, regardless of the technology used, this requires data standardisation across systems, such as common risk measurement methodologies, common data definitions, common reference data and common data sourcing.

Effective data quality governance has a number of strands. These include data standards and data design governance, data quality measurement and data issue management. The first of these entails agreeing standards with stakeholders and ensuring that new IT

Figure 13.1 Data adaptability illustration

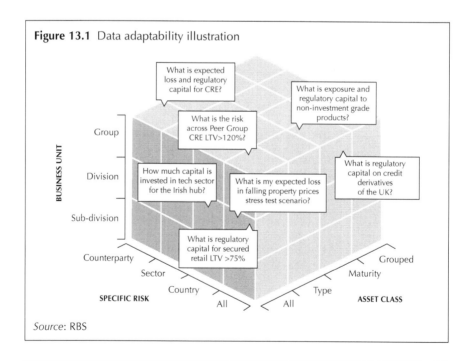

Source: RBS

investments or enhancements comply with those (including minimum documentation requirements, data lineage requirements, reference data standards and requirements for consistency of data definitions).

Data quality measurement entails measuring the completeness, accuracy and consistency of data. This includes periodic reconciliation to the balance sheet where appropriate, with the reconciliation frequency and accuracy criteria clearly defined (based on the data usage). Given the breadth of data items used to manage risk, data quality measurement efforts (over and above reconciliation) need to be focused on the most important data items, defined in accordance with their business uses and the materiality of the risk. Data sampling is also a useful complementary tool, allowing for a greater range of data areas to be covered over time and for them to be looked at in more depth – for example, cross-checking data against files or validating data with subject matter experts.

Data issue management entails communicating, monitoring and championing the resolution of data issues identified through the metrics, sampling or in the course of business. Effective governance requires senior management sponsorship and the engagement of data consumers and data providers, who can speak with authority, drive activity within their respective areas and provide a clear escalation mechanism to a senior governance forum where necessary.

Risk reporting practices

Risk is reported at many levels within an organisation in order to support specific risk management processes. Firms should understand the suite of reports that they have, their users, their purpose and the relationship between reports. The suite of reports should operate effectively and coherently together, with each report having a distinct and clear purpose, with duplication minimised, standardisation across similar business maximised and a clear hierarchy of reports defined (see Figure 13.2).

Reports should be tailored to the needs of their audience and regularly reviewed with users to ensure they remain fit for purpose. Metrics should include forecasts and stress outcomes where relevant, not just historical data. Risk should also be shown in the context of both appetite and profitability. For most audiences, and particularly senior management, reports should include insight and

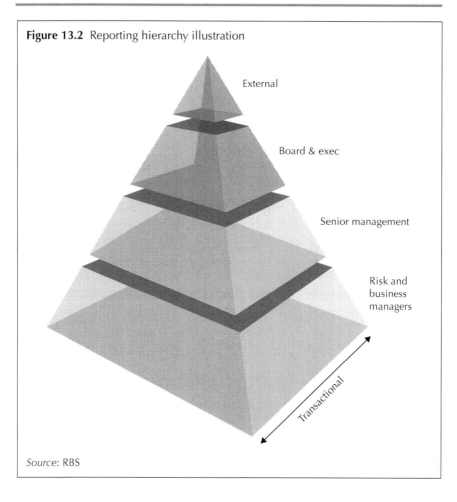

Figure 13.2 Reporting hierarchy illustration

External

Board & exec

Senior management

Risk and business managers

Transactional

Source: RBS

recommendations, or action plans, alongside metrics rather than leaving readers to interpret and draw their own conclusions. It can be a challenge to select and supply the appropriate aggregate risk report content for a senior audience without overwhelming them with information. Content cannot be exhaustive, but should focus on a range of key performance indicators (KPIs) linked to risk appetite while providing more in-depth analysis of the top and emerging risks that the users are responsible for managing. This should include risks identified through management judgement, not just metric-driven reporting. Finally, the frequency of risk reports should be agreed with users and specific triggers for more frequent reporting considered.

Supervisory review tools and cooperation

The Basel Committee have set guidance for regulators to: (i) encourage an appropriate focus on this topic given its importance, and conduct regular supervisory reviews; (ii) ensure regulators have appropriate tools to drive remedial actions, such as limits on risk or new business and capital add-ons; and (iii) (for home and host regulators) cooperate to share knowledge and ensure supervisory review activity is coordinated by the lead supervisor. Supervisory cooperation on this topic is welcomed by banks and limits (although does not eliminate) divergence between regulators, who have different emphases and expectations that reflect their local market dynamics and culture.

CHALLENGES IN ACHIEVING EFFECTIVE RISK DATA AND IT

The multifaceted nature of risk is a key challenge. The breadth of risk types (eg, credit, market, operational, conduct, liquidity, enterprise) and multiple lenses through which we assess them (eg, single name, country, sector, counterparty) mean there is a wide range of information needs that must be met. This makes execution more complex. Furthermore, risks are often managed by specific groups of subject matter experts. As a result, few individuals understand the full range of risks and the interconnections between them. This often leads to the isolated development of systems and a lack of common standards. Establishing IT governance across the risk function helps build broader understanding, identifies synergies and connections, and enables the effective prioritisation of IT investments.

The complex and often subjective nature of risk means there are many valid approaches to measuring specific risks. In the case of credit risk, for instance, it is reasonable to measure current, potential (worst case) and expected exposures, as well as losses. Risk can also be measured before or after risk transfer and/or provisions. Care must be taken to appropriately define risk measurement for each product type. If this aspect of measurement is not properly controlled, a multitude of competing measures can spring up within a firm. Defining a suite of core standard risks measures, with guidance as to how the measures should be used, is key to developing a consistent understanding of risk across the firm. This does not have to mean that no other specific measures are permitted for specific products or businesses where there is a genuine need, but does mean that a common language must exist so that risk can be widely understood, analysed and compared across businesses. Risk measures also often differ from the accounting treatment and measures used by the business for valid reasons (eg, gross versus net). Nonetheless, this creates a reconciliation challenge that risk managers need to tackle if risk measures are to be understood and used appropriately across the organisation, and with stakeholders externally.

Risk taking is at the heart of banking – every loan, deposit or trade generates risk. The data needed to measure and manage risk thus originates from the core transactional systems and operational processes of banks (although this can have a risk-specific lens or calculation applied). As a result, the requirement to draw out the correct data has to be embedded in many different operational systems and processes. The lack of standardisation across organisational systems – which may include many legacy and third-party systems – and the lack of front-to-back process design are fundamental challenges to getting an accurate aggregated view of risk. In addition, risk information is used at different levels of the organisation – in accordance with different timelines and in different locations – to support a wide range of core business processes, such as credit sanctioning, anti-money laundering and fraud checks, through to portfolio management, external disclosure and stress testing. This breadth of demand, with differing priorities, creates real challenges in developing coherent but manageable solutions. Given the way that risk management practices have evolved over time, solutions have often been implemented piecemeal to meet specific needs, rather than designed as a coherent whole.

As a result, risk functions are major stakeholders in organisation-wide data architecture, although they may only own some discrete components, such as credit grading models. This means risk functions have limited direct control over their own architecture, but are critical partners in their firms' IT strategies, driving and leveraging core IT infrastructure planning. To ensure that risk requirements are considered in all IT initiatives, firms must put in place effective data and IT architecture governance. Even where a risk function owns specific systems, other areas – business units or, increasingly, the finance function – are often the predominant users. In many firms, IT architecture historically has been federated with limited central control or governance. Establishing this governance and driving alignment across the firm requires senior sponsorship, and takes significant and scarce human and financial resources. Firms need to debate and agree an appropriate operating model to manage risk infrastructure and the risk interest in the broader organisational architecture. How much of the governance is managed by the risk function and how much by the broader IT function? How is business support for the governance and alignment best achieved?

Dialogue between risk and finance functions is important. Agreeing the relationship and degree of alignment between their architectures is important but particularly challenging, given the breadth and complexity of activity they both support. The growing use of risk-related data for financial and regulatory reporting, alongside the rising standards being set for risk data, has led to demand for increased integration. However, there are also significant discrete sets of requirements and divergence in how and when these functions use data. Risk has a greater emphasis on timely data to support day-to-day risk management activities, while many finance function processes tend to support periodic reporting. Therefore, firms must develop architectures that can meet both sets of demands while making the reconciliation and combination (eg, risk–return metrics) of both sets of data as straightforward as possible. Shared systems are therefore not always the appropriate strategy. Useful alignment strategies can include coordinating data sourcing and adjustments, employing common reference data, including necessary data keys in risk systems to facilitate reconciliation, and ensuring finance systems are sufficiently granular and timely to permit appropriate reconciliations.

Most risk managers and regulators recognise there are issues with the reliability and consistency of risk information. Evidencing these alone is difficult, although it is critical to generating support for the necessary remedial activity or investment and to ensure prioritisation of the appropriate resource. Challenges include the complexity of the risk data architecture, which makes issues difficult to identify. Differences in risk exposure amounts calculated by discrete systems may be small on a net basis, for example, but have a significant impact on the understanding of a given risk profile (eg, credit grade, sector, country). Identification of issues requires a well-thought-out framework of data quality metrics to measure completeness, accuracy and consistency. Selecting and developing appropriate metrics requires knowledge of risk data usage, risk assessment methodologies, individual systems and data flows across them. Deployment of data profiling tools and access to large volumes of data from multiple systems are also needed to implement the metrics.

Measuring data accuracy is particularly challenging. How can you confirm the accuracy of specific data items given this is generally proprietary information with no, or limited, external reference points? For example, to check the loan-to-value (LTV) ratio of a real estate loan one might compare valuation trends to publicly available indexes, but the latter lack detail and are therefore not directly comparable. As a result, the comparison may generate a material number of apparent anomalies to investigate.

Accuracy checks often also generate additional data demands, as the data required to perform the check may not be available in the reporting system and so require further data sourcing or joining across systems. Again, to test the LTV ratio of a real estate loan, it might be necessary to check that the valuation was carried out in accordance with the internally required frequency and method, which is likely to vary by customer segment/loan size. Quantifying the impact of data issues is also complicated given the multiple uses of data and the fact that the correct data value may not be known, so estimates may have been used. In some cases, the impacts are driven by a qualitative regulatory assessment (ie, there is no clear formula for costing) or the cost may not be transparent (eg, a regulator may apply conservative assumptions in a regulatory stress test where data inputs are missing). Ultimately, many data issues originate in upstream business processes and systems – therefore, being able to articulate the issue and its impact is critical to drive the correct process enhancements or remedial action.

CONCLUSION

Risk data and IT are key enablers for risk measurement and thus, in turn, risk management. Risk measurement underpins the understanding of current risk profile relative to risk appetite, generating a forward-looking risk profile that includes stress testing and the assessment of risk management performance. Historically, many banks have not adequately invested in, or coordinated, these capabilities across their firms to ensure they have robust, comprehensive and timely capabilities, particularly across business units. Reasons vary from firm to firm, but factors include failure to fully integrate acquisitions, complex legacy IT estates, federated business models and the lack of a strong risk management culture. These shortcomings were evident to regulators, investors and firms during the financial crisis, and have spurred greater interest in improving capabilities, on the part of regulators as well as the businesses themselves. New regulatory standards and increased recognition of the importance of these capabilities represent a permanent, not a temporary, change for the industry and firms must respond accordingly.

In order to define their requirements, firms need to debate the capabilities, methodologies and standards appropriate to their business. These must be documented and formally agreed in order to establish the necessary level of governance. The results of this process underpin their risk data and IT architecture.

Naturally, this should be done in light of industry best practice and trends. These requirements should be revisited regularly to take into account changes, not only in the wider industry but within the firm itself. Clarity and consensus on requirements makes the task of assessing the current state, driving remediation across the bank and securing necessary investment much easier.

Risk data and IT across the firm must operate as a comprehensive and coherent activity across entities within the firm and across risk types, where appropriate. This requires much greater coordination and, in many cases, changes to operating models to bring together previously disparate teams. Responsibility for the coordination of activity across the overall framework also needs to be clearly allocated and adequately resourced.

Data aggregation solutions vary from firm to firm. This depends on individual requirements and current state, but there is a trend towards building large firmwide data warehouses, often one for each risk type, supporting multiple processes in order to meet aggregation demands and adaptability expectations. Data aggregation is dependent on clear data definitions and the availability of appropriate data across the firm. For this to be effective, organisations need clear target architectures, enhancement roadmaps where necessary and good ongoing design governance. Data lineage must be understood for key data items. Firms also need effective data quality management, including metrics to measure data completeness and accuracy, and then rigorous governance to deal with any identified issues.

Finally, risk reporting needs to be more coherent across each firm, and more forward looking. The suite of risk reports should be managed and understood as a whole to ensure they provide comprehensive and consistent measurement of risk. Reports should meet users' needs rather than report what is readily available, and there should be a regular dialogue between users and producers of reports to ensure this is the case. In addition, reports should focus more on forward-looking information such as scenarios and stress testing.

There are many practical challenges associated with achieving high-quality risk data and IT. The multifaceted and pervasive nature of risk within banks means that this is not a simple task. Success entails meeting a complex set of requirements with dependencies throughout the firm, affecting core business processes and systems. The complex and often subjective nature of risk means that there are multiple risk measures to support. Firms also need to balance formalisation of their capabilities with maintaining risk management agility and innovation. Risk therefore needs to step up and play a major role in influencing and shaping organisation-wide data and IT infrastructure, ensuring this is well co-ordinated and controlled. If they are unable to do this, the capabilities needed for effective risk management cannot be developed adequately. Doing this successfully will require the investment of resources in explaining requirements, current shortcomings, the consequences of not addressing those and the potential commercial opportunities. This focus supports improved risk management and also helps the firm realise longer-term benefits through increased operational efficiency and greater commercial insight.

Meeting these expectations requires cultural as well as practical change. This change must take place both within the risk function and across the wider firm. The investment and management attention given to risk data and IT reflects the firm's broader risk culture and the importance attached to effective risk management. There are a number of key themes across the industry that can support this broader cultural change – for example, the focus on capital management, stress testing, risk appetite and resolution planning; the increased management focus on operational efficiency and cost management; the continued rapid evolution of information technology; and the competitive threat from technology-led challengers. Leveraging the interest and opportunities arising from these and other broader themes facing the industry is crucial in terms of gaining the necessary support and maximising the value of the solutions to the firm. Effective risk data and IT capabilities are a valuable resource for the firm, and can often have broader usage than just risk management.

Many firms have made significant progress since the financial crisis. Introducing new policies and procedures for managing data and IT going forward – and addressing specific gaps in data aggregation capability or targeted data quality management – can be undertaken in the short-to-medium term. However, given the complexity of banks, their legacy IT estates and the commercial challenges facing the industry, the full journey of data standardisation and architecture rationalisation will take many years.

1 Harrington (1991).
2 Jones and Bearley (1996).

REFERENCES

Basel Committee on Banking Supervision, 2013, "Principles for Effective Risk Data Aggregation and Risk Reporting".

External Disclosure Task Force, 2012, "Enhancing the Risk Disclosures of Banks".

Harrington, H. James, 1991, Business Process Improvement: The Breakthrough Strategy for Total Quality, Productivity, and Competitiveness (New York, NY: McGraw-Hill).

Jones, John E. and William L. Bearley, 1996, *360 Degree Feedback: Strategies, Tactics and Techniques for Developing Leaders* (Human Resource Development).

Propper, Carol, Simon Burgess and Denise Gossage, 2008, "Competition and Quality: Evidence from the NHS Internal Market 1991–9", *The Economic Journal*, 118, pp 138–70.

Senior Supervisors Group, 2008, "Observations on Risk Management Practices During the Recent Market Turbulence".

Senior Supervisors Group, 2009, "Risk Management Lessons from the Global Banking Crisis of 2008".

Senior Supervisors Group, 2010, "Observations on Developments in Risk Appetite Frameworks and IT Infrastructure".

14

The Role of Whistleblowing in Risk Culture and Effective Governance

Carol Sergeant

Public Concern at Work

"The world is a dangerous place to live; not because of the people who are evil, but because of the people who won't do anything about it."

Albert Einstein

As we have learnt from earlier chapters, it is the role of boards and senior executives to set what used to be called "vision and values", now re-named variously as risk appetite, risk culture and "tone from the top".

Even the best-run organisations face the risk that, at some point, something will go badly wrong. Formal audit and risk processes often fail to identify major issues, or fail to do so at an early enough stage. Typically, the first people to know about risks and wrong-doing will be those who work in or with the organisation, and they are often people in more junior positions. However, these people can be afraid to speak up (sometimes with good reason) and do not always know where and how they can raise issues safely and confidentially. When they do speak out, they are frequently ignored and no action is taken, and in some cases they suffer serious adverse personal consequences, including dismissal, blacklisting and victimisation by colleagues. Gagging clauses, particularly in settlement agreements, are still reported to be widespread.

Whistleblowing is a vital source of information that is often not properly encouraged or effectively deployed. A culture of silence can have a very corrosive effect on any organisation. Boards and senior executives need to ensure that there are safe and effective ways for people working in and with their organisation to raise concerns, and that the concerns raised are listened to and acted upon.

This chapter sets out the legal, regulatory and practical arrangements in the UK, the latest research on attitudes to whistleblowing and the effectiveness of the current regime, including the key recommendations of the UK's Whistleblowing Commission, which reported in November 2013.[1] It explains the barriers to effective whistleblowing faced both by individuals and organisations, and how these can be addressed in the design and implementation of workplace whistleblowing arrangements so that it will be easier for individuals to raise concerns, and more likely that organisations will listen and take action. Whistleblowing arrangements are a board-level responsibility and this chapter sets out the questions boards should ask. Although focusing on the UK as a case study, the experience and learnings provided have wider application.

WHAT IS WHISTLEBLOWING?

Whistleblowing is the raising of a concern, either within the workplace or to external parties, about a danger, risk, malpractice, wrongdoing or illegal act that is having, or could have, a negative impact on their own organisation, its customers or others. The UK government has defined it as follows: "Whistleblowing is when a worker reports suspected wrongdoing at work. Officially, this is called 'making a disclosure in the public interest'. A worker can report things that aren't right, are illegal, or if anyone at work is neglecting their duties."[2]

Organisations use a number of other words to describe this activity – for example, "speak out policies" and "speak up arrangements". They are all aimed at encouraging workers to raise concerns about wrongdoing. The term "whistleblowing", which has now gained wide acceptance in the UK, will be used throughout this chapter.

WHY WHISTLEBLOWING MATTERS, AND THE COST OF GETTING IT WRONG

The failure to encourage and respond to the early warnings that whistleblowing brings has had disastrous consequences in many sectors and industries, including major financial losses, market manipulation, severe reputational damage and unnecessary loss of life. Regulators, particularly in health, social care, the media and financial services, have also been criticised for failing to respond to whistleblowing reports they have received and failing to ensure the sectors they regulate have adequate whistleblowing arrangements.

There are numerous examples of cases where effective whistleblowing would have prevented or mitigated severe harm. Some of the more notorious examples are set out below. These cases provide examples of the absence of effective arrangements and process to encourage whistleblowing, key messages being lost in middle management, and senior executives and boards themselves failing to listen and take action.

In 1987, the *Herald of Free Enterprise* sank off the coast of Zeebrugge because it had set sail with its bow doors open, causing the death of 193 passengers and crew. The Sheen Inquiry into the tragedy found that staff had raised concerns about the safety risk of this practice on five separate occasions, but that their warnings were lost in middle management.

The UK National Health Service (NHS) has seen a number of cases where effective whistleblowing could have prevented unnecessary suffering and death. The public inquiry into the poor quality care and deaths at Mid Staffordshire NHS Foundation Trust (the Francis Inquiry, February 2013) found that: "[The board] did not listen sufficiently to its patients and staff or ensure the correction of deficiencies brought to the Trusts attention. Above all, it failed to tackle an insidious negative culture involving a tolerance of poor standards and a disengagement from managerial and leadership responsibilities".[3]

In his report, Robert Francis QC recommended that:

> Reporting of incidents of concern relevant to patient safety, compliance with the law and other fundamental standards or some higher requirement of the employer needs to be not only encouraged but insisted upon. Staff are entitled to receive feedback in relation to any report they make, including about any action taken or reasons for not acting.[4]

The Care Quality Commission (CQC), the regulator of health and social care in England, was also found wanting. CQC whistleblower Amanda Pollard told the Francis Inquiry:

> In my view those leading (the) CQC are more concerned with how they and the organisation are presented in the press rather than listening to those working within the organisation. This is something to worry about. The organisation becomes dangerous when driven

by reputation management, for example by promising to deliver annual inspections when this is simply not achievable; what suffers is the quality of the inspection.[5]

In an earlier inquiry in 2004 following the conviction of Dr Harold Shipman, a general practitioner who had killed at least 215 of his patients over a period of 24 years, Dame Janet Smith, a High Court Judge, commented in her report:

> To modern eyes, it seems obvious that a culture in all healthcare organisations that encourages the reporting of concerns would carry with it great benefits. The readiness of staff to draw attention to errors or "near misses" by doctors and nurses, and the facility for them to do so, could have a major impact upon patient safety and upon the quality of care provided.[6]

Later in her report she goes on to say that this "could make a greater contribution to patient safety than any other single factor."[7]

The financial services industry has also faced cases where malpractice has gone unreported, reports have been ignored, or where concerns raised within the organisation have failed to reach senior management or result in action being taken. In 2012, the UBS rogue trader Kweku Adoboli was sentenced to seven years imprisonment for one of the largest frauds in UK history. By the time his positions had been unwound, UBS had lost US$2.3 billion. The bank was subject to a significant fine from the UK Financial Services Authority and was subject to sanctions and restrictions on its business by the Swiss Financial Market Supervisory Authority (FINMA) (which did not have fining powers). UBS suffered severe reputational damage, leading to the resignation of a number of senior executives, including the chief executive Oswald Grübel. Many colleagues were aware of Adoboli's activities and reported discrepancies and limit breaches, but the reports were ignored or not properly investigated, in some cases because Adoboli appeared to be making significant, even extraordinary, profits. Others who were aware of the activities remained silent. One colleague reported Adoboli's excessive risk taking and secret account to superiors, but no action was taken. Adoboli got to hear of his colleague's confidential report, causing difficulties for the colleague on the trading floor, so when the excesses continued and escalated the colleague chose to stay silent.

The UK Parliamentary Commission on Banking Standards (PCBS)

was set up to review and report on professional standards and the culture in the UK banking sector in the wake of the London Interbank Offered Rate (Libor) fixing scandal and mis-selling of retail products. In its report "Changing Banking for Good", it stated that:

> The Commission was shocked by the evidence it heard that so many people turned a blind eye to misbehaviour and failed to report it. Institutions must ensure that their staff have a clear understanding of their duty to report an instance of wrongdoing, or "whistleblow", within the firm. This should include clear information for staff on what to do. Employee contracts and codes of conduct should include clear references to the duty to whistleblow and the circumstances in which they would be expected to do so.[8]

The as-yet unconcluded worldwide investigations into Libor and FX rate fixing suggest that the practices were known about, questioned and in some cases reported, including to regulators, but no action was taken. The UK Treasury Committee's second report into the fixing of Libor, "Fixing Libor: Some Preliminary Findings", found that a senior manager at Barclays had flagged the potential conflict between those derivative traders with risk positions and those who submit Libor rates. According to the report, "No questions were asked of Manager E or the Submitters in relation to this issue, no action was taken by Compliance and no systems and controls were put in place to deal with the potential conflict."[9] The Treasury Committee concluded that there were "serious failures of governance for which the board is responsible."[10]

In all these cases and many more, people did speak out, but were not listened to and no action was taken. This has resulted in tragic and unnecessary deaths and personal harm, as well as significant financial loss and incalculable damage to reputations, confidence and trust.

In many other cases, people are not willing to speak out at all. Research for the Institute of Business Ethics has shown that more than half of employees (52%) who are aware of misconduct at work stay silent.[11] Where there is no confidence in an organisation's internal whistleblowing procedures, people will sometimes eventually report a serious concern to the media, often after considerable delay, thus depriving the organisation of the opportunity to put an end to damaging activities at an early stage and put their own house in order. In the case of Serco's out-of-hours GP services, the National Audit Office (NAO) report found:

> Whistleblowing policies are insufficient if organisational culture does not support them. Whistleblowers raised important concerns about Serco's out-of-hours GP services in Cornwall. Serco has a whistleblowing policy and a range of channels for staff to raise concerns with management. However, the whistleblowers expressed fears about the consequences if they raised concerns internally.[12]

The NAO report went on to recommend:

> The Department of Health should take the lead in making sure that whistleblowers are, and feel, protected throughout the NHS (National Health Service). Whistleblowers are a valuable source of intelligence and should be encouraged to come forward ... The Department should also make sure local NHS bodies hold managers to account if whistleblowers suffer reprisals.[13]

THE LEGAL POSITION

In the UK, as in most countries that have whistleblowing legislation, the law is focused only on providing protection and compensation for *bona fide* whistleblowers who have suffered discrimination and financial loss as a result of speaking out. It is of course very important to have legislation protecting the position of whistleblowers, but this will not lead to effective whistleblowing unless there are also requirements on organisations. In the UK there is no legislation requiring organisations to have effective whistleblowing arrangements. Very few UK regulators have imposed whistleblowing requirements on the organisations they regulate or sanctions for failure to meet standards, and those that do set requirements have generally only introduced them latterly, often under pressure from public inquiries. Although there have been some promising developments, it is too early to know whether and when the various recommendations will be implemented and what impact they will have.

Legal position: Protection for the whistleblower

The UK first introduced legislation to protect whistleblowers in 1998 via the Public Interest Disclosure Act (PIDA).[14] The law, which was and remains world leading, protects workers who speak out in the public interest about wrongdoing or malpractice they have witnessed in the workplace.

PIDA offers protection to a broad range of workers in the private, public and charity sectors, including contractors, subcontractors and agency workers. However, there remain some significant gaps and uncertainties about what is covered (for example, partners, interns, non-executive directors, some general practitioners may not be covered). With increasingly flexible and changing work patterns, regular updating of the definition of worker is required.

The current categories of wrongdoing are set out in Section 43B of PIDA:

(1) In this Part a "qualifying disclosure" means any disclosure of information which, in the reasonable belief of the worker making the disclosure, is made in the public interest and tends to show one or more of the following:

  (a) that a criminal offence has been committed, is being committed or is likely to be committed,
  (b) that a person has failed, is failing or is likely to fail to comply with any legal obligation to which he is subject,
  (c) that a miscarriage of justice has occurred, is occurring or is likely to occur,
  (d) that the health or safety of any individual has been, is being or likely to be endangered,
  (e) that the environment has been is being or is likely to be damaged, or,
  (f) that the information tending to show any matter falling within any one of the preceding paragraphs has been, is being or is likely to be deliberately concealed.

PIDA seeks to strike a fair balance between protection of whistle-blowers that act in the public interest and the protection of employers from false, malicious and unfairly damaging reports. Lord Nolan (Appeal Court judge and founding chairman of the UK Committee on Standards in Public Life) praised PIDA for "so skil-fully achieving the essential but delicate balance between the public interest and the interest of employers."

PIDA does this by having a tiered disclosure regime, which encourages internal whistleblowing to the employer but also provides for external whistleblowing to regulators and to the wider public, including the media, where internal whistleblowing is not effective. However, it sets more onerous tests and thresholds for reporting externally. In reporting to a regulator, the discloser must reasonably believe the information and any allegation within it to be substantially true. Disclosure to the wider public (including the media) is subject to more onerous and complex conditions. It must be reasonable in the circumstances to make the disclosure, and the disclosure must not be made for personal gain. There must be a valid reason to disclose more widely – for example, reasonable fear of detriment if the disclosure is made to the employer, or that disclosure has already been made to the employer but no action has been taken, or there is no regulator (as prescribed in PIDA) that the worker can disclose to. Fear of a cover up, or if the failure is of an exceptionally serious nature, also provide protection to the discloser. However, a disclosure will not be protected if by making it the worker commits an offence, such as breaching the Official Secrets Act or misconduct in public office.

PIDA also prohibits "gagging clauses" in settlement agreements and other contracts that would prevent a worker speaking out in the public interest. However, gagging clauses are reported to be widespread in many sectors, and the fear of forfeiting often substantial financial and other benefits by breaching a gagging clause is a major deterrent to potential whistleblowers. Gagging clauses have therefore been banned in the UK national health sector.[15] However, there is concern that workers are still not receiving adequate advice on their rights with respect to gagging clauses, and that the drafting of this section of PIDA is insufficiently clear.

Changes were made to PIDA under the Enterprise and Regulatory Reform Act 2013 (ERRA).[16] This gives further protection to employers by requiring whistleblowers to demonstrate a reasonable belief that the disclosure was made in the public interest, and provides that a discloser who has acted in bad faith can have any compensation awarded reduced by up to 25%. ERRA also provides increased protection for workers by introducing a vicarious liability for employers, so that an individual who has suffered detriment from a fellow worker as a result of blowing the whistle may bring a claim against the employer. The definition of worker has been broadened somewhat, and more importantly future changes can be made more easily by way of secondary legislation.

Notwithstanding these amendments, in 2013 the Whistleblowing Commission found that PIDA was not working as intended and is complex and difficult to understand.[17] It made a number of recommendations designed to make the legislation clearer and easier to apply, including: defining wrongdoing more widely and including gross waste or mismanagement of funds and serious abuse of authority;[18] clarifying the anti-gagging provision and ensuring it is adhered to;[19] and making more use of the ability to update the definition of worker via secondary legislation – in particular, amending it to deal with blacklisting by covering job applicants.[20]

Legal position: Requirements on organisations and regulators

While a great deal of attention has been focused on securing legal protection for whistleblowers, there are no legal requirements for organisations to have effective whistleblowing arrangements. Some regulators recommend and encourage whistleblowing arrangements, but it is very rarely a mandatory requirement and in most cases there is no review of whether organisations are complying and no sanctions if they fail to comply.

The only exception is the International Civil Aviation Organisation (ICAO), which has for some time required whistleblowing procedures (referred to as "internal reporting systems") as part of mandatory safety reporting systems. In order to be licensed within the aviation industry, organisations and individuals must comply with mandatory reporting system regulations.

Many of the UK's major public inquiries and reports have recommended more and better oversight and intervention by regulatory bodies in the UK to whistleblowing may be about to see significant change. Most of the major public inquiries in the 2010's recommended more and better oversight and intervention by regulatory bodies, including appropriate sanctions to enforce good whistleblowing practice. In 2013, there were recommendations both from the PCBS to banking and financial services regulators and from the Health Select Committee in respect of the CQC, the regulator for the health and social care sector.

The PCBS criticised the Financial Conduct Authority (FCA) for having "little appreciation for the personal dilemma that whistleblowers may face",[21] and recommended that the UK's financial regulators should:

(a) periodically examine a firm's whistleblowing records, both in order to inform itself about possible matters of concern and to ensure that firms are treating whistleblowers' concerns appropriately;
(b) determine the information banks should report on whistleblowing in their annual reports;

(c) require senior persons within banks to have an explicit duty to be open with regulators where they become aware of possible wrongdoing regardless of whether they are in direct contact with the regulator; and

(d) provide feedback to the whistleblower and to consider enforcement action against an individual or firm if a whistleblower is victimised.[22]

The PCBS also recommended that the regulators should require information on whistleblowing to be disclosed in annual accounts.

The UK financial services regulators the FCA and the Prudential Regulatory Authority (PRA) encourage firms to have whistleblowing arrangements in place, and mirror PIDA by suggesting the use of internal procedures in the first instance, where possible. If there are no internal procedures, or whistleblowers are not confident in them, or there has been an inadequate response from the firm, then staff are encouraged to make reports to the regulator's whistleblowing hotline. The number of reports made to the FCA has been increasing significantly. Between November 2012 and October 2013, reports increased by 35%, from 3,183 to 5,150.[23] There is now good evidence that the FCA is following up on the individual reports it receives, but little evidence so far that the regulators are reviewing the effectiveness of firm's own whistleblowing arrangements. In the future, European regulations (for example, the draft European Union Market Abuse Regulations) may make whistleblowing arrangements and their oversight by regulators mandatory.

Firms in other (non-financial) sectors are also encouraged to have whistleblowing arrangements. In its UK Corporate Governance Code 2012, which applies to companies listed on the London Stock Exchange, the Financial Reporting Council (FRC) recommends that listed companies should have whistleblowing policies in place or explain why they did not have them. It says: "The audit committee should review arrangements by which staff of the company may, in confidence, raise concerns about possible improprieties in matters of financial reporting or other matters."[24] However, there is no review of whether companies are following the guidance and no sanctions for non-compliance.

In the government sector, health has been a particular focus of attention. The Health Select Committee recommended that the CQC should review the whistleblowing arrangements of those that it registers:

> While it is essential that proper procedures are established to support whistleblowers who report cases to the CQC, in most cases it will be important for staff in the first instance to raise issues through accessible procedures at their place of work. We have noted earlier in this report the importance which CQC inspectors should attach to making an assessment of the professional culture of organisations which provide health and social care. A key element of this assessment should be a judgement about the ability of professional staff within the organisation to raise concerns about patient care and safety issues without concern about the personal implications for the staff members concerned. An organisation which does not operate on this principle does not provide the context in which care staff can work in a manner which is consistent with their professional obligations. It should therefore be refused registration by the CQC.[25]

It is not yet clear how the CQC will respond to this recommendation.

The Leveson Report into the culture, practice and ethics of the press recommended that a whistleblowing hotline should be established for journalists who feel under pressure to act unethically and contrary to the Editor's Code. Lord Justice Leveson said: "My overall assessment is that a series of pragmatic solutions need to be devised to maximise the chance that genuine whistleblowers will use confidential avenues in which they have faith ..."[26]

The Whistleblowing Commission concluded that it would be undesirable at the present time to have statutory requirements for organisations to have whistleblowing arrangements.[27] However, it did make a number of recommendations with significant implications for regulators:

(a) that PIDA be amended to authorise the Secretary of State to issue a Code of Practice on whistleblowing arrangements, and provide that such a code must be taken into account by courts and tribunals whenever it is relevant to do so;

(b) that the government should do more to persuade regulators to require or encourage those they regulate to have in place effective whistleblowing arrangements that meet the standards of the Code of Practice;

(c) that the licence or registration of organisations that fail to have in place effective whistleblowing arrangements should be reviewed;

(d) that regulators have a clear procedure for dealing with whistleblowers who come to them, including the provision of feedback; and

(e) that regulators include whistleblowing in their annual reporting mechanisms, including accountability hearings before parliament (The Whistleblowing Commission made detailed recommendations on the information that should be published annually).

SOCIETAL ATTITUDES TO WHISTLEBLOWING ARE BECOMING MORE POSITIVE

When PIDA was first introduced in 1998, it was described in the media as the "snitcher's charter". However, since then, the public attitude to whistleblowing in the UK has become much more positive. Research by the University of Greenwich in 2012 showed that four out of five people in the UK thought that workers should be supported in revealing wrongdoing, even if it means revealing confidential information,[28] and a YouGov survey commissioned in 2013 by Public Concern at Work (PCAW), the whistleblowing charity, found that 74% of working adults considered the term "whistleblower" to be positive or neutral.[29]

However, despite this very helpful development in attitudes, which has been reflected in politics and the media, there remain significant challenges and barriers to effective whistleblowing.

BARRIERS TO EFFECTIVE WHISTLEBLOWING: FROM THE EMPLOYEES' POINT OF VIEW

PCAW runs a confidential independent advice line that provides legal and practical advice to whistleblowers. In 2013, together with the University of Greenwich, PCAW analysed 1,000 recent case studies from its advice line, covering all sectors, and identified the following trends:[30]

❏ 83% of whistleblowers will raise a concern twice, mostly internally, but only very few will do so a third time, so organisations get just two chances to listen and act;

❏ 15% of whistleblowers raise an issue externally;

❏ 74% of whistleblowers say nothing is done about the wrongdoing;

❏ 60% of whistleblowers receive no response from management, either positive or negative;

❏ the most likely response (19%) is formal action (disciplinary or demotion);

❏ 15% of whistleblowers are dismissed;

❏ senior whistleblowers are more likely to be dismissed; and

❏ newer employees are more likely to blow the whistle (39% of whistleblowers have less than two years' service).

Fear of reprisals from current and future employers (including formal and informal blacklisting) is a major and well-founded concern and barrier for whistleblowers. For many years, the construction industry ran a secret and well-organised blacklist of workers who had raised safety concerns, and informal blacklisting approaches still apply in many sectors and industries.[31]

Fears of reprisals and victimisation from colleagues can also be a big concern. This was an issue in the the Mid-Staffordshire NHS Trust case. Fellow workers may either have been a party to the wrongdoing or turned a blind eye. Most employers have done little or nothing to protect whistleblowers from fellow workers. It is too soon to know whether the recent amendment to PIDA (see above) to include vicarious liability for employers will change this.

Even without any fear of adverse consequences, it is often unclear to employees where and how a concern can be safely and confidentially reported. They will typically feel very vulnerable and isolated, and in many cases do not have access to truly independent and confidential advice about how to proceed and how to protect their own position. This also is a significant barrier.

ORGANISATIONAL BARRIERS TO EFFECTIVE WHISTLEBLOWING

One very obvious barrier is that addressing the whistleblower's concern could get in the way of meeting short-term personal and organisational targets and objectives. The report is therefore either deliberately ignored or covered up (with the source of the report often undermined and sometimes dismissed), or there is a subconscious rejection because the issue raised does not fit the organisational norm and set of beliefs about itself. Targets and objectives exist in all sectors (public, private, mutual and charity), and senior management and boards need to be very conscious of the unintended consequences of targets and monitor these carefully.

Another barrier is the inability to "think the unthinkable". This is a particular danger in some of the better-run organisations, which think they have paid a lot of attention to good culture and process and cannot believe that there can possibly be any serious malpractice.

Many organisations, and the people in them, have very poor listening and understanding skills, especially when confronted with something that does not fit the official organisational norm or their own personal experience and beliefs. The impact and materiality of the report is quite literally not understood.

There is also a tendency to suspect the motives of whistleblowers. Most are courageous people with entirely altruistic motives, but even those that have more complex motives may still be raising vital issues and should be listened to.

Simply putting in place whistleblowing policies and helplines does not make for effective whistleblowing. As has been made clear in many of the inquiries where things have gone badly wrong, these whistleblowing tools will only work if they have senior sponsorship and are embedded in an open and honest culture.

These are all complex behavioural and cultural issues that boards need to consider in all aspects of their work and not just in the whistleblowing context. The "it could not happen here" syndrome is a big impediment to active listening and constructive action.

DESIGN OF WHISTLEBLOWING ARRANGEMENTS

In designing whistleblowing arrangements, it is very important to take into account the behavioural aspects outlined above. Human beings like to be part of a herd. Speaking out, or whistleblowing, is lonely and tough. It requires conviction and considerable courage, particularly when everyone else is either ignoring the issue or perhaps complicit in it. Hearing and responding to something about your organisation that you do not want to believe is true, perhaps something quite shocking, is also tough, even for people with the highest ethical standards. It is important therefore to design whistle-blowing arrangements that take account of human behaviours, and that encourage and support both the whistleblower and the key listeners and decision-takers in the organisation.

A code of practice for effective whistleblowing

The Whistleblowing Commission has published a "Code of Practice for Whistleblowing", which seeks to address the barriers identified and provides practical guidance for employers, workers and their representatives.[32] It sets the standards against which organisations can be measured.

Good communications about whistleblowing with trade unions or staff organisations, where they exist, also typically leads to more

PANEL 14.1: CODE OF PRACTICE FOR WHISTLEBLOWING

There should be written procedures, which are clear, readily available, well publicised and easily understandable. These should:

❏ identify the types of concerns that can be raised (with examples);
❏ provide a sufficiently broad list of people and bodies to whom workers can make reports (including non-executives and regulators);
❏ give assurances that the worker will not suffer detriment for having raised a concern, unless she/he has knowingly provided false information;
❏ provide assurance that her/his identity will be kept confidential if the worker so requests unless disclosure is required by law; and
❏ require that the worker be told how and by whom the concern will be investigated; how long it will take; the outcome (if this is possible); be told to report if they believe they are suffering any detriment as a result of raising the concern; and that she/he is entitled to independent advice.

The Code also addresses training, review and oversight. The organisation should:

❏ ensure appropriate training at all levels;
❏ identify the person with overall responsibility for effective whistleblowing arrangements;
❏ periodically audit the arrangements, the audit to include: numbers and types of concerns raised and outcomes of investigations; a review of other adverse incidents where staff could have made reports but did not; feedback from whistleblowers; complaints about victimisation or failure to maintain confidentiality; a review of staff awareness, trust and confidence in the arrangements;
❏ ensure independent oversight and review by the board, audit or risk committee or equivalent, this body to set the terms of reference for the periodic audit;
❏ include information in its annual report or equivalent about the effectiveness of its whistleblowing arrangements; and
❏ finally, the Code makes clear that settlement agreements should not include a clause that precludes a worker from making a protected disclosure under PIDA.

effective whistleblowing, not least because employees are more likely to have confidence in the arrangements. Staff organisations will also have good knowledge and advice about how best to frame the arrangements to meet the needs of the people they represent and may even play a role in receiving whistleblowing reports.

Many of the organisations that have experienced terrible failures had whistleblowing policies and helplines in place, but there was no substance behind them. They were not effectively communicated, owned and monitored, and did not have the confidence of the staff. A genuinely well-functioning approach to whistleblowing is a powerful indicator of good culture and requires considerable investment of time and effort. Experience shows that those organisations where the board, and in particular the chairman, takes a very close interest in whistleblowing are the most effective (this is "tone from the top" in action).

FROM THEORY TO PRACTICE: QUESTIONS BOARDS SHOULD ASK

There are a number of practical and straightforward questions a board should ask to judge whether arrangements really are effective. The board should also demand to see evidence.

- ❏ What do we do to proactively encourage whistleblowing?
- ❏ Does everyone in the organisation know where and how to make a confidential report? (just having this written into a whistleblowing policy is not sufficient evidence!)
- ❏ Is it truly confidential and safe to make a report?
- ❏ Do employees have confidence in the arrangements? Have we asked them?
- ❏ What happens to whistleblowers? How are they treated, are they ever disciplined or dismissed?
- ❏ What do we do to protect whistleblowers from victimisation by colleagues?
- ❏ Can employees easily access truly independent and confidential advice on how to protect their own position if they speak out?
- ❏ Does the organisation provide regular feedback to whistleblowers to explain what is being done about their concern?
- ❏ Who on the executive is responsible for ensuring the right conditions for effective whistleblowing? Are they sufficiently capable, independent and senior? Do they have easy and regular access to independent non-executive directors?
- ❏ Where is the oversight at non-executive level, and does it work? How often does the board review the effectiveness of whistleblowing arrangements?
- ❏ Are the whistleblowing arrangements regularly independently audited?

❏ Does the organisation have adequate training for effective whistleblowing and active and open-minded listening skills?

❏ On the basis that "what gets measured gets done", is there sufficient monitoring and reporting on the effectiveness of whistleblowing arrangements, including the protection and support provided to whistleblowers, and does this information get to the right levels in the organisation at the right time?

❏ Are the levels and types of whistleblowing reports plausible for that type of organisation? What actions are taken in response to reports?

❏ Does the organisation publish whistleblowing statistics externally, for all of its stakeholders to see? If not, why not?

CONCLUSION

A healthy and open culture is one where people are encouraged to speak out, confident that they can do so without adverse consequences for themselves, confident that they will be listened to and confident that appropriate action will be taken. Organisations that claim to never receive whistleblowing reports should be a concern.

Unlocking the vital information and early risk indicators that are sitting in any organisation, often unrecognised, and making good use of them will make for a safer and more successful organisation. To the extent that all organisations impact on the rest of society via markets, products and people, there are also wider societal benefits. Having a good "culture", strong values and good intentions is necessary but not sufficient. It requires proactive and detailed attention from the chairman down, very careful monitoring, and constant renewal and refreshing. This is very much a board-level accountability.

1 The Whistleblowing Commission: Report on the effectiveness of existing arrangements for workplace whistleblowing in the UK', The Whistleblowing Commission, http://www.pcaw.org.uk/files/WBC%20Report%20Final.pdf, November 2013.

2 See https://www.gov.uk/whistleblowing/overview.

3 Letter to the Secretary of State, The Mid Staffordshire NHS Public Foundation Inquiry, volume 1, p 9 (available at http://www.midstaffspublicinquiry.com/sites/default/files/report/Volume%201.pdf, February 2013).

4 ibid, Recommendation 12, p 243.

5 Evidence of Amanda Pollard to the Mid Staffordshire Inquiry, WS0000078138ñ139, volume 2, paragraph 93.

6 Fifth Report of the Shipman Inquiry, 2004, "Safeguarding Patients: Lessons from the Past – Proposals for the Future", December 9, paragraph 11.50, p 329.

7 Fifth Report of the Shipman Inquiry, 2004, "Safeguarding Patients: Lessons from the Past – Proposals for the Future", December 9, paragraph 81, p 23.

8 Parliamentary Commission on Banking Standards, 2013, "First Report of Session 2013–14, Changing Banking for Good", June, paragraph 142, p 48 (available at http://www.publications.parliament.uk/pa/jt201314/jtselect/jtpcbs/27/27.pdf).

9 House of Commons Treasury Committee, "Fixing Libor: Some Preliminary Findings: Second Report of Session 2012–13", paragraph 37, p 21 (available at http://www.parliament.uk/documents/commons-committees/treasury/Fixing%20LIBOR_%20some%20preliminary%20findings%20-%20VOL%20I.pdf).

10 ibid, paragraph 38, note 8.

11 Institute of Business Ethics, 2005, "Ethics at Work: A National Survey".

12 National Audit Office, 2013, "The Role of Major Contractors in the Delivery of Public Services", November 12, p 51 (available at http://www.nao.org.uk/wp-content/uploads/2013/11/10296-001-Delivery-of-public-services-HC-8101.pdf).

13 Report by the Comptroller and Auditor General, HC 1016, Session 2012–13, 2013, "Memorandum on the Provision of the Out-of-hours GP service in Cornwall: Summary", March 7, Recommendation F, p 7 (available at http://www.nao.org.uk/wp-content/uploads/2013/03/Out-of-hours-GP-services-Cornwall-Executive-Summary.pdf).

14 Public Interest Disclosure Act 1998 (available at http://www.legislation.gov.uk/ukpga/1998/23/contents).

15 Department of Health, 2013, "Patients First and Foremost: The Initial Government Response to the Report of the Mid Staffordshire NHS Foundation Trust Public Inquiry", March, paragraph 2.36, p 47 (available at https://www.gov.uk/government/uploads/system/uploads/attachment_data/file/170701/Patients_First_and_Foremost.pdf).

16 Enterprise and Regulatory Reform Act 2013 (available at http://www.legislation.gov.uk/ukpga/2013/24/contents/enacted).

17 ibid, paragraph 73, p 17, note 1.

18 ibid, Recommendation 9, p 17, note 1.

19 Recommendation 17, Page 22, ibid note 1.

20 Recommendation 10, Page 19, ibid note 1.

21 Parliamentary Commission on Banking Standards, 2013, "Changing Banking for Good", June, paragraph 793, 796 and 799 (available at http://www.parliament.uk/documents/banking-commission/Banking-final-report-vol-ii.pdf).

22 ibid, paragraphs 789–805, note 20.

23 Information obtained by Kroll from the Financial Conduct Authority under the Freedom of Information Act, January 2014 (available at http://www.kroll.com/news/press-releases/?getPressRelease=62137).

24 Financial Reporting Council, 2012, "The UK Corporate Governance Code", September, paragraph C.3.5., p 19, (available at http://www.slc.co.uk/media/78872/uk-corporate-governance-code-september-2012.pdf).

25 Health Select Committee, 2013, "Report of Accountability Hearing of CQC 2012", January 13, paragraph 58 (available at http://www.publications.parliament.uk/pa/cm201213/cmselect/cmhealth/592/59209.htm).

26 Second Volume of Leveson Report, 2012, November, paragraph 8.9, p 993 (available at http://www.official-documents.gov.uk/document/hc1213/hc07/0780/0780_ii.pdf).

27 ibid, paragraph 47, p 12, note 1.

28 Wim Vandekerckhove, 2012, "UK Public Attitudes to Whistleblowing", November 15 (available at http://ssrn.com/abstract=2176193 or http://dx.doi.org/10.2139/ssrn.2176193).

29 PCAW commissioned a YouGov survey, June 2013 (available at http://www.pcaw.org.uk/whistleblowing-commission-sources-yougov-survey).

30 Public Concern at Work and the University of Greenwich, 2013, "Whistleblowing: The Inside Story – A Study of the Experiences of 1,000 Whistleblowers", research project, May

(available at http://www.pcaw.org.uk/files/Whistleblowing%20-%20the%20inside%20story%20FINAL.pdf).

31 The matter has been the subject of a report by the Scottish Affairs Select Committee, March 26, 2013: "Blacklisting in Employment: Interim Report" (available at http://www.publications.parliament.uk/pa/cm201213/cmselect/cmscotaf/1071/1071.pdf).

32 ibid, pp 28–30, note 1.

Index

(page numbers in italic type refer to figures and tables)

A

Adamson, Clive 165
Adoboli, Kweku 298
AIB Group 185–6
AIG 99
Asian airline crash 52
Association of British Insurers
  (ABI) 127
  "Principles of Remuneration" of
  242
Association for Financial Markets
  in Europe (AFME) 264

B

Banque de France 263
Barclays 262
  and Libor scandal 26, 47
Barings Bank 17, 20, 91, 95, 186
BCCI 92–3
Bear Stearns 252
Bernanke, Ben 94
BlackRock 125
BNP Paribas 262
bonus steering committee 244
  see also remuneration
BP 140–2, 144
  and Deepwater Horizon 5, 26,
  140–2

values articulated by 141
Buffett, Warren 71–2
business units, legal entities and
  products 91–3

C

Cadbury, Sir Adrian 240
Capital Requirement Directive
  (CRD) 263, 264
Capital Requirements Regulation
  (CRR) 263, 264
Care Quality Commission (CQC)
  297, 303, 304–5
Carney, Mark 99
Carroll, Cynthia 52
cascading risk appetite
  118–19
  see also risk appetite
Cecilia Malmström 185
Challenger launch 25–6
Chambers, Peter 126
"Changing Banking for Good"
  (PCBS) 299
chief risk officers (CROs):
  change practices and challenges
  for 25–44; *see also* risk
  culture
  different "voices" of 40–1

dilemmas and trade-offs faced
by 40
as "partnering overseers" 41
as "partnership builders" 40
remuneration committee decides
on package of 245
and risk function, organisational
footprint of 39–42
role of, as set out by Legal &
General 244
and SIE principles 112–13
Citibank 252
City HR Association 14, 144–5, 147
clawback and malus 153, 232,
248–51
disclosure of 249
enforcing 249–50
"Code of Practice for
Whistleblowing"
(Whistleblowing
Commission) 308–10
see also whistleblowing
codes of conduct 34, 58–9, 299
Columbia Accident Investigation
Board 7
Committee on Standards in Public
Life 301
Companies Acts 240
Comprehensive Capital Analysis
and Review (CCAR) 277
conduct:
influencing risk of, means of
achieving 168–73
cultural change, achieving
172–3
customer-centric approaches
168–9
drivers of culture 172
incentives 170–1

simpler products/smarter
business methods 170
value to customers, evaluating
169
whistleblowing 171
reducing likelihood of failures in
161–87
board's role in 178–9
board's structure and
approach 179–83
and board's top priorities,
review of 181
and business standards
committee 181–2
and conduct sub-committee,
establishing 181–2
and customer service,
appointment of executive
with responsibility for 181
ensuring NEDs are
independent and actively
engaged 180
and future successful
organisations 178
understanding conduct
agenda 179–80
regulatory focus on 162–8
and change in tools and
indicators 174–7
issues and implications 166–8
"Conduct Agenda" (FCA) 162–3,
164, 168, 170, 172, 178–9,
181
Corporate Governance Code 48–9,
240, 243, 249, 304
corporate risk management,
shareholder expectations in
127–8
Cranfield University 77

Crosby, Gilmore 19
culture indicators, development of
69–70

D
data and IT 275–93, *282–3*, *284*, *286*
and Basel reporting principles
282–3
characteristics of 280–7
aggregation capabilities 281–5
overarching governance 280–1
effective, challenges in achieving
287–90
and governance–culture link
277–80
and risk reporting practices
285–6
supervisory review tools and
cooperation 287
Deepwater Horizon 5, 26, 140–2
disaster myopia 3
Dodd–Frank Act 75, 91, 256

E
Einstein, Albert 295
Enhanced Disclosure Task Force
(EDTF) 261–2, 267, 269,
277
enhancements to internal audit
approach to reflect risk
203–10, *204*
reporting 209–10
testing 206–9
broadly based bottom-up
207–8
of culture in each audit
assignment 209
of governance and control
environment 207

enhancements to internal audit
staffing 210–12
Enron 144
Enterprise and Regulatory Reform
Act (ERRA) 302
Equitable Life 99
Euro Secured Notes Issuer (ESNI)
264
European Financial Services
Round Table (EFR) 264
European Market Infrastructure
Regulation (EMIR) 256
European Securities and Markets
Authority (ESMA) 134
explanatory panels:
clawback consultation 250
"Code of Practice for
Whistleblowing" 309
FSB definitions 109
risk appetite statement 115–16
view from Alfred P. Sloan 75
view from Warren Buffett 71–2
external disclosure 259–71
as key to market discipline
259–64
room for improvement in 264–71
mandatory, set by regulator
264–6
voluntary, by institutions
266–71
see also risk transparency

F
Figaro 220
figures:
bank's changing business,
evolution of *90*
data adaptability illustration
284

enhancements to internal audit
approach to address risk
culture *204*
FSB's risk appetite framework
86
map of current state versus
target state *210*
performance roadmap, path
taken by *149*
PRA's risk framework *84*
reporting hierarchy illustration
286
risk culture, bandwidth model of
30
risk culture, critical components
of *201*
Financial Conduct Authority 153,
303–4
"Conduct Agenda" of 162–3, 164,
168, 170, 172, 178–9, 181
and "joining the dots" in risk
culture templates 34
and reward mechanisms 153
see also Financial Services
Authority
Financial Industry Regulatory
Authority (FINRA) 164,
166–7
Financial Market Supervisory
Authority (FINMA) 298
Financial Reporting Council (FRC)
49, 123, 128, 129, 130–1, 132,
133, 239, 243, 249, 304
Financial Services Authority 153,
298
and incentive schemes 8
and RBS 247
see also Financial Conduct
Authority

Financial Stability Board (FSB) 1,
276
on compensation practices 215
consultation paper from 165
and Europe versus US 224–5
"Guidance on Supervisory
Interaction …" report of 2,
165
peer reviews carried out by
224–5, 234–5
principles and standards of
220–3
progress report from 107
on RAF, creation of 95
regulators' expectations set out
by 193
risk culture definition given by
84
supervisor guidance from 84
Supervisory Intensity and
Effectiveness (SIE) group of
108–9
examples of responsibilities
under principles of 111–13
"Thematic Review on Risk
Governance" report of 9
Financial Times 220
"Fixing Libor: Some Preliminary
Findings" (Treasury
Committee) 299
Flint, Douglas 124, 167
Francis Inquiry 297–8
Francis, Robert 297
French Revolution 235
Fukushima nuclear disaster 4

G
gagging clauses 295, 302
Gecko, Gordon 140

Girl Scouts 51
Glasser, William 148
global financial crisis, and poor
    and inappropriate culture
    51–2
Global Financial Stability Report
    (GFSR) 271
goal alignment 17
"gold-platers" 36
Greenwich, University of 306
Grímsson, Ólafur Ragnar 162
Group of Thirty 58
"Guidance on Supervisory
    Interaction with Financial
    Institutions on Risk Culture
    (A Framework for Assessing
    Risk Culture)" (FSB) 2, 165
"Guide to Board Effectiveness"
    (FRC) 49, 145
Gulf of Mexico, oil spill in, *see*
    Deepwater Horizon

H
Halliburton 5
Hayward, Tony 141–2
HBOS 82
Health Select Committee 304–5
Herald of Free Enterprise 297
Hesselbein, Frances 51
Hester, Stephen 161
HIH Insurance 98
HM Revenue and Customs
    (HMRC) 250
Holder, Eric 164
Horta-Osório, António 161
HSBC, and SIV bailouts 6
human-resource management and
    risk culture 37–9
    see also risk culture

I
Icelandic banking crisis 162
individual risky behaviour 8
internal audit 191–213, *210*
    and authority and stature 195–6
    board-level sponsorship for, to
        report on risk culture
        198–200
    response 197–8
    and risk culture assessment
        framework 200–3
    risk reflected in enhancements to
        203–10, *204*
        reporting 209–10
        testing 206–9
    role of, in risk governance
        193–5
    staffing, enhancements to
        210–12
internal disclosure 257–9
    see also risk transparency
International Civil Aviation
    Organisation 303
International Corporate
    Governance Network
    (ICGN) 123, 127–30 *passim*
Investment Management
    Association (IMA) 127, 132
IT and data 275–93, *282–3, 284, 286*
    and Basel reporting principles
        282–3
    characteristics of 280–7
        aggregation capabilities
            281–5
        overarching governance 280–1
    effective, challenges in achieving
        287–90
    and governance–culture link
        277–80

and risk reporting practices
285–6
supervisory review tools and
cooperation 287

J
Japan, property prices in 4
JLT Group 155
"joining the dots" approach 34–5
JP Morgan Chase 25

K
Kerviel, Jérôme 140
King's Cross underground fire 4
Kochan, Thomas 52
Leeson, Nick 17, 20, 91, 95, 98, 140,
186
see also rogue traders

L
legal entities, business units and
products 91–3
Legal & General 244
Lehman Brothers 140
Leveson, Lord Justice 305
Leveson Report 305
Libor, scandal involving 26, 47,
140, 162, 164, 299
Liikanen Report 263
Lloyds Banking Group 54, 161
London Whale 25, 26

M
Malmström, Cecilia 185
malus and clawback 153, 232,
248–51
disclosure of 249
enforcing 249–50
Market Abuse Regulations 304

Mid Staffordshire NHS Trust 8, 26,
47, 207, 297, 307
monitoring culture at board level
66–70
and culture indicators,
development of 69–70
and personal contact with key
players and throughout the
organisation 67
and survey data on culture
67–9
mortgage-backed securities, global
exposure to 4

N
NASA 26
National Association of Pension
Funds 127
National Audit Office (NAO) 300
National Commission on the BP
Deepwater Horizon Oil Spill
and Offshore Drilling 5
National Criminal Intelligence
Service 185
National Energy Board of Canada
141
National Health Service (NHS) 162,
165, 169, 171, 177, 180, 297,
300
and whistleblowing 297
Nolan, Lord 301
Norges Bank Investment
Management 125, 135

O
Office of the Comptroller of the
Currency (OCC) 107, 185
Old Mutual 244
Owen, Judge 99

P

panels:
  clawback consultation 250
  "Code of Practice for
    Whistleblowing" 309
  FSB definitions 109
  risk appetite statement 115–16
  view from Alfred P. Sloan 75
  view from Warren Buffett 71–2
Parliamentary Commission on
    Banking Standards (PCBS)
    96, 97, 99, 124, 139, 161,
    298–9, 303–4
PAYE 250
Penrose, Lord 99
performance management 60–2
  framework 60–1, *61*
  and risk-based remuneration
    14–15
  values-driven 137–60
    and boards 145
    challenges in achieving 157–8
    characteristics of *151*
    and consistent behaviour, lack
      of 158
    and corporate culture 138–44
    defining, and expected
      behaviours 140–2
    and functional specialisms 146
    and monitoring of external
      factors, lack of 158
    normalising 147–55
    and organisational alignment,
      lack of 158
    and organisational
      development or HR lexicon,
      lack of 157–8
    and people risk, defining
      138–44

and performance roadmap
    148–55, *149*; *see also*
    performance roadmap
  questions to consider for:
    identifying values 155
  questions to consider for:
    measure for values 156
  questions to consider for:
    recruit, select and induct for
      values 156
  questions to consider for:
    reinforcement 157
  questions to consider for:
    understanding culture 156
  responsibilities for 144–6
  and senior executive teams 146
performance roadmap 148–55, *149*
  and values:
    employee engagement 153–5
    identification of 148–9
    individual career equation
      153–5
    leading and embedding
      149–50
    measure for 150–2
    reinforcement of 152
    reward mechanisms 152–3
    selecting for 150
    whistleblowing procedures
      152
Piper Alpha 26
Polaroid 140
Pollard, Amanda 297
press, Leveson Report into 305
Prime Collateralised Securities
    (PCS) initiative 264
"Principles for Effective Risk Data
    Aggregation and Risk
    Reporting" (BCBS) 276

"Principles of Remuneration"
(ABI) 242
products, business units and legal
entities 91–3
ProNed 240
Prudential Regulation Authority
(PRA) 153, 172, 250, 251, 304
and reward mechanisms 153
risk framework of *84*
role of 81–4
views of, on risk culture and risk
governance in banks and
insurers 81–101
and bank's changing business
90
and banks and insurers,
culture or risk culture for
98–100
and business plans 89–90
and business units, legal
entities and products 91–3
and defining rick capacity
86–7
and identified risks 87–9
and PRA's role 81–4, *84*
and risk limits 93–6
and role of board and
executives 96–8
and Senior Management
Regime (SMR) 96–8
Public Concern at Work (PCAW)
306
Public Interest Disclosure Act
(PIDA) 300–2, 306

R
raising concerns, speaking up and
whistleblowing 60
see also whistleblowing

recruitment and clearance policies
64–5
regulatory focus on conduct
162–8
and change in tools and
indicators 174–7
issues and implications:
conduct 166–7
higher capital requirements
167–8
reputation 167
see also conduct
remuneration:
committees, *see* remuneration
committees
critical appraisal 235–6
deferring 248–9
insufficiency of 251–2
development of new regulatory
approach to 216–26
European versus US approach
224–5
to intervene or not to
intervene 216–17
and "intrusion" of regulators
and legislators 219–24
and public state aid 225–6
transparency and governance
217–18
effective governance of 220–1
and factoring risk into
performance measures and
targets 246–8
FCA/PRA code on 153
incentive-compatible structure
for 226–34
alignment of risk and
compensation: corporate
framework 227

deferral and clawback 232–3
  instruments for payout 233–4
  performance measurements
    227–9
  risk measures, incorporation
    of 229–32
  size of pool 229
and incentives 14–15
industry progress 234–5
initial pillars of public policy in
  217–19
and link between policies and
  risk management 241–3
and malus and clawback 153,
  232, 248–51
  disclosure of 249
  enforcing 249–50
risk-based, and performance
  management 14–15
as shares 248–9
  insufficiency of 251–2
remuneration committees 14, 234
  and CRO's remuneration
    package 245
  and emerging UK good practice
    239–53
  and deferrals into shares,
    insufficiency of 251–2
  deferring remuneration and
    paying in form of shares
    248–9
  factoring risk into
    performance measures and
    targets 246–8
  and policies–risk management
    link 241–3
  history and role of 239–40
  reporting risk to 243–6
  responsibilities of 240–1

"Review of Corporate Governance
  in UK Banks and Other
  Financial Industry Entities",
  see Walker Report
risk:
  and compensation 215–37
    critical appraisal 235–6
    effective governance of 220–1
    industry progress 234–5
    and new regulatory approach
      to remuneration 216–26; see
      also remuneration
    and public state aid 225–6
  culture of, see risk culture
  enhancements to internal audit
    approach to reflect 203–10,
    204; see also internal audit
    reporting 209–10
    testing 206–9
  factoring of, into performance
    measures and targets 246–8
  funds at 252–3
  knowledge about, appetite for 37
  quantification of , in appropriate
    format 252
  reduction of, employees fail to
    prioritise 7
  reporting of, to remuneration
    committee 243–6; see also
    remuneration; remuneration
    committees
  senior management fail to
    uncover 6–7
  trade-offs lead to too much 5
  transparency, see risk
    transparency
risk appetite 10–12, 35–7, 129, 252
  and appetite for knowledge
    about risk 37

cascading 118–19
defining 109
different meanings of 103–4
history of regulatory and
    private-sector initiatives on
    104–8
and risk culture 35–7; *see also* risk
    culture
and risk culture, regulatory view
    of 103–21
    and RAFs, meanings and
        definitions of 108–10
statements, qualitative and
    quantitative 114–16
risk appetite framework (RAF):
    board's setting of 84
    description of 116–17
    FSB definition of 85
    FSB's *86*
    and link with
        culture/embedding 119–20
    meanings and definitions of
        108–10
    and wider culture 11
risk-assessment techniques,
    improved 20–1
risk-based remuneration 14–15
risk capacity, defining 86–7, 109
risk concentrations, better
    approaches to assess 21
risk culture:
    appropriate, creating 10
    and accountability 17
    and goal alignment 17
    and incentives 14–17
    and incentives: wider 15–17
    and performance management
        14–15
    and risk appetite 10–12

and risk-based remuneration
    14–15
and transparency 18–22
and values and behaviours
    12–14
assessing 9
assessment framework 200–3
board-level sponsorship for
    internal audit to report on
    198–200
board's role in 9, 47–78
    and agenda, risk on 76–7
    and behaviour, common
        issues with 73–6, *74*
    and board as role model 71–2
    and board composition 72–3
    and culture indicators,
        development of 69–70
    and FSB SIE group's
        principles, examples of
        responsibilities under
        111–13
    and monitoring 66–70
    and own culture 70–7
    and personal contact with key
        players and throughout the
        organisation 67
    and survey data on culture
        67–9
    and that of senior executives
        96–8, 110–13
    and trends at board level 77–8
board's setting of 52–8
    obstacles to 54–5
    through communication and
        training 55–8
    values 53–4
changing: industry initiatives
    31–9, *33*

and compensation, and
"intrusion" of regulators
and legislators 219–24
critical components of *201*
and data and IT, importance of
275–93, *282–3, 284, 286*
characteristics of 280–7
data–IT, governance–culture
links 277–80
effective, challenges in
achieving 287–90
risk reporting practices 285–6
supervisory review tools and
cooperation 287
developing, through
communication and training
55–8
and disaster myopia 3
discussed and defined 1–24,
27–31
tabulated definitions of *27*
essence of 2
external 259–71
failure of, understanding 3–8
employees' lack of
prioritisation concerning 7
and failure of senior
management to uncover
risks 6–7
and individual risky
behaviour 7–8
lack of focus 3–4
and trade-offs leading to too
much risk 5
FSB definition of 84
human-resource management
and 37–9
indicators of, developing 69–70
internal 257–9

and internal audit 191–213; *see
also* internal audit
and authority and stature
195–6
investor's perspective on 123–36
and risk governance 129–30
and risk reporting 130–2
and shareholder expectations
in corporate risk
management 127–8
shareholder time horizons and
investment approach 123–6
and UK Stewardship Code
132–4
and "joining the dots" 34–5
and limits of limits 117–18
model factors, by organisation
33
monitoring, at board level 66–70
multi-dimensional "bandwidth"
model of 29–30, *30*
policies and processes that
reinforce 58–66
codes of conduct 58–9
and monitoring key talent
65–6
performance framework,
monitoring use of 62–3
performance framework to
support desired culture 62
performance management
framework 60–1, *61*
raising concerns, speaking up
and whistleblowing 60
recruitment and clearance
policies 64–5
sanctions 63–4
succession and key-person
risk 65–6

poor and inappropriate, and
  global financial crisis 51–2
RAF's link with, and embedding
  119–20
and risk appetite 10–12, 35–7
and risk appetite, regulatory
  view of 103–21
  history of regulatory and
    private-sector initiatives
    104–8
  and RAFs, meanings and
    definitions of 108–10
and risk governance, PRA's
  views on 81–101, 84
  and bank's changing business
    90
  and banks and insurers,
    culture or risk culture for
    98–100
  and business plans 89–90
  and business units, legal
    entities and products 91–3
  and defining rick capacity
    86–7
  and identified risks 87–9
  and PRA's role 81–4, 84
  and risk limits 93–6
  and role of board and
    executives 96–8
  and Senior Management
    Regime (SMR) 96–8
selected definitions of, tabulated
  27
training programs to develop
  56–8
and transparency 255–72
  background to 256–7
transparency seen as essential to
  257–64

UK regulators focus on 25
understanding, within
  organisation 192–3
see also risk
risk function, organisational
  footprint of 39–42
risk governance:
  and culture, investor's
    perspective on 129–30
  and culture, PRA's views on
    81–101, 84; see also
    Prudential Regulation
    Authority
  and bank's changing business
    90
  and banks and insurers,
    culture or risk culture for
    98–100
  and business plans 89–90
  and business units, legal
    entities and products 91–3
  defining risk capacity 86–7
  and identified risks 87–9
  and risk limits 93–6
  and role of board and
    executives 96–8
  and Senior Management
    Regime (SMR) 96–8
  and data–IT, governance–culture
    links 277–80
  role of internal audit in 193–5; see
    also internal audit
risk reporting 130–2
risk transparency 18–22, 255–72
  background to 256–7
  essential to robust risk culture
    257–64
  external 21–2, 259–71
  high-risk areas, exploring 20

internal 257–9
openness to information 19
risk-assessment techniques,
improved 20–1
risk concentrations, better
approaches to assess 21
and testing risks against appetite
11
rogue traders 8, 16, 140, 167, 185–6,
298
Kerviel 140
Leeson 17, 20, 91, 95, 98, 140, 186
Rusnak 185–6
Royal Bank of Scotland (RBS) 82,
124, 126, 161
scorecards used by 247
Rusnak, John 185–6
see also rogue traders
Rustenburg platinum mine 52

S
Salomon Brothers 248
Salz Review 139
San Francisco airport 52
"sandbox guardians" 36
Santander 262
Sants, Hector 165
Securities and Exchange
Commission (SEC) 164, 166
Senior Management Regime (SMR)
96–8
Senior Supervisors Group (SSG)
105, 275–6
Serco 300
shareholder expectations in
corporate risk management
127–8
Shareholder Rights Directive 123,
133

shareholder time horizons and
investment approach 123–6
Sharman, Lord 131
Sheen Inquiry 297
Shipman, Dr Harold 298
Singapore International Monetary
Exchange 186
Sloan, Alfred P. 75
Smith, Dame Janet 298
Smith New Court 248
Société Générale 140
space shuttle 7, 25–6
Stafford Hospital, *see* Mid
Staffordshire NHS Trust
Stewardship Code, UK 132–4
survey data on culture 67–9

T
tables:
Basel data and reporting
principles overview *282–3*
board behaviour, common issues
with *74*
performance management
system, design features for
61
risk culture model factors by
organisation, summary of *33*
risk culture, selected definitions
of *27*
values-driven performance
management system *151*
"Thematic Review on Risk
Governance" (FSB) 9
"three lines of defence" (TLD)
structure 26, 42
Times 99
Toyota 141
Transocean 5

Treasury Committee 299
Tucker, Paul 233

U
UBS 140, 164, 298

V
Vickers Report 263

W
Walker, Sir David 52
Walker Report 52, 75, 139, 241
Washington Consensus 161–2
Washington subway incident 7–8
Wheatley, Martin 163
whistleblowing 60, 120, 152, 171,
    295–313
  barriers to:
    from employees' point of view
    306–7
    organisational 307–8
  design of arrangements for
    308–10

code of practice 308
explained 296
and fears of reprisals 307
and gagging clauses 295, 302
importance of, and cost of
    getting it wrong 296–300
legal position on 300–5
  organisations and regulators,
    requirements on 303–5
  protection 300–3
and National Health Service
  297
questions boards should ask
  310–11
societal attitudes to 306
Whistleblowing Commission 296,
  302–3, 305
  "Code of Practice for
    Whistleblowing" issued by
    308–10

Z
Zhou Enlai 235